Great Photographic Essays from LIFE

Commentary by Maitland Edey
Pictures Edited by Constance Sullivan

New York Graphic Society • Boston

Library of Congress Cataloging in Publication Data

Main entry under title:

Great photographic essays from Life.

   1. Photography, Documentary. 2. Journalism,
Pictorial.   I. Edey, Maitland Armstrong, 1910–
II. Sullivan, Constance.   III. Life.
TR820.5.G7   779'.092'2   78-7070
ISBN 0-8212-0742-3

Designed by Dianne Smith/Designworks Inc.

New York Graphic Society books are published by Little,
Brown and Company; published simultaneously in Canada by
Little, Brown and Company (Canada) Limited.
Printed in the United States of America   First Edition

Acknowledgements

"Franklin Roosevelt Has a Wild West" photographs copyright © 1936 by the Estate of Margaret Bourke-White; text copyright © 1936 by Time Incorporated. "A Woman Photographs the Face of a Changing City" photographs copyright © 1938 by Berenice Abbott; text copyright © 1938 by Time Incorporated. "Country Doctor," "Spanish Village," and "Drama beneath a City Window" photographs copyright © 1948, 1951, 1958, respectively, by W. Eugene Smith; text copyright © 1948, 1951, 1958, respectively, by Time Incorporated. "A Last Look at Peiping" photographs copyright © 1949 by Henri Cartier-Bresson; text copyright © 1949 by Time Incorporated. "Winter in Maine" photographs copyright © 1951 by Black Star; text copyright © 1951 by Time Incorporated. "Three Mormon Towns" photographs by Dorothea Lange copyright © 1954 by The Oakland Museum; photographs by Ansel Adams copyright © 1954 by Ansel Adams; text copyright © 1954 by Time Incorporated. "Irish Country People" photographs copyright © 1955 by The Oakland Museum; text copyright © 1955 by Time Incorporated. "In a Dutiful Family Trials with Mother" photographs copyright © 1959 by Cornell Capa; text copyright © 1959 by Time Incorporated. "The Era of Sentiment and Splendor" photographs copyright © 1960 by Clarence John Laughlin; text copyright © 1960 by Time Incorporated. "Displaced Germans," "The Private Life of Gwyned Filling," "Fight Trainer," "A Portfolio of Distinguished Britons," "The Prairie," "A New Way to Look at the U.S.," "The Spirit and Frenzy of Olympian Efforts," "The Lash of Success," "We Are Animals in a World No One Knows," "The Shakers," and "A Family of His Own" copyright © 1945, 1948, 1951, 1952, 1952, 1952, 1960, 1962, 1965, 1967, 1971, respectively, by Time Incorporated.

Our thanks to the photographers and many others who helped obtain prints for this book. We are especially grateful to the following persons at Time Incorporated: Ralph Graves, Corporate Editor; Mary Jane McGonegal, Editorial Services; Doris O'Neil, Picture Collection; and George Karas, Herbert Orth, and the technicians of the Photo Lab.

Maitland Edey
Constance Sullivan

Contents

In the fall of 1936 the photographer Margaret Bourke-White was sent by the editors of the about-to-be-launched *Life* Magazine to Fort Peck, Montana, to photograph a dam being built there. Miss Bourke-White had come to eminence in the early 1930s as a leading architectural photographer, and the dam itself was the principal target of her camera. But she was a restless and notably enterprising woman. She took it upon herself while at Fort Peck to photograph some of the goings-on she observed in a couple of nearby boom towns that had sprung up.

On November 23 the first issue of *Life* came out. On its cover was Bourke-White's portrait of the dam, an arresting arrangement of monolithic concrete shapes, strongly composed, and with two tiny figures at the bottom to give it scale. It has since become one of the best-known architectural studies ever made by an American photographer.

Inside the magazine were — as it would turn out — some even more significant pictures. These were selections from the rest of her take, a candid close-in look at a dusty, rawboned, false-fronted shantytown and the people in it. The photographs' subjects included families on relief, construction workers, roustabouts, taxi dancers, bartenders and drifters — the kind of population that has bloomed over and over again in the United States, watered by the refreshing rain of money from big construction projects, withering when the jobs run out. This was the American frontier, the quick new chance. Thumbing through Bourke-White's pictures, one could catch a strong whiff of that temporariness, of a brawling life with rough edges and few illusions and no amenities. She caught it all, and for a photographer trained to do other things, it was a remarkable achievement. Equally important, it was also caught by the new editors of the magazine. One of those, Daniel Longwell, having been wired by Bourke-White about what she was up to, sent back encouragement, saying he thought her pictures would make a good "Party" in the back of the magazine. John Shaw Billings, the new managing editor, recognized with a rush of relief that they would provide the strong opening story he had been hoping for.

Billings had not been in on the planning of *Life*; he was the editor of *Time*. But when the editorial direction that was responsible for getting out the first issue of *Life* broke down, Billings was summoned by Henry Luce, the head of the company, to cut through the chaos and get volume 1, number 1 out on schedule. This did not suit Billings at all. Brought up as a newspaperman, he was interested in news, and was happily running the most successful news magazine in the country. He had little or no experience with pictures beyond the one- or two-column cuts that he was accustomed to sprinkling through the pages of *Time*. Nevertheless he agreed to the shift and went to work. Up to his neck in other matters, he was not shown the Bourke-White take when it came in. Instead, it was brought to the office of Henry Luce by Ralph Ingersoll, another member of the original staff. Ingersoll began spreading pictures on the floor of Luce's office, saying: "There's your lead story." He and Luce had it pasted up. Only then did Billings see it. It is ironic that the man who would almost literally create the photo essay had little hand in creating the first one. His only contribution was to suggest the layout of the final spread.

Luce and the others did not realize it at the time, nor did anyone else in the excitement and turmoil attending the birth of *Life*, but they had just created the first true photographic essay ever made: a collection of pictures on a single theme, arranged to convey a mood, deliver information, tell a story, in a way that one picture alone cannot. Selection and arrangement are all-important. A successful photo essay is always greater than the sum of its parts. It has a life of its own. It says more, has a greater impact than any single picture in it.

The Fort Peck story adhered to those criteria. Luce, Ingersoll, and Billings all had the journalist's instinct for a strong story line. They also shared a powerful, though undeveloped, visual sense, combined with a strong interest in American history. Given a chance to use pictures creatively, they jumped at it. They recognized the "frontier" element in Bourke-White's take, and realized also that its effect could not be captured in two or three pictures — so they used seventeen. If another group, with a different set of ideas and editorial convictions, had been there instead, a different-looking photo essay would have emerged — or perhaps no photo essay at all, and credit for the "first" would have gone to someone else.

That it would have gone to somebody very quickly is certain. Candid photography was booming. Its penetration into journalism was becoming increasingly strong. The very fact that a picture magazine like *Life* was on the boards is indicative of that, as was the spawning of *Look, Pic, Click, Picture, Peek*, and others now forgotten. Given that sudden burst of picture magazines, it was only a matter of time before some enterprising editor or designer would see the immense potential in groups of pictures and break out of the shackles that had hitherto prevented their combination into essays. The surprise is that it had not happened before.

Photo essays require good "sets" of pictures. When it is recalled that these have existed ever since Matthew Brady began working on Civil War battlefields, it is reasonable to ask why they were not made into photo essays at the time. The answer is that there was no way of mass-producing them. The printing industry had yet to find a method of transferring a photographic image — the gradual changes from black to white that make up the picture — from a photographic print to another piece of paper.

Brady could do it himself, of course, slowly, one picture

1

at a time in his darkroom. But newspaper editors could not, in numbers large enough to satisfy their needs. All they could reproduce were pen-and-ink drawings whose tonal effects were sharply made by discrete lines that could easily be transferred to a wooden or metal plate by an engraver. The engraving could then be put on a printing press for runs of thousands of impressions.

Photographs have no such sharp lines. They are brought into being by the action of light on an emulsion containing silver that has been spread and then left to dry on a transparent backing. Since the material in an emulsion has no "edge," the images left on it have no edge either. Their changes in tone are gradual and subtle. There is no way of mass-printing them unless their tones are transformed into very fine lines or small dots.

It was the dot that metamorphosed the photograph from a one-at-a-time studio portrait to a ten-thousand-an-hour newspaper picture. Someone hit on the idea of rephotographing the photograph through a fine screen. The result was an image broken up into very small dots. The photograph had been transformed into a line drawing — or, if one prefers, into a dot drawing.

The halftone had been born. Anyone looking through a strong magnifying glass at a photograph reproduced in one of today's newspapers or magazines will instantly see that, while it gives an impression of being made of lines, it is actually a complex pattern of minute dots. In the darkest parts of the photograph the dots will run together to form areas of solid black. As the tone becomes lighter, the dots will shrink in size until, in the white parts, they disappear altogether.

That was what Brady and his contemporaries lacked: a way of mass-producing photographs. If they were to be reproduced in quantity at all they first had to be turned into drawings by fast-working artists employed by newspapers. The work of early photographers could appear in illustrated publications only after it had been transformed into line-drawings by specialists in this work. One was Winslow Homer, who supported himself in his early years by making lively drawings for *Harper's Weekly*, an illustrated magazine that was enormously popular in the United States between 1857 and 1916.

Harper's Weekly is a fascinating subject for anyone interested in the development of pictures as an adjunct to journalism. Its editors experimented with all sorts of layout devices: cookie-cutter shapes; comic-strip sequences; action-filled, eye-stopping, double-page spreads. Week after week Homer would supply a "double-truck" picture, and it would be featured in the magazine's centerfold. In a large sense *Harper's Weekly* was the *Life* Magazine of its day. It depended on pictures, and exploited them ingeniously, but it had to do without photographs.

Men like Homer could also supply *Harper's* with something that photographers could not: action. The bulky cameras and the glass plates and the slow emulsions and slower lenses of the day made anything resembling candid photography impossible. Brady's photographs are monuments of immobility. His studio portraits, of course, did not pretend to convey immediacy or action. But his field pictures would have if they could have. Brady's pictures of General Grant and his staff, or of Lincoln seated in a field tent at the front, give some impression of immediacy because of their background, but they are wholly static. So are the shots of men standing in trenches or lounging in quarters. There is no sense of movement in any of them. Nor is there in the views of battlefields with their scatter of spread corpses; those men will never move again. Equally still — dead and uninhabited — are the ruins of Atlanta, the stacks of supplies, the motionless ships tied to empty wharves. In a Brady photograph, no one runs, shouts, or even waves his hand.

For a lively street scene, of horses galloping, of people strolling and talking, of scampering little boys, the picture-minded editor had to fall back on the artist. Before action could be fixed on a photographic negative, faster cameras and faster film would have to be devised.

Both came. In the years before, during, and after World War I, thanks to the halftone screen, newspapers had begun using photographs, but in a very primitive way. For one thing, newsprint was pulpy stuff and could not take a fine-screen halftone. The best it could handle was a coarse dot structure made from a screen with about 60 lines to the inch. For a truly rich reproduction, for something that resembled the original photograph, a screen of 150 to 200 lines was required. In their efforts to get better quality in their printing of photographs, editors began putting inserts of special smooth-surface paper, something known as coated stock, into the Sunday editions of their newspapers. These were the rotogravure sections, haphazard collections of the week's best news pictures, assembled into patterns on the page.

By the end of World War I many large-city papers had their "roto" sections, the pictures usually printed in a chocolate-colored ink that was thought to give them greater richness. The ink and the smooth paper stock instantly separated the roto section from the rest of the paper. Its pictures often were well reproduced. To the visually unsophisticated readers of the time they were rewarding in and of themselves: single glimpses of what had been happening during the previous week. Each was treated as an entity, with no effort toward organizing them into larger stories. This was partly due to the limitations of the pictures themselves. They were almost uniformly static. A press photographer sent out to cover the dedication of a bridge

would ask the principals to arrange themselves in a group facing the camera, scissors and ribbon prominently displayed. No action shown. None possible. He would take one picture and then head for the next assignment. If that happened to be an indoor banquet the preparation would be even longer. He would have to fire off a magnesium flare, a small pile of powder set on a tin reflecting tray and sending up a large cloud of smoke when it was ignited. There were no such things as flashbulbs.

For editors accustomed to working with pictures taken under these conditions, there was not much they could do with them beyond arranging them into tasteful patterns on their roto pages. Even with the gradual development of more flexible and faster press cameras, the *thinking* of editors was not flexible enough to demand anything different. Only occasionally, like a dim flash of heat lightning low on the horizon, did some warning of the visual excitement to come manifest itself. In November 1918, for example, the editor of the *Illustrated London News* decided to cover the celebration of the Armistice with a double spread of pictures collected from all over London. Here was a glimmer of the photo essay of the future, with one of its ingredients at work: a group of pictures on a single theme. But their treatment was still the old "roto" treatment. The form of the layout was not dictated by the content of the pictures but by the desire for an overall pattern, a symmetrical arrangement of shapes — some rectangular, some round, some overlapping others — the pattern further emphasized by heavy black-and-white borders around each picture. A primitive effort but an effective one. For all the similarity of the pictures, the very repetitiveness of vehicles festooned with people, smiling crowds and waving flags made for a sense of festivity and excitement. That came through despite the straitjacket layout.

In the 1920s came a breakthrough comparable almost to the development of the halftone: truly fast candid cameras. The first of these was the Ermanox, scarcely larger than a modern Nikon, and with a lens capable of getting pictures under natural-light conditions at banquets, conferences, and other places where older slower equipment simply would not work. In the hands of a German, Erich Salomon,

the Ermanox brought candid photography into being.

Salomon's pictures, when they began appearing in European journals, caused a sensation. Often the subjects did not know they were being photographed. They would be caught in vivid, sometimes awkward or unflattering attitudes, but looking *real*, not posed, as Salomon clicked away unobtrusively in the corner of a palace or a courtroom. He made one famous picture of the prime minister of France, Aristide Briand, at a state banquet in 1931, snapping his shutter at the very instant Briand discovered him in the room and pointed a finger at him.

Salomon's work electrified a whole generation of young European photographers, many of them Germans. It helped stimulate the development of even better and smaller cameras than the Ermanox, notably the Leica — again German. It sparked the publication of picture magazines like the *Munich Illustrated Press.* Editors, for the first time, began experimenting with picture-story layouts in which the content of the pictures dictated the layout instead of being ignored in favor of a constricting overall design. It was in this ferment that talk of starting new picture magazines began in the United States, helped along by the fact that some of the best of the emerging European photographers were Jews seeking work here, far from Nazi persecution.

Salomon was a news photographer. Although he was an accomplished artist also, his real interest was in current events, in catching people off guard, in penetrating places and revealing things that people had never seen before. It was not so much art as a kind of astonished "My God, look at this, in a photograph!" that propelled his work. That influence was so powerful that it is not surprising that there should have been an unconsciously strong news bias in the use of pictures when *Life* first came out — even aside from the fact that most of the early *Life* staff had been recruited from *Time,* a news magazine.

For all that, *Life*'s original prospectus statement was a prophetic one, promising more than the magazine initially delivered. Whoever wrote it was able to see beyond the short and snappy, beyond the tricks and pictorial sensations and the fast coverage of events that the new candid technique was making possible, to a nobler vision of what photography, creatively used in journalism, might ultimately do. It was, without realizing it, talking about picture essays when it stated its purpose:

To see life; to see the world; to eyewitness great events; to watch the faces of the poor and the gestures of the proud; to see strange things — machines, armies, multitudes, shadows in the jungle and on the moon; to see man's work — his paintings, towers and discoveries; to see things thousands of miles away, things hidden behind walls and within rooms, things dangerous to come to; the women that men love and many children; to see and take pleasure in seeing; to see and be amazed; to see and be instructed.

To see. To see in a sudden burst of seeing, in a dazzling explosion of new pictorial revelation. That was what shot *Life* into orbit. Eventually it made good on all the promises in its prospectus. To do so, its editors had to familiarize themselves with photo-essay techniques, and then refine them, rather than blundering into them instinctively as they had done with that first Bourke-White essay. They had to learn to shake themselves free of Salomon-dictated concepts of news: to distinguish between what was essentially news coverage and other subtler, more difficult concepts that required not only the skills of candid news photography but a mental and aesthetic approach that was entirely different.

The difference, of course, was that news has its own imperatives. There is no shaping. What happens happens. It does not repeat itself. There can be no retakes. The photographer, no matter how cleverly he may have prepared himself, is at the mercy of events. He cannot be in two places at the same time. And yet he must get the story. That is why — in a strictly news sense — one man cannot cover an event like the coronation of a queen. An experienced picture editor, with a journalistic responsibility for getting that story whole, will dispatch a team of photographers to cover it: one man inside Westminster Abbey for the actual ceremony, another in the streets for close-up crowd reaction, another on top of a building to get an overall of the procession, and so on. The result, blended by a skillful editor, could be considered an essay of sorts, but it is not a true one. Its energy is dissipated by having been filtered through the minds (and the lenses) of too many people. The concentration of emotion, or insight, or beauty, the coherence of a single point of view that is brought to a true photo essay — these things come into being when a set of pictures is the work of one man. A photo essay should have singularity.

Singularity is a relative term. As we examine the photo essay further, we will find that *no* essay is truly singular. The word must be applied only to the work of the photographer, and must be elastic enough to accept the intrusion of others into the essay-making process.

Looking at photo essays complete, shaped and published in magazines, one is tempted to regard them as pictorial Athenas, sprung whole from the inspired brows of photographers. That is far from so. While photographers do take the pictures, that is only part of the process. Photographers are congenitally poor editors. They are unable to look at their own work dispassionately, and have a regrettable tendency to value a picture by the difficulty experienced in obtaining it: "How can you throw out that one? I waited hours — I froze myself stiff getting it!" They see qualities in many of their pictures that others don't. They want more pictures used. They argue bitterly with editors about that. "You are killing my story. You can't do justice to it in eight pages. You need sixteen." Probably the most famous argument of this sort occurred when Eugene Smith came back from Lambaréné, Africa, with a huge stack of photographs of Albert Schweitzer. The editors of *Life* laid out twelve pages. Smith said the story could use sixty. He suggested that the entire issue might be devoted to Schweitzer. As a photographer he had a point; he had taken dozens of superb pictures that were not going to be used. Worse, the story having been commissioned by *Life*, the pictures were *Life*'s property and might never be seen by anybody. Smith lost that argument. He was thinking about individual photographs and not about photo essays. The two are not the same.

Which is not to say that the photographer is not sometimes right; the label "editor" does not confer infallibility on the man who is trying to shape a bundle of pictures into a coherent essay. Sometimes he fails, and butchers a take that deserved a better fate. Therein lies the tension — the chanciness — that turns the art of the photo essay into such a gamble. More than one intellect, more than one set of prejudices and aesthetic standards are involved in its creation. I can think of no other visual aesthetic form in which this plurality of influences prevails. With a painting, the selection of a frame, even the choice of where the picture is hung in a room, may fleetingly affect the quality of the aesthetic response that it evokes. But those matters are really nothing but frames: edge considerations, peripheral concerns. In the long run they have no bearing on the painting itself. But the framework, the architecture, of a photo essay is as much a part of the final work as the pictures themselves. In a large measure, the framework *is* the essay. One really has to go outside of the visual arts entirely to find an analogy. The best one I can think of is music, in which there must be a partnership between composer and performer before there can be a meaningful aesthetic experience.

The making of photo essays is a joint affair, always involving two people (photographer and editor) and sometimes as many as seven. The majority of the essays in this book reflect the work of six or seven different people, which justifies a short description of how *Life* was set up.

Being a news-oriented general-interest picture magazine, *Life* had to have a pool of staff photographers ready on short notice for all sorts of assignments, not only fast-breaking news stories but small features of various kinds: fashion, sports, nature, medicine and the like. Those areas of interest were the responsibility of departmental editors. It was up to the sports editor, for example, to produce a stream of publishable sports stories. These, as they were assigned and shot, would go into the hopper with stories from all the other departments, from which the managing editor made his selections each week in putting together a magazine. That made the various departments competitive with one another for space. A resourceful editor learned not only how to think of all sorts of ways to cover his beat, but also learned how to improve his chances of producing superior stories by trying to get good photographers assigned to them, for nothing killed a good idea faster than poor photographic execution.

A good departmental editor also thought beyond the week-to-week coverage of his beat, cudgeling his brains for ways of doing larger and more ambitious stories that did not have news pegs: in short, photo essays. For example, the sports editor, rather than covering the Army–Navy football game as a specific event, might decide to attempt an essay on football itself. Marshall Smith, *Life*'s sports editor, did just that in 1962. He decided to capture something of the mood of tough high-school football as played in the Pennsylvania steel towns, with its down-in-the-trenches flavor, its splinted fingers and muddy bandages. Such a story would be timeless; it would not be about a particular team or a particular player. It could be shot anywhere, any year. It would give a photographer a chance to make a personal statement about the essence of football. He could do it with faces, with hands, with empty locker rooms, with crowd reactions, with racing, blurred figures — the possibilities were nearly endless, and the choice was up to him. But he could not start unless he was sent.

On this particular story a photographer *was* sent: Mark Kauffman. Kauffman shot a marvelous essay that would have been included here if the negatives and glossy prints had not been lost.

So, right at the outset, we find people other than photographers intruding on the photo-essay process. Kauffman did not think of the football story. Smith did. What is more, he wrote a shooting script for it, a description of what he had in mind and what he hoped the photographer would be inspired to capture. Therefore it must be nailed down quickly that the decision to create a photo essay on a certain subject and expressing a certain mood comes, in more cases than not, from an editor. The concept is then presented to a photographer, whose job it is to realize it. Sometimes he must be cajoled into taking it on. Always his imagination must be engaged by the originality or the persuasiveness of the script, for if he is to do his job properly he must add something of his own to it. In actual fact, staff photographers seldom had to be talked into doing photo essays. They were more apt to complain that their energies were being sapped by short inconsequential one- or two-page stories, and that the essay plums were going to others.

Some of the complaint was unjustified. Many *Life* staffers were reliable photographers who could be depended on to go out and make an acceptable shot of a new playground or an amusing sequence on a new fad like the hula hoop, but whose imaginations and abilities were not up to the insights, either photographic or psychological, or even to the sustained creative effort that a photo essay demanded. Still, there were staff photographers who probably could have made fine essays if given the chance — or who might have profited by what they learned in initial failure if given a second chance. Those second chances did not come often. The photographic staff was large, and bulged with conspicuous talent jostling for attention. Every assignment was a gamble, often an expensive one. The photographic editor, whose responsibility was managing that stable of photographers and doling out the assignments, minimized the risks as well as he could. He was answerable to the managing editor, and he could not afford to make many mistakes.

When I was breaking in at *Life* the photo editor was Wilson Hicks. His role in the shaping of a picture essay was pivotal. It was he, for example, who selected W. Eugene Smith to shoot the "Country Doctor" essay shown on page 65. Smith may have talked it over privately with an editor, and may even have given him some ideas to help sell the shooting script to Hicks, for Hicks had to be sold. He was constantly being hit from all sides by proposals for stories of every conceivable dimension, from a request for a single picture of a medicine bottle to one for several thousand miles of travel throughout the Mediterranean to retrace the wanderings of Ulysses. Hicks had to decide not only which stories to assign but also to whom they would be assigned. When he chose Smith to photograph the life of a country doctor, he put an indelible stamp on that story. Another photographer, a different result.

Hicks was a difficult man. Editors and photographers alike were afraid of him because he had the power to starve them professionally by failing to assign work to them. A young editor could be rendered literally helpless if his picture scripts piled up on Hicks's desk without action. Sooner or later the managing editor would become aware that the youngster was producing nothing, and he would be fired.

5

Similarly, the photographer who went weeks without assignment, or, when he got one, found himself working on something so marginal that there was little chance that even one of the staff stars could do anything with it, would gradually begin to assume the coloration of a loser.

Hicks was well aware of the power he had, and he exploited it. Most of the time he did it for positive reasons. Part of his responsibility, he felt, was making sure his photographers were not made to work uselessly. He took it upon himself to teach aspiring editors that they were not to write up preposterous scripts that were either physically impossible to execute or else so hopelessly long-drawn-out as to be impractical, or — worst of all — just plain dull. He did nothing about these; he let them gather dust on his desk. If the editor finally came in to complain — or, rather, to ask, for one did not complain to Hicks — he would then be treated to a fatherly lecture on script writing. If he listened politely and earnestly, and in succeeding efforts seemed to have been learning from Hicks, he was treated more indulgently. Editors could get around Hicks in this way and become pets. He was not above playing favorites.

With photographers the situation was similar but worse, because Hicks was directly in charge of them. An editor was part of the central chain of editorial command that went straight up to the top, to Billings. Anything that came in to Hicks with Billings's imprimatur on it was automatically assigned. But Hicks hired the photographers himself, assigned stories to them, evaluated their work, and had what amounted to a life-and-death control over their careers. What saved him from being a capricious tyrant was an abiding love for photography. He was passionately interested in it and, by extension, in the careers of photographers. Many photographers complained bitterly about Hicks. Some hated him. The truth is that he made many more careers than he stunted. He was always on the lookout for new talent, and when he found it he nursed it along. It was he who spotted the potential in Leonard McCombe as a maker of in-depth, psychologically intense photo essays. He did the same with many others. He even went so far as to make an occasional bizarre leap — assigning a photographer whose specialty was pretty girls to a political convention or a baseball game — in an effort to stretch the potential of someone he suspected had more than had yet been shown. In that way he often got bizarre but fascinating results from seemingly routine assignments. He talked for hours with photographers, analyzing their work, making suggestions to them, encouraging them when they felt down. On one occasion he rescued a photographer from what amounted to near peonage. Alfred Eisenstaedt, unworldly and obsessed with photography to the exclusion of nearly everything else, had, on arriving in the United States, signed a contract with a photo agency that was more rewarding to the agency than it was to him. Moreover, he had signed for life. Hicks, hearing about this, got in touch with the head of the agency and explained that as long as that arrangement prevailed, no photographer represented by that agency would ever get another *Life* assignment. The contract was torn up, and Eisenstaedt's bondage ended.

On balance Hicks was a strongly positive influence in the history of photojournalism.

So now we have three people involved in the production of an essay: departmental editor, photo-assignment editor, and photographer. A good script has been written, a good match-up between script and photographer has been found, the photographer has gone out and shot his story. What happens then?

Enter number four, the negative editor.

Life photographers learned early to cover themselves. Enough of them had been in on layout sessions and seen how editors and designers treated their pictures to know that it was always a good idea to have a long wide arrangement of a key picture as well as a tall thin one, just in case the designer's whim called for the former. This is an oversimplistic reference to what was actually a far more complex matter — the relationship between photographer and designer during the laying-out of photo essays — but the lesson for photographers was clear: take lots of pictures.

Life photographers did take lots of pictures. They became notorious for it. Freelancers, who had to buy and process their own film, were not only jealous of the free film and free processing that the *Life* staffers were given, but they were actually scornful of their overshooting. "Anybody can get a good picture if he hangs around long enough and shoots hundreds of them. I go out and I think. I decide what to take. I see six pictures, so I make six exposures." For salon or advertising work, perhaps enough. But for a photo essay, not enough. I must keep repeating that a photo essay is different. It is not just a group of photographs. It is something more, made from a particular arrangement of certain selected photographs. Just as the photographer exercises a critical selectivity in the pictures he chooses to make, so does the designer exercise an equally critical selectivity in the ones he chooses to use — and selectivity again in how he decides to use them. It stands to reason that the more flexibility the photographer gives the designer, the easier the latter's job will be. Wise *Life* staffers provided plenty. They habitually overshot, not only for variety, but also to avoid the possible later charge of having missed something obvious. "For God's sake, you *knew* this story was about a homecoming soldier. Where is the shot of him opening the icebox for his first piece of mom's apple pie?"

The result of these pressures was that when photographers came back to the office they usually had enormous quantities of exposed film with them. This not only had to be processed, but the good pictures in the take had to be selected and then enlarged to 8 × 10 or 11 × 14 size so that the physical exercise of putting them together into a layout could be accomplished.

Out of a thousand exposures, how does one select forty that tell the story? That is the responsibility of the negative editor. The title derives from the function: she edits negatives. She has a light table for looking directly at negatives or color transparencies. She has a complete set of contact prints and a large magnifying glass. It is her job to boil down the sprawling take of the photographer into a workable bundle of the best pictures. Best means not only the best from a pure photographic point of view but also the best from the point of view of how they push the story along and fill in its details. A quick look at the essays in this book will reveal that many of them are not just collections of super photographs. There is a judicious sprinkling in of "point" pictures, ones that make a telling or needed comment that helps glue the story together, expand it, and also provide variety in the layout.

That the majority of pictures selected for inclusion in a successful photo essay should be striking photographs goes without saying. However, they have to be recognized as striking. It may appear foolish even to suggest that this is a problem, but it is, and can sometimes be a serious one. If the good pictures in a photographer's take are submerged in a huge pile of mediocre ones, or if there are so many minimally different versions of one subject that the designer, when he comes to make a layout, has his critical sense numbed by looking at them — if, in short, the good is blurred and lost in a haystack of the near-good and the downright bad — then the chance of digging the good out of the haystack is significantly reduced. It is the job of the negative editor to distill the best from a large set of pictures, to shrink it down to its most potent form.

For many years *Life*'s chief negative editor was Peggy Sargent, a woman of great tact and patience. She had started her career in photojournalism as an assistant to Margaret Bourke-White. Experienced in looking at contact prints, she was hired by *Life* and quickly developed a

phenomenal skill at picking out the best and the essential from any take. In this work she had the help of the departmental editor, if she needed it, to make sure she missed nothing. She seldom did. She also had the help of the photographer, which she usually did not need. He would stand at her elbow, urging that she mark for printing many more pictures than she otherwise might have. Over the years Peggy used extraordinary diplomacy in her relations with photographers. Her office was a natural hangout for them, and she became intimate with almost all of those on the *Life* staff, and with a good many freelancers as well. For one and all she performed the priceless service of making them look better than they were. Their technical failures — and there were thousands of them — never saw the light of day. Unimaginative shots, stupid shots, vulgar shots (unless the story was supposed to be vulgar) were discreetly discarded. Only the cream was kept, and Peggy was a master at finding the cream. The result, even with such super novas as Eisenstaedt, McCombe, Kessel, and Elisofon, was tighter, leaner, more impressive stories, ready for the all-important next step: layout.

In the early days of *Life* much of the layout was done directly by the managing editor, John Billings. Every managing editor, sooner or later, works out his own way of organizing things. Being *Life*'s first, Billings had a clean slate. Also he had a small staff. It was easier for him than for some of his successors to go any way he chose. His way was to do everything himself. By everything, I mean everything narrowly connected with the actual putting together of a magazine once a week. The finding of personnel, the organization of duties, their departmentalization, the staff meetings to discuss future work, the agreement on stories, the shooting of them — those things Billings delegated. "You do all that," he said, in effect, to his deputies. "I don't want to be bothered with it. I want a steady stream of good material passing over my desk every week. It is your job to supply it. I will decide what I like, what to throw away. I will lay it out. I will place it in the magazine. I will decide how much space it should have. I will edit the copy that is written about the pictures. And on Saturday night at six o'clock I will put on my hat and go home."

That is what he did. For ten years, barring illness and

vacations, he put out one issue of *Life* after another almost single-handedly. He was a genius — impatient, arbitrary, an elemental editorial force who through shyness kept a distance between himself and most others. His staff admired him extravagantly, and most of them were intimidated by him. I was frightened to death of him, but I, too, admired him extravagantly. Like everyone else, I learned not to waste my time on stories about American Indians; they bored him. Better by far to try and think up ways of doing stories on railroads; Billings was crazy about railroads.

His testimony is those first ten years of *Life*. His tastes, his prejudices, his inspirations, his weaknesses are all there in the five hundred magazines he created. Those early ones are fascinating to look at. They reveal the mind of a man suddenly wakening to the enormous strength of photographs when used in new ways. Almost anything that looked exciting or original Billings put into *Life*. As a result *Life* vibrated visually. Those early issues were crude but powerful, radiating a kind of raw young energy that may be felt even today, and that tended gradually to become diluted as the magazine (and its readers) grew more sophisticated.

Part of the early vitality derived from the fact that almost everything *Life* did at first was new. It simply had not occurred to journalists thinking in one-picture terms to go to certain places and look at certain things and then tell their stories in photographs, *assigned* photographs by men sent out to get them. It had not occurred to them to write long information-stuffed captions describing the photographs; or to look beyond and behind the photographs for others that might have been taken years before or thousands of miles away, but that could be troweled in for background enrichment of the story; or to look aside from the main event entirely to emphasize a humorous or pathetic sidelight to it.

Billings did all this with unflagging and often irreverent gusto. As I have noted, he was a newsman, and the early issues of *Life* literally quivered with news — in pictures. Much of his material was hatched right in the office and shot by the photographic staff, but a respectable amount of it came in over the transom or through the wire services. As a result, a great deal of *Life* was artfully stitched together by clever use of seemingly unrelated pictures. Billings's elephantine memory served him well there. If a picture caught his eye he would set it aside, and remember it months later when another to complement it crossed his desk. He was endlessly resourceful in rescuing items with pictorial zing but not enough of it to stand by themselves. By clever match-ups and play-offs he would build up the zing. His layouts were bold and straightforward. They went directly to the meat of the story. No fooling around.

Although any early issue of *Life* would teach much the same lessons, I choose here to describe the issue of May 30, 1938. There is nothing special about that one, only my feeling that it shows Billings at work at his most typically "Billingsish." The first story that week bears his stamp: a raw piece of contemporary Americana — marathon dancers — chosen to get the issue off to a fast start because the pictures were arresting. They show slumping people literally out on their feet, falling to the floor, being supported by their partners, being revived. They were shot by an outsider, but Billings wanted more, so a staffer, Bernard Hoffman, filled out the story. The text description was sardonic, Billings's way of justifying this seamy look at a seamy holdover from the Great Depression. He understood the fascination the seamy had for people, and he exploited it, but tried to take the edge off it with humor. He liked to shock, and did so over and over again, with pictures of brain operations, with the first pictures ever published in a general magazine of the birth of a baby, with murders, warfare, concentration camp victims. World War II gave him endless opportunity to shock, and he exploited that too, but in a high moral way because it was part of a great cause that the entire country was wrapped up in and whose nightmare quality its citizens could fully understand only if it was hammered home to them in pictures.

For all this, Billings was prudish. *Life* was full of pictures of busty, bare-legged girls, but their exposure had its limits. The deeper cleavages and wholly transparent nightgowns were touched up with an airbrush in the layout room by a man with the nickname of "the nipple obliterator." I remember once being given a chance to put together an issue of *Life* and inserting a short story on a dog's head, one severed from its body but kept alive in a laboratory to demonstrate Pavlovian or other scientific phenomena. It was a grisly story, sure enough, but I was well aware of Billings's injunction to keep the readers "jumping along," as he put it. This would make them jump, so I put it in. Billings, who was monitoring my struggles from an upstairs office, reacted instantly. "This is repulsive," he said. "Remove it." I tried to defend my choice. He turned his back on me in his swivel chair and refused to speak.

The bounds of taste — his bounds — were clear. Collapsing marathon dancers staggering about under the gaze of people who paid to watch their suffering: that was an easy one, made easier by the inclusion of a press-agent gag shot of an unconscious woman getting her hair waved. The story ended on that grim/funny note and was followed by the week's lead news story, a staff-assigned one on a sharply contrasting subject: factories under construction. Henry Ford planned to enlarge auto capacity and, as the headline put it: "Take a $35,000,000 Crack at Depression." Then came several spreads of miscellaneous news, followed by a mixed bag of small features: one on a beauty contest (that week's excuse for cheesecake); one on the new fad of dark glasses, and featuring another Billings trademark: emphasis on information (prominent in the layout was a box describing eight different types of sunglasses, their advantages and disadvantages, and their cost); and three or four others. The Billings mix: a generous portion of news, information, variety, several changes of pace, visual excitement, and some humor.

Then Billings rolled up his sleeves and really went to work. The feature story in that week's issue was a sixteen-page study of Czechoslovakia, extremely timely because it was in the final throes of its effort to resist being swallowed by Hitler. It is an intriguing mixture, part news story, part picture essay, wholly absorbing. It starts boldly on a double spread, with pictures of the countryside and two large headshots of the men contending for control of Czechoslovakia: Beneš, the president, and Konrad Henlein, leader of the Sudeten Germans in Czechoslovakia and Hitler's man for disrupting and ultimately taking over the country.

If asked, Billings probably would have labeled it as a photo essay. If so, it was a double one for it was shot by two staffers, Margaret Bourke-White and Peter Stackpole, and is made uneven by the inevitable differences in their ways of looking at things. Billings took advantage of those differences by using them to impart pace — one unexpected visual jump after another.

That story really is a sixteen-page cram course in everything one should know about Czechoslovakia. Billings assumed the reader knew nothing, and then proceeded to tell him a great deal. The opening spread is followed by a crudely drawn but informative map. Then comes a spread on political rallies, livened by three pictures of a woman selling sausages. Next a spread on the living conditions of the Sudeten Germans. Then one that is pure Billings: four large pictures that have nothing whatsoever in common, except that by the use of clever headlines they are related. And so on — through the Czech munitions industry, its peoples, its history and culture.

Later editors of *Life* would have scorned to do such a story — I should say: scorned to do it in that headlong, scrappy, unvarnished way. The layouts are not tasteful. There are jarring differences in the scale of some of the photographs, many of which are disfigured by having ugly headlines pasted on them like labels. Nevertheless it has great power. For all its crudity it is a wonderful story, with a kind of jumping vitality, and stuffed with information. The reader, finishing it, could certainly have said: "I know what I need to know about Czechoslovakia. I also know what it and its leaders look like."

Why bother to describe this story in such detail? Indeed, why bother with all the other stories in the issue? Because

in it, and in them, are revealed so many of the devices and attitudes, the growing appreciation of what can be done with pictures, that were gradually refining and fusing themselves into what would become the classic *Life* photo essay. The Czechoslovakia story was an essay in transition. If it had been done ten years later it almost certainly would have been slanted more self-consciously toward news, and printed boldly and baldly in the news section at the front of the magazine. Billings's genius, and his limitation, was that he did not distinguish as clearly as later editors would between news and features, between the informative and the essentially decorative, between the timely and the timeless. Almost everything he used was timely, or bent by him to become timely. In one way or another it reflected what was going on in the world around him, what people were talking about that week. Aesthetics, both in the pictures he used and in the way he used them, were secondary to impact, to his insistence that the reader be grabbed by the lapel and forced by the sheer power and inventiveness of an issue of *Life* to read it from cover to cover. Millions did.

What was invaluable to Billings in his remorseless progress through one set of pictures after another was an unrivaled memory, and the ability to assemble into coherent patterns in his head the elements of a photo essay as he went along. By the end of his first run-through of a set of pictures he usually had a pretty good idea already of what he would do with them. Each one registered on him, not only as an interesting photograph or a dull one, but also as a hastener or retarder of the story that was forming in his mind.

Carl Mydans, a *Life* staff photographer for many years, remembers a typical Billings virtuoso performance. Mydans and his wife had been caught at Bataan by the Japanese invasion at the start of World War II, and had spent a long time in Japanese prison camps before being freed by the recapture of the Philippines. Back in the United States, and his strength fairly well restored, Mydans was sent to California to photograph a story on Japanese internees at Tule Lake. Billings wanted to see the pictures immediately and refused even to let the news editor arrange them in proper order. He asked that Mydans be on hand to do any explaining that was necessary.

None was. Mydans remembers standing behind Billings, marveling at how he went through the set, methodically, silently, looking briefly at each picture, setting aside those that Mydans himself realized were the key pictures in the take. After going through them once, Billings pushed back his chair, congratulated Carl on a fine job, swept up the dozen he had selected, and said: "I'll use these. They'll make nine pages. Now, let's go to lunch and finish up when we get back."

Returning to the office, he asked Mydans if he had

9

omitted any pictures that Carl particularly liked.

"One," said Carl, "the one of the man playing the guitar."

"I remember it," said Billings. He riffled through the pile of rejects, found the picture, threw out another he had chosen, called in a layout man, and laid out the story in about a minute and a half.

Billings's preoccupation with pace and impact, and his practice of laying out all stories himself, relegated the designer to a distinctly secondary role. He had one, of course. Over the years he had several. But once the basic look of the magazine was set, its overall design module and type selection frozen, there was not much for designers to do. They functioned more as layout men than designers. They put together what Billings told them to and in the way he said. They contributed little themselves.

Billings was propelled by people and events. The incongruities of the world, its daily follies, guffaws, and disasters were what ignited him. A shy man, he met the world vicariously in pictures. He wanted to see and know everything, and pass on that seeing and knowing. Those elements, plus his insistence on a hard, driving story line, were, in my opinion, the enduring features that he bequeathed to the photo essay. He gave it thrust and coherence, he gave it visual wallop, and he gave it timeliness. He did not give it beauty, nor a frame in which photographic quality could be exhibited for its own sake. The latter — except in rare cases — he considered effete salon stuff, not relevant to the more robust, red-blooded world of photojournalism.

Billings was succeeded as managing editor of *Life* by Daniel Longwell, who had served throughout Billings's editorship as his principal idea man and energizer of all the departmental editors. Longwell was an Etna of ideas. He fizzed with them seven days a week. He made a peculiar and involuntary contribution to the photo essay. Many of his ideas were cloudy, or seemed so, for Longwell was a notably incoherent speaker. He was given to spouting out phrases, often single words that his listeners clung to desperately, trying to extract meaning from them. "Girls," he would say. "College girls. Got to be something there about college girls. Time to — Ivy. Shoes. Those new — uh —"

Such adjurations were often so vague as to appear almost useless. But they were surprisingly effective. The editor would go back to his office, shaking his head, wondering what he had been told to do. He would sit down and begin to chew over the subject of college girls. Without the constriction of too precise direction he was free to aim as high or as wide as he chose. An astonishing number of Longwell's fuzziest and most fragmentary suggestions ended up in the magazine as photo essays, many of them coming

from small news stories he had clipped from the daily papers; his pockets were always adrift in newspaper clippings. A good many of these stories were about high-school and college life. Others were about horse shows, society, and the entertainment world, for Longwell's mind was essentially that of an entertainer, not a thinker.

Longwell's function as an idea factory was of enormous importance to *Life* because his greatest influence was felt during World War II and in the year immediately following — a period when the grim challenge of covering the war and its aftermath was occupying so much of *Life*'s energies. Longwell kept the magazine lively and frothy, zipping in all directions. During 1945 alone *Life* published photo essays on the Waldorf-Astoria Hotel (Eisenstaedt), the Mohawk Valley (Ruohomaa), the University of Chicago (Myron Davis), Harry Truman's Missouri background (Eisenstaedt), the Charter of the United Nations (Mili), Neiman-Marcus (Nina Leen), the Missouri Valley Authority (Hans Wild), high fashion (Eileen Darby and Philippe Halsman), and a spate of stories on such subjects as teenage boys, high-school fads, and fan clubs. These were shot with a high degree of skill by able photographers and some of them contained memorable photographs, but they lacked the mark of greatness. I believe there are two reasons for this.

First, for all the yeastlike heaving of Longwell's mind, he lacked Billings's visual conviction. He was not a photojournalist at heart, but a stirrer-up of people and things. He considered himself a catalyst, the keeper of the country's pulse, quick to spot its moods, its tastes and frivolities. His role in determining what flowed over Billings's desk had been a pivotal one. But when he became managing editor he failed to put a stamp of his own on *Life*'s essays. They became ersatz Billings.

Second — and this was something that Longwell had no control over — was the growing competence of departmental editors. As they came to understand better and better the potential of the photo essay and began competing more and more aggressively for large space in the magazine, they began writing more ambitious and tighter and tighter shooting scripts. This tended to constrict the photographer, draining his energies into numerous "point" pictures that he was ordered to make, forcing him to think in terms of single photographs at the expense of the entire story. It was an unhealthy moment in the evolution of the photo essay, a time when the editor had almost too much to say about its shaping, a time when the designer had not yet begun to have enough to say. Moreover, high-school fan clubs, no matter how skillfully shot, were an irrelevancy when stacked up against Bastogne or Buchenwald. So were such staff-concocted ideas as showing in a single picture everything that a family of four ate in a year: so many hundred

quarts of milk, so many dozen steaks, so many cans of coffee, all arranged in a picture that took nearly a week to assemble. That story actually ran in *Life* and fascinated its readers, but it and the editorial thinking that produced it were not the spring from which great photo essays flowed.

Longwell recognized his limitations. He was uncomfortable carrying the multiple responsibilities of managing editor and accepted them with the understanding that they would be his on an interim basis while two younger men, Joseph Thorndike and Edward K. Thompson, were being considered for the job.

Thorndike got the nod. He was totally unlike Billings. He had come to *Life* directly from Harvard, and unless editorship of the *Harvard Crimson* can be considered a newspaper career, his experience in news journalism was nil. Unlike the beefy, extremely physical Billings, who took a Falstaffian delight in the pictorial shocks he was concocting, Thorndike was slender, quiet, and cool. He lacked the relentless sureness of Billings. He mulled things over, had second thoughts about how stories should be laid out. He sought other opinions. He could be argued with.

Under Billings, "no" had meant "no." An ambitious photo essay — perhaps one that a departmental editor, researcher, and photographer had labored over for months — would be set in front of him. He would flip through the stack of glossy prints, turning them deliberately with an enormous thumb, occasionally tossing one aside as ideas about how to lay out the story began to form in his head. The team responsible for the story would stand silently behind him in a small nervous group. I can recall a growing sense of dismay as Billings neared the bottom of a set of pictures I had prepared for him and failed to toss aside a single one. We all learned to put the best ones on top because Billings was not above turning away if he had flipped through half a dozen and seen nothing that interested him. He would push the rest aside unlooked-at and say: "What else have you got?" There was no reprieve, only a dreadful sinking sense of failure. So swift and sure were his judgments, so Jovian, that it was not for us to imagine that he was ever narrow-minded or guilty of bad judgment. Failure by him was unthinkable. By us it was chronic.

Thorndike listened. He always looked at all the pictures in a set, and patiently heard out the argument of the editor as to why it was a superior story. He was more interested in ideas than Billings, more interested in culture. He regarded *Life* as a vehicle for bringing culture to the masses. Under his editorship ambitious essays on art, religion, and cultural history began appearing in *Life*. Its tone became more elevated, although the cheesecake was still there. It was just made smoother and better looking: fewer press-agent shots of Miss Community Chest, and more staff-assigned stories on fashion or Hollywood starlets. In fact the entire magazine became better looking. Thorndike had a keener aesthetic sense than Billings and was determined to express it in more tasteful layouts, a greater variety and subtlety in type styles, more attention to white space. He began to clean *Life* up.

With these preoccupations the designer's importance began to grow. Charles Tudor, an artist and layout man who had worked more or less anonymously under Billings, began to play a larger role under Thorndike and ultimately emerged on the masthead as art director. He held that post for a number of years. As a result of his influence photo essays improved in appearance; *Life* as a whole began to look more polished.

Six people have now been identified as having a hand in shaping a *Life* photo essay: departmental editor, picture editor, photographer, negative editor, designer, and finally managing editor. The seventh person was the researcher, for it was he (actually, usually a she) who had to dig up most of the raw material for a story. If a decision was made to do an essay about a student nurse from a small town coming to the big city to work in one of its municipal hospitals, it was the researcher who had to start the wheels rolling to find a suitable subject, make sure the girl would consent to have her life anatomized, make sure she was pretty enough to satisfy the standards of the magazine, that she did indeed have interesting and varied hospital duties, also a life outside the hospital, and that there were no ugly secrets in the latter that might erupt embarrassingly after the story had been published. The researcher also had to go out on location with the photographer, make notes on all the pictures he was taking, getting down in her notebook names, dates, places, clothing, food, conversation, and a hundred other things, for the writer of the story would surely ask her for that information later on and she had to make sure that every picture was fully captioned. She had to help the photographer in the actual taking of his pictures, holding lights, smoothing clothes, finding objects — vases, chairs, pets, whatever he asked for — cajoling people, reassuring the person being photographed, persuading her to hold still for retakes, running out for sandwiches, hot drinks, cool drinks, supplying a handkerchief in case of tears, getting written releases to guard against the possibility of lawsuits for publishing unauthorized photographs. On and on. The researcher's duties were endless. Most *Life* photogaphers came to rely so heavily on researchers that they could scarcely work without them.

An eighth might be added to the aforementioned seven: the writer. But he should not be. All of the others had a hand, directly or indirectly, in the making or the selection of the photographs; the writer did not. He may have written his story brilliantly, but his contribution was mere glue. The beating heart of a photo essay is pictures. The writer plays no role visually. Therefore he is not a part of the process.

Thorndike's concept of how to run *Life* was markedly different from Billings's. Not only were his priorities and interests different — he was basically more interested in features than he was in news — but his method of getting what he wanted was different. Whereas Billings had insisted on looking at raw sets of photographs and making up his mind about how to lay them out, Thorndike delegated the actual laying-out of most feature stories to the departments that originated them.

The Thorndike approach aided the further development of the photo essay in two ways. It encouraged the departmental editor to think in photo-essay terms. It also gave him an opportunity to see his own pictorial ideas realized. Heretofore he had been a silent, often agonized, observer as an essay was being put together. Now his own creative flashes about how the pictures should be organized would have a chance. Again, the musical analogy returns. The editor with unlaid-out stories is as shackled as the composer with unperformed works. Each may have gorgeous ideas in his head. But if they get only as far as being musical notes on sheets of paper, or stacks of unorganized pictures on a shelf, they are nothing.

Thorndike's preference that he be shown laid-out stories brought into being many that under Billings would not have got past the thumb-flipping stage. It is true that many of these might have been better off left on the shelf. But the very act of making them, learning the hard way that it is impossible to create a good layout from a faulty set of

pictures, taught many departmental editors a great deal about what was really needed to get photo essays off the ground, something that Billings knew instinctively but that others had to learn: there must be dramatic photographs, but there must also be a story line, a way of building those photographs into an essay.

Free to make layouts, editors made many, and the work in the layout room expanded exponentially. Assistant designers were gradually added to the staff: Michael Phillips, Bernard Quint, David Stech, and, later, Robert Clive. Of these, Quint was the most innovative. His early work on *Life* had been limited to helping departmental editors lay out small feature stories, but he proved so skillful at this, so good at finding the appropriate picture to start a story off, so resourceful at dressing up even the most insignificant little items, that he inevitably found himself working on more ambitious projects. As Tudor, the art director, was drawn deeper into the multiple-issue cultural projects that Thorndike was bent on developing, Quint gradually became the man who laid out the single-issue photo essays. He brought formidable credentials to his job. He knew type. He knew a great deal about the history of design. He knew a great deal about photography and photographers. He understood what was needed in an incoherent mass of pictures to make sense out of them. He drew on all those resources to produce a flood of vivid, aesthetically pleasing and clear photo essays. I emphasize clear. A story that leaves the reader in any doubt along the way about what it is trying to say is a failure.

Quint's ways of achieving the effects he was after reflected an instinctive good taste bent to the needs of the moment by steps that were always logical and crystal clear to him but often not so to others. His instructions to the paste-up people in the layout room were detailed. Pictures were to be cropped exactly as indicated, not approximately. The positioning of a headline was precise: right here, as marked, not two millimeters to the left. To him, more than to anyone who had preceded him, essay design was an art form; he cared passionately about all those small details because they were the difference between something routine and something truly moving. Inasmuch as the bulk of the work that was flowing over the paste-up tables was cut-and-dried material that conformed to half a dozen familiar modules that were used over and over again, Quint's miniscule refinements often went unnoticed. Mistakes in paste-up enraged him. Inability to comprehend what he was trying to accomplish also enraged him. The scheme that he worked out for Smith's "Spanish Village" embodied layout devices that had not been tried on *Life* before, and he was enraged that neither Tudor nor Thompson seemed able to understand what he was doing. In that case he finally, and triumphantly, got his way. Creativity flowed from him as steadily as sap from a tree. He could be choking with anger at some insanity, and yet capable of tackling another taxing layout problem with all his energies intact. Perhaps the two went together, his temperamental outbursts a measure of his commitment. He was not the world's easiest designer to work with, but he was the most gifted I have ever met. He was not above pointing out to photographers their stupidities and omissions, and then explaining how he was going to circumvent them. This prompted Gjon Mili to say drily to him once: "Bernard, when you talk like that you convict yourself. You are a culprit. You cover up mistakes by making them look good."

Quint succeeded Tudor as art director of *Life* in 1961, a position he held until 1969. He is now a freelance designer. His influence on the evolution of the photo essay and on the look of much of the other material that went into *Life* was a profound one, and has never been properly acknowledged. This was partly because staffers worked anonymously at *Life*. The originator of a story did not get his name on it, nor did the designer. As time went on and as the photo essay continued to flower, not only as an art form being perfected right there in *Life* but also as a showplace for the talents of a growing group of truly gifted photographers, it became the practice to put the photographer's name on any photo essay that was considered outstanding enough to justify its getting a byline. That practice enhanced the glamour that had always attached itself to photographers. They were the bright stars of the show, the ones who traveled to far places, who met royalty and presidents and got their autographs (Alfred Eisenstaedt), who risked their necks in war and sometimes got killed, who actually landed on the ice at the North Pole (George Silk), who were imprisoned at Bataan (Carl Mydans), who disappeared for months at a time in Africa and came home with trunks full of primitive art (Eliot Elisofon), who dawdled in Hollywood with the world's most glamorous women (Bob Landry), who parachuted in midwinter into the front lines of Korea during a catastrophic marine retreat (David Douglas Duncan), who hobnobbed with Picasso, Dufy, Matisse, Pablo Casals, Isaac Stern, and a dozen other world-known painters and musicians (Gjon Mili), who could go anywhere and do anything, and leave subjects captivated with a mixture of broken English, broken French, broken Yiddish, broken Italian, broken German (the world's only Jewish Cossack, Dmitri Kessel).

The *Life* photographer was a celebrity in his own right, and, like an opera prima donna, was excused a certain amount of temperamental display. This was often harmless, sometimes comical, occasionally serious — as in the case of Eugene Smith, whose relations with *Life* became so strained that they broke, and Smith's career suffered as a result.

For all these reasons the *Life* photographer was con-stantly out front, highly visible, usually raising a cloud of dust wherever he was working. Margaret Bourke-White had the singleness of purpose and the self-assurance to get her bags routinely carried by brigadier generals whose commands she was visiting during World War II — occasionally by major generals. In 1949 Frank Lerner succeeded in having the Sistine Chapel in Rome closed down for several months while he photographed its ceiling in sections, working from a moving scaffolding that ran along a railroad track he had built on the floor — the only way to match the edges of the photographs exactly because the floor itself was uneven. His lights used so much current that they finally overloaded the Vatican electrical system, leaving the Pope in momentary darkness. In 1957 Peter Stackpole managed to divert an entire squadron of U.S. destroyers to help him search for the *Mayflower* replica ship that was somewhere west of Bermuda on its trip from England to the United States. Stackpole wanted pictures of the vessel at sea. He also had to pick up the take of another *Life* photographer, Gordon Tenney, who was on board, so that the pictures could be hurried to New York and published in the magazine on the day the ship landed at Plymouth. The Navy obliged him.

Balloons, oil tankers, football teams, factory shifts. All stood still or turned round for the *Life* photographer. His power and his visibility were at their height when public appreciation of photography as an art form began to grow. It was in the 1950s that a few enterprising galleries in New York began exhibiting the work of photographers, sometimes in groups, sometimes as one-man shows, following the lonely pioneering work of Alfred Stieglitz begun decades before. People began increasingly to collect photographs. Critic and collector alike started to look for the first time at certain *Life* photographers as artists rather than as mere journalists. A few of them began to slip over into the niche already occupied by "serious" photographers like Stieglitz, Edward Steichen, Ansel Adams, Edward Weston, Imogene Cunningham, and others.

That kind of recognition was some time in coming, as it also was in the case of fashion and advertising photographers. Both photojournalist and commercial photographer were considered tainted by having to do things on assignment for other people, rather than being free to hack out their own artistic trails, and tainted also for making money, sometimes in very large amounts. Nevertheless, recognition of sheer merit began to come, and with it an obsessive overconcentration on the photographer of photo essays at the expense of the designer. It was this climate of thought — the gradual public elevation of the *Life* photographer to the status of artist (on top of the glamorous figure he already cut) — that tended to obscure the collaborative nature of photo essays. That, I think, is why the work of

13

men like Bernard Quint has been underestimated to the point where, in some quarters, it is completely ignored. Underestimate if we must; after all, it *is* the photographer who takes the pictures and there could be no photo essay without him. Nevertheless the designer must be given his due. Those who will not give it to him, who direct their attention only to the photographic quality of the pictures in a photo essay, do not understand photo essays.

Quint came into his own during the editorship of Thorndike. Some of the most notable essays ever made were put together by him. That is not to say that Thorndike abdicated his own responsibility. Rather, he considered himself the polisher, the final arbiter. He felt that he could more quickly arrive at what should be done with an essay by putting his own critical faculties to work near the end of the process, and escape a good deal of unavoidable preliminary labor: sorting out the material so that a coherent story line is established; breaking down the pictures into groups that seem to fit themselves both logically and visually into separate double-page spreads; finding the right opener, one that will seize the reader and at the same time set the tone of the story and state unmistakably what it is about; identifying the real stoppers, the pictures whose effectiveness is so strong that they must be "played big"; finally finding the ender, another strong picture that winds the story up. Experienced photographers kept those needs in mind while they worked. They were always looking for openers, enders, double-trucks. The most experienced had it within them almost to dictate the shape of a layout by the kinds of pictures they took. But even they were sometimes frustrated to find their stories unfolding under the designer's hand in ways they had not imagined, with some of their surest bets either used small or not used at all. That could lead to fights, occasionally nasty ones.

An ambitious essay usually went through several transformations before it was ready to be presented to the managing editor. Certain spreads might be laid out two or three ways to see which looked best when photostats of the pictures had been reproduced to the proper scale and pasted to layout sheets the exact size of a double-spread in *Life*, along with captions, headlines, and text blocks of dummy type so that they looked exactly the way they would when published.

When an essay layout was completed it would be thumbtacked — spread by spread — to the cork-covered office wall of the managing editor, the alternate spreads also displayed above or below the others, which, in the case of an ambitious essay, might run along the wall for twenty feet or more. This all-in-one viewing was essential. There was no other way of evaluating a photo essay than by pasting it all up and then looking at it as a whole.

Thorndike worked over those pseudo-completed essays slowly and carefully. He would ask for the reject pictures and go through them. Sometimes he would leave an essay as it was. More often he would change it slightly, usually condensing it. Not only was competition for space in the magazine ferocious, but designers — even the best of them — tended to make essays too long. They were powerfully affected by photographs. They responded to them almost as strongly as their takers did, and were as reluctant to omit good ones. The most ambitious and complex takes tended to become unwieldy in layout. Occasionally this was deliberate. Knowing Thorndike's propensity for shortening, and feeling that a given story could not be properly told in under ten pages, a designer might lay it out for twelve or fourteen, with the expectation that it would be shortened to ten, and thus avoid the real blood-letting of being cut to eight. But that ploy was a dangerous one. Stretched too thin, a story would begin to look thin, and would wind up at the bottom of a pile of other essays waiting to be used. Most of the time, however, the best essays, laid out by the best designers, were made to what designers thought was the best length.

The pile of reserve photo essays was known as the essay bank. Sitting in the bank by no means spelled the death of a photo essay. All managing editors liked to have on hand a full bank on the widest possible variety of subjects. When I resigned from *Life* in 1955 there were between one hundred and two hundred photo essays in the bank. Some had been there for several years. One that I remember in particular was "British Coal." Henry Luce had the idea that the economic woes and political turmoil of a Britain emerging from a devastating war could be cured by improving the efficiency of the British coal industry by ten percent. But to explain that meant excursions into geology, machinery, the structure of the Labour Party, the class system in England, the rise of Japan and Germany — the subject was endless. One photographer after another broke his lance on "British Coal," and the layouts for that one essay became a bank in themselves.

Wide choice was important. Each week *Life* had two major features besides the photo essay: a big news story and a text article. If the managing editor had already decided that the text article would be on politics and knew that the news lead that week would probably be a story on the World Series, he would look for a photo essay as far removed from sports and politics as possible. He had to make his choice early in the week, on Monday or Tuesday, so that the essay could be written and closed, clearing the decks in the copy room, the layout room, and the typists' room for the flood of news stories that would hit them on Friday and Saturday. The presses, of course, had to be cleared too. *Life* was printed on special presses in Chicago. They printed nothing else. They were enormous, seeming

to me, the only time I visited them, to be a couple of blocks long. The amount of printed material that they spewed out was tremendous, and had to be coordinated with the collating and binding operations, the baling of magazines into bundles and loading them into trucks and freight cars so as not to cause jam-ups along the way. Those mammoth presses had to be kept operating more or less steadily, and that need was reflected back in New York by a schedule that called for the progressive closing of various parts of the magazine, beginning on Monday and continuing through Saturday night. The advertisements, particularly the color ones, would have been printed in advance.

The first thing the managing editor did when he came to work at the beginning of the week was to take a look at that week's mock-up, a long sheet of paper that, in effect, described the actual issue that he would be working on. The mock-up told him how many pages that week's magazine would have, where the advertisements fell, and where the open spaces for picture stories would be. The choice of a photo essay would depend, to a certain extent, on the actual size of the magazine. *Life* tried to maintain a balance between advertisements and editorial matter. Consequently, if a given issue had a large number of advertisements in it, the number of editorial pages would also be large. By adroit shuffling about of the advertisements, the editor could sometimes clear out an extra-large well of space to accommodate an overlong essay. But that shuffling was not always easy. Extra-large essays, by their very size, were much less likely to be used. That explains why most of those in this book are eight to ten pages long.

Moving advertisements around in the magazine was like playing with an ingenious and often intractable puzzle. *Life* was printed on separate large sheets of paper, on several presses simultaneously. Those sheets were then folded, trimmed, and gathered into sets of four, eight, sixteen, or thirty-two pages, depending on the size of the original sheet. Those sets of pages, or "forms," were then stacked one on top of another in proper sequence, the ones containing advertisements falling in here and there in assigned places, until an entire issue had been assembled. A cover was then added to the pile, the whole thing was fastened together down the center with three staples, folded double, and — presto, a copy of *Life*.

Reading matter that is put together that way, by dropping forms in one on top of another, is nothing more than a bunch of separate sheets of paper piled up and then folded together into a booklet. Obviously, the second sheet in the pile is going to have one of its halves as the second page in the booklet; the other half will be the next-to-last page. It was the same with *Life*. Move around some pages in the back of the magazine, and some pages in the front would also move.

A difficulty was that some ad pages could not be moved; they had been pre-sold by the advertising department on the guarantee that they would occupy certain preferred positions in the magazine. This occasionally caused unexpected problems in layout and essay selection. Consider the dilemma of the managing editor who was determined to use a photo essay on the poaching of big game in Africa, only to discover that his last picture, a powerful full-page stopper of some natives butchering a hippopotamus, fell opposite a four-color ketchup ad showing a man biting into a juicy hamburger. The advertiser would surely object to such a juxtaposition. If the ad could not be moved, and if the editor could not find a more acceptable closing picture, another essay would have to be substituted. Occasionally, through no fault of their own, worthy photo essays would be jettisoned three or four times. The freshness or shock appeal of their pictures would wear off, the layouts would get dog-eared, and enthusiasm for them would wither.

A final problem having to do with the ad mock-up was that some essays literally shouted to open on a two-page spread, and such an opening space was not always available. A shift would then have to be made to an essay that opened on a single right-hand page — or the essay would have to be laid out differently. What this book does not show — and cannot, because the originals have long since been lost — are the compromises in layout that were forced on the editor by the intractability of the mock-up.

Thorndike was skillful at reorganizing the ad mock-up of an issue to accommodate the stories he wanted to put into it, but he did not match Edward K. Thompson, who succeeded him as managing editor in 1949 after Thorndike had resigned in a dispute over editorial policy. Thompson was raised in a farming town in North Dakota, broke in as

15

a reporter on small local papers, then moved to Milwaukee as picture editor of the Milwaukee journal. During *Life*'s earliest days, when the staff was still small and still dependent on outsiders to supply it with material, Thompson moonlighted as a Milwaukee stringer for *Life*. He sent in so many pictures and picture-story ideas that he was hired and brought to New York by Wilson Hicks to serve as his assistant. He did not stay there long. Almost effortlessly he moved out from under and began working his way up the editorial ladder.

Thompson was a born photojournalist. A throwback to Billings, he had Billings's visceral approach to pictures, Billings's sense of newsiness, of timeliness, of immediacy and wallop. Unlike Billings, he inherited a magazine with a talented design staff in place, considerable sophistication in photo-essay techniques, a strong orientation toward in-depth features, and a growing willingness on the part of management to pay whatever it had to to get what it wanted, whether it was the memoirs of Churchill or Eisenhower, lavishly illustrated and printed serially over many issues, or, later, the exclusive rights to the stories of the astronauts and their wives, *Life*'s own inside look at the space program.

Thompson took full advantage of all that bounty. He was interested in nearly everything, possessed boundless energy and an almost indestructible physique. Unlike the superficially hearty but actually very private Billings, Thompson was unabashedly gregarious and sentimental. He cried easily. He got angry easily and recovered easily. He behaved outrageously at times and felt badly afterwards. He intimidated his staff and cosseted it. He abused it but was forgiving and indulgent. Working for him was like living on a roller coaster. He was a professional hick, a deliberate country hayseed contending with a lot of smooth Ivy League types. He took in some people with that, and with his innocent baby expression and his odd western hats, but he was actually an extremely knowing and sophisticated man, the best magazine editor I have ever encountered.

Thompson's way with *Life* was a blend of Billings and Thorndike. Like Billings, he was at his best when facing a large and taxing news challenge, one that involved a great many people, photographers sent to dozens of places, helicopters hired, portable photo labs set up, extra crews standing by for work all Saturday night and on into Sunday morning. Occasionally he would take an entire staff with him to Chicago for a late closing so that he could gain a day, working there all Sunday and on into Monday. The physical effects of those marathons were brutal to everybody else, but Thompson thrived on them.

For all the three-ring circus city-desk flavor of Thompson's regime, he retained Thorndike's interest in features

and his respect for good design. Tudor and Quint both flourished under Thompson and were given every opportunity to innovate with photo-essay ideas. They did it in two ways. First, they emphasized the aesthetic content of a set of pictures, by making essays that concentrated more and more strongly on establishing a mood rather than telling a story. Contrast Leonard McCombe's "Gwyned Filling" on page 51 (a "story" essay) with Alfred Eisenstaedt's portrait gallery of distinguished Britons on page 118 (a "mood" essay). McCombe's is one of the marvels of its kind. Nothing quite like it had ever been attempted before: a round-the-clock probe into the joys and sorrows of an obscure young girl who comes to the big city to make a start in life, a breakthrough combination of photographic virtuosity and psychological insight. Part of the essay's greatest skill is the subtlety with which the designer has used headlines and other layout devices to soft-pedal the photographic virtuosity and emphasize the story. The reader becomes so wholly absorbed by the latter that he does not really notice what wonderful pictures are being used to tell it. In the Eisenstaedt essay the reverse is true. A formal, measured layout is chosen, with small chaste headlines and discreet captions. Nothing is done to detract from the impact of the portraits themselves. The mood is brooding and still; those noble and thoughtful faces are what remain in the mind. There is no "story" at all.

Under Thompson mood was encouraged in a second way also, by the introduction of work by outside photographers who were not photojournalists. *Life* never became a gallery for the display of salon photography but it edged in that direction. During the 1950s it ran photo essays by such internationally known photographers as Ansel Adams, Henri Cartier-Bresson, and Dorothea Lange. Lange was a documentary photographer whose talents easily lent themselves to essay use; witness her marvelous story on Irish country life on page 167. But Adams was not. He was a one-shot man if there ever was one, taking infinite pains with every photograph he made, demanding of each picture that it stand on its own feet with no support from others. The meld of those disparate talents in the joint essay on page 155 is absolutely fascinating. Cartier-Bresson was something else again. He also expected his pictures to be complete in themselves, but they were more fleeting. In an extraordinary way he managed to mix timelessness and evanescence, glimpsing life as it flowed past all around him. He worked quietly and discreetly, waiting to catch the deepest essence of meaning in moments of exchange between people, of women thinking alone, of men going about their business, of children unaware that they are being watched. His work is candid photography carried to a pinnacle of refinement, "the decisive moment caught," as he put it. The magic of those decisive moments is that they can be sewn together into eloquent photo essays that glisten with perception, like the one on page 77.

Thompson went a step further. He was not above printing the work of photographers who did not have international reputations and on subjects that were wholly static, simply because he thought they were beautiful. The essay on architecture by Clarence John Laughlin on page 209 is a case in point. But that is about as close to salon photography as Thompson was willing to go, and he did not go there often. If a set of pictures held together in one way or another, if they satisfied the prime requirement that together they were greater than the sum of their parts, then they belonged in *Life*. If not, they didn't, and attempts to use them might draw an editor into dangerous ground, into a seductive field of snares where designers' ideas took over and became ends in themselves, turning the photographs they used into mere instruments for their personal aesthetic expression. More than one magazine has foundered because it has wound up being run by its art director and not by its editor.

Thompson was too much of a journalist to get lost in aesthetics. Most of the photo essays produced during his editorship were strongly story-oriented. But there was that increasingly large injection of mood, much of it expressed in color. New, fast four-color printing presses were being developed. Color photography began to play a larger and larger role in the thinking and planning of *Life*'s editors. Ultimately the most ambitious and innovative work of its best photographers was no longer being done in black-and-white. That is a wry paradox. At the moment when the photo essay reached its highest development in its purest form — black-and-white photography — it was beginning to drown in a wave of color.

Getting out *Life* was a killing business. Billings, a powerful and disciplined man, lasted just under ten years on the job. Thompson lasted a phenomenal twelve before moving up into an advisory post and turning the editorship over to George Hunt. Thompson's timing was perfect. He had run *Life* during its greatest days and had been responsible for much of its greatest success. He left before the pictorial overkill of television began to make *Life* irrelevant.

Hunt not only had a hard act to follow, but he had to do it at a hard time. From the beginning it had been clear that *Life* lived or died by photographs. Originally it had been oxygenated by the sheer novelty of photojournalism, later through increasingly ambitious and innovative exploitation of it. But a time came when the shine began to wear off. The public eye became so jaded from constant exposure to remarkable photographs that even the extraordinary pictures failed to excite. Ironically, advertising contributed to this. Advertising had floated *Life*, had paid for all those glittering editorial extravagances, had made so much money

that throwing away a hundred over-the-hill photo essays at one swoop during a periodic housecleaning of the essay bank was nothing more than an inconsequential financial write-off (except to those who had made the essays). Now advertising added to the photographic glut by appropriating many of *Life*'s own pictorial innovations. Advertisers had always used photography. Now they used it with a drum-rattle insistence. *Life*'s editors had to set up more and more stringent rules to restrain advertisers, to make sure the reader could tell what was an advertisement and what was not. The rules did not always work. I remember once on an airplane talking to a man who said, when he learned I was a *Life* editor:

"I sure do love those picture stories in *Life*. I look forward to them every week." Flattered, I asked him what were his favorites.

"The adventure ones."

"Adventure ones?"

"Yes. Those strange adventures. You have one every week — on the back cover."

I realized then that he was talking about a series of four-color Canadian Club whiskey advertisements, sickeningly corny ones that aped *Life*'s story-telling techniques and that we on *Life* were contemptuous of. What a comedown for the lofty editor. But it did hint at what was happening to the public eye.

As an editor moving with the times, Hunt took full advantage of the improved color capability of *Life*'s presses. The magazine had always used some color. Its editors were proud that from the earliest days they had been able to run four-color stories on art and on historical and scientific subjects. But the presses that made that color were small and slow. Anything printed on them had to be sent to Chicago far in advance of publication. In the late 1940s and early 1950s the lead time for closing a color story in *Life* was about seven weeks.

By the time of Hunt's accession that time gap had shrunk dramatically, and before his resignation in 1969 he was able to close large color stories on a current schedule — i.e., during the same week that the rest of the magazine went to press. That enabled him to indulge in such extravaganzas as hiring a Boeing jet and flying an entire crew of editors, photographers, layout men, and darkroom technicians to England to cover the funeral of Winston Churchill in color, and develop the pictures, lay out the story, and write it on the flight back to New York. In old-fashioned picture-journalistic terms this was a fantastic coup: printing an ambitious news story in color and distributing it nationwide the week it happened. Ironically, though it impressed professionals, its impact on a jaded public was nothing compared to the impact made by earlier less ambitious black-and-white issues of *Life*.

Hunt was a painter of considerable skill and he was visually oriented, perhaps as strongly as any editor of *Life* had been. He responded particularly keenly to color, and the color revolution in printing suited him admirably. He reveled in it. He liked his color pictures big and he liked them bold. Moreover, they helped him cope with several interlocking and ominous problems that were threatening *Life*. One was that large color advertisements had become so blatant that strong injections of editorial color were needed to offset them. Another was that color was beginning to appear in better quality and with increasing frequency in other publications: *Life* felt it had to keep ahead of them. A third was television. TV was already riveting the public eye in the way *Life* once had, but it was still largely a black-and-white medium. A color-filled *Life* could supply something that TV could not.

Hunt used a great deal of editorial color, and he used it with great skill. Some of the best photo essays he published were in color. Unfortunately they cannot be shown here, in a book that is confined to black-and-white. That exclusion does not trouble me, since my own preference is for black-and-white essays. The two are quite different, the difference going beyond the mere addition of tints to photographs. Color essays require different thinking on the part of the photographer and different treatment in layout by the editor. I cannot explain the end effect on me of those differences. I can only register it. Black-and-white essays touch me deeply in ways that color essays do not. The former are for me an art form. The latter, too often, are just collections of photographs. Part of the trouble, I believe, lies in printing. A black-and-white photograph, reproduced with care, can come quite close in richness and subtlety to the original. A color photograph, printed in a magazine, is a sorry substitute for the brilliant transparency from which it was made. Anyone who takes color transparencies — and I do — will have difficulty being satisfied with their reproduction on paper.

George Hunt's stature as an editor of *Life* cannot be properly evaluated without color; nor can that of his successor, Ralph Graves. More serious is the exclusion of the work of certain photographers. Some of the most gifted who ever worked for *Life* are not represented here. For several, that is because they were specialists in news photography. For others, the nature of the subjects assigned them did not have the stuff of great photo essays. An example would be fashions. Philippe Halsman made dozens of essays on fashion, using beautiful models and producing luscious photographs, but their subject matter is too vapid to qualify them for greatness. Most staffers were extremely versatile and their work, on all kinds of subjects, appeared in all parts of the magazine. It does not appear here because the best of it — after about 1960 — was in color. That

eliminates a huge chunk of Gjon Mili's finest work. Nothing of his is in this book. Nor is anything by Dmitri Kessel. Both men were devoting more and more of their time to culture, to its reflection in painting, architecture, and sculpture; those subjects are best photographed in color; painting, obviously, cannot be literally reproduced any other way. The careers of men like Mili and Kessel, and others like Carl Mydans, were inextricably bound up with *Life*, to whose success they made incalculable contributions. Other notable talents like Eliot Elisofon and Alfred Eisenstaedt are represented by one photo essay each; they made scores. Larry Burrows, a superlative photographer who was killed in Vietnam, is not represented. There are equally painful omissions: Tom McAvoy, Edward Clark, Ralph Crane, Loomis Dean, David Douglas Duncan, Andreas Feininger, Fritz Goro, John Dominis, Nina Leen, Yale Joel, Ralph Morse, Peter Stackpole, Gordon Parks, Mark Kauffmann, John Phillips, to name a few. Hard choices.

As the grip of TV on the public consciousness strengthened, *Life* began to sicken. Advertising, which had once been a visual problem, now began to be a financial problem. It dried up. Before the advent of TV, national consumer advertisers had nowhere to show their wares — well printed, well laid-out, enticingly described — except in national magazines. Now there was an alternative that spoke and moved, and advertisers deserted the magazines in droves. *Colliers*, at the moment it had achieved the largest circulation in its history, went bankrupt. *The Saturday Evening Post* staggered on for several years, draining its parent corporation, the Curtis Publishing Company, of almost every drop of financial blood, and then went under. *Look* followed shortly after. That left *Life*, the last and largest and most successful of the great general-interest dinosaurs.

Loss of advertising began to be a serious problem during Hunt's editorship. It was interpreted by some as reflecting a decline in the freshness and vigor of *Life*, by others as a signal that the very concept of a national picture magazine was no longer a valid one. Everything, it was said, had been done. That is not so. A run-through of the issues published during the middle and late 1960s will reveal an enormous amount of ingenuity and originality in its news coverage and in the creation of a stream of interesting photo essays. Nevertheless the criticism was there — in the company's balance sheet — and Hunt struggled courageously with it. Despite his own predilection for pictures he became persuaded that *Life* would have to become a weightier publication, one that readers would not so much skim through as linger over. The way to slow the reader down, of course, is to decrease the emphasis on photographs and increase the emphasis on text. Hunt became interested in

investigative reporting. Long articles about political corruption in New Jersey and about the Mafia began to appear. There were even assaults on the photo essay itself.

In 1966 *Life* put together an after-the-fact story on the murder of a Kansas farming family by two young drifters. The news peg was the publication of Truman Capote's *In Cold Blood*, a detailed account of the murder, its effect on the community, finally the catching and eventual conviction of the killers. It was a grisly and enthralling story. *Life* covered it by dispatching Richard Avedon (shades of Wilson Hicks and his capricious assignments; Avedon was a prominent fashion photographer) to Holcomb, Kansas, to photograph its citizens, the courthouse, and other elements that provided the background for Capote's book. To slow the story down and give it depth, long columns of text were printed with it, and a follow-up article by a *Life* staffer, Jane Howard, on how Capote came to write the book and why it took him six years to do so. For sheer interest, combined with the shock value of Avedon's portraits of the principals, this story is hard to beat, and certainly justifies the text-and-picture blend that Hunt was seeking. But it is not a photo essay. It is an illustrated article. It has three good pictures, one of Capote, and one each of the two murderers. The rest is filler. A decade earlier all the stops would have been pulled out to make this a true photo essay. That is not to say that it would have been any better, only that the top editorial management was having serious doubts about the validity of *Life*'s original premise: to see.

Hunt's efforts did not succeed. Despite riveting coverage of the Vietnam war (so much better in *Life* than what was being served up by television that the comparison each week was embarrassing), despite the excitement and turmoil caused by the campus revolution of the late 1960s, *Life* continued to bleed. In 1969 Hunt relinquished the managing editorship. He was succeeded by Ralph Graves, whose entire professional career had been spent on *Life* in a wide variety of editorial posts, and who probably was better prepared for the job professionally than any of his predecessors. Graves was an outstanding editor, tough-minded, pictorially innovative. In a different climate he could have become one of *Life*'s greatest.

Graves abruptly turned the emphasis of *Life* around again. It was a picture magazine, he said, and would have

to live as one. He did some brilliant things during the two years he was in charge, but he was presiding over a wake. The annual deficits grew enormous. Some of the last issues of *Life* were pathetically thin; they had almost no advertisements in them at all.

I have commented on the visual problem created by too many advertisements during the big fat days of the 1950s and early 1960s. Lack of advertising also presents a problem. It cuts down on the number of permitted editorial pages, sentencing the editor to some hard choices. With very little space provided him, will he attempt to achieve variety and pace with a number of short, shallow stories, or will he shoot for impact and depth with only a couple of more ambitious efforts? One way that a larger, healthier *Life* had captured and held a wide audience was by offering such a generous mixture of stories that almost anybody could find something that interested him in every issue. That luxury was denied Graves. At the end *Life* seemed skimpy and starved.

Graves also had to deal with the political turmoil and antiestablishmentarian campus attitudes of the late 1960s and early 1970s. That problem is too complex to get into here, but it hastened the inevitable for what was perceived by a whole generation of young people to be an establishment monument. In December 1972 an announcement went out to staffers that publication was being suspended.

That announcement turned out to be news of worldwide interest. I happened to be in Africa at the time. I had been on a six-week camping trip, and the first thing I did on returning to Nairobi was to buy a paper to catch up on what had been going on in the world during those six weeks. The lead story in the Nairobi paper was that *Life* had perished. What a shock. All of us who worked on *Life* remember, just as everybody else does about Pearl Harbor, exactly where he was and what he was doing when he got the news. I got it in the lobby of the Norfolk Hotel.

Life was published for just over thirty-six years. Between November 23, 1936, and December 29, 1972, and including a few special year-end issues, more than eighteen hundred numbers of the magazine were produced. Each had a photo essay in it, some had two. Others had photo essays labeled as news stories. The total runs to about two

19

thousand. Arbitrarily choosing from that enormous stock can never do justice to the range of talent it contains.

But it can do a few things. It can reflect the changes in attitude that took place over the years as to what a photo essay should be. It can reflect a greater and greater latitude in the kinds of subjects covered, and in the diversity of photographic talents that produced them. It can trace a gradual swing away from emphasis on news. It can reflect the growing weight of the designer's hand in the layout of an essay, and with that an increasing respect for the photographs as photographs.

There, if anywhere, I believe, lies the most significant element in the evolution of the photo essay: the emergence of a true partnership among editor, photographer, and designer. At the beginning the photographer, no matter how gifted or what his virtuosity, was a creature of the editor. Like the court musician commanded to produce occasional compositions for his patron, the photographer produced pictures on order. The editor used them for entertainments of his own, to tease, delight, shock, inform — with wild shapes and juxtapositions — counting on his own ingenuity and daring to exploit the photographs to their utmost. It was the editor's ideas behind the pictures that held them all together and turned them into essays. Gradually designers tamed this rip-snorting tendency. Essays became smoother, layouts less cluttered. It had been recognized from the beginning, of course, that a big picture on a page is more compelling than a small one. Certain pictures had always been played big for their sock. But their sock had often been diluted by their having been surrounded by smaller point pictures to make the story busy and informative. Respectful of the quality of the photographs they were working with, designers gradually began making pictures larger and larger.

These tendencies, with some interesting exceptions, are identifiable in the essays selected for this volume. So are the elements that appear to be common to all great essays. If any of the examples included here lacks one, it will possess most or all of the others: photographs that individually are arresting enough to stand by themselves but which interact with each other to make larger statements; something original in the point of view or the technique of the photographer; psychological insight on the photographer's part, clearly expressed in his pictures; a strong story line or a strong mood or, best of all, both; a layout approach that is sensitive to the above elements and exploits them.

Despite what I have said about the team effort that was responsible for *Life* photo essays, in the last analysis all gets back to the photographer. Editors and designers can make superb essays out of good photographs and they can make poor ones out of superb photographs, but they can make only mush out of poor photographs. Two or three arresting shots do not a great photo essay make — although it was attempted often enough. The pages of *Life* are full of examples of this: failed assignments rescued by just enough striking pictures so that an acceptable layout can be arrived at by playing the best ones very big. That often salvaged essays but never made memorable ones.

Those selected here have none of that thinness. The pictures in them are uniformly interesting — whether technically, informationally, or aesthetically — even the small ones. And the test is to blow up some of those small ones to see how they would look played big. For the restless-fingered, it is an interesting exercise to rearrange the photographs on a given spread, or even on a series of spreads, and try to find a better design. If all the pictures are strong (as they are in Eugene Smith's "Spanish Village," for example), good substitute layouts will be easy. It is astonishing how many valid changes can be rung on a set of half a dozen photographs. Whether the new layout will be better than the old — well, that will be a matter of opinion. It is there that the whole business of making photo essays is so enthralling. There are no final judgments.

Photographs being the basic ingredient, it is also interesting to consider what kinds of photographs — or, rather, what kinds of photographers working on what kinds of subjects — made the finest essays. As I have already indicated, subject matter inhibited many. A Halsman can make beautiful set pieces out of fashion assignments. He can make arresting covers (he made 101, many more than any other photographer). A Fritz Goro can solve extraordinary technical problems in his efforts to make scientific processes visible, dreaming up ways of showing things that nobody has thought of before. Both men contributed mightily to *Life* but they did not produce memorable essays because their material was wrong. Looking at the photo essay from a distance, starting one's selection by snatching the easy ones, those that stand out in the memory as great even before any attempt is made to define greatness, one realizes rather quickly that the greatest photo essays have to do with people: with human dilemmas; with human challenges; with human danger or suffering; with the places that humans can return to as part of their own experience, whether it be the streets of New York or a winter night in Maine — where memory lives. The view can be as narrow and intense as the problem of one old lady without a home of her own. It can be as sweeping as a series of aerial views of the United States. So long as we can recognize it as an extension of ourselves, as something we feel, remember, long for, agonize over, laugh at, it can qualify as a great essay. If the pictures measure up and if the designer has not failed, it will be one.

Of the great ones, the greatest, in my view, tell stories. And they do it with a personal involvement that shines out of the layout, that transcends technique. Smith's "Country Doctor" is such a story. Cornell Capa's on the homeless old lady is another. Leonard McCombe's on an adopted boy is another. Those, for me, are the essence of what photographic essays should be. And they are the most difficult to bring off. They require the most patience; the most tact; the deepest psychological insight; the Cartier-Bresson quickness to seize the decisive moment, motor quickness to freeze action, intuitive quickness to catch emotion. Most important of all, they require sustained creative involvement. The photographer who cannot keep himself "up" day after day on a complex story cannot succeed with it.

Such essays are also the hardest to lay out. Unless the designer is responsive to the particular flavor of the interplay between photographer and subject, the delicate bond that has been forged between a person living and a person recording that living — and those bonds are not always the same; sometimes they are forged by discretion and self-effacement, sometimes by intrusion — if the designer is not sensitive to these things, and to the underlying vision that propelled the photographer from the beginning, he will have failed him. When he does not, when all the elements fuse, the rewards are the greatest.

But think how sated the audience would have become if *Life* had fed it a "Country Doctor" every week. Variety was the spice of *Life*, and that need for variety compelled the spurts in all directions that make up the balance of this book. There is not a weak essay in it. There is not one that did not have half a dozen others shouting for substitution. It may be argued that there is too much Smith and too much McCombe. I do not think so; they are the men whose talents were most suited to the creation of essays. Furthermore, Smith's "Country Doctor" is, in its conception and its execution, a world apart from his "Spanish Village." Both are light years away from his "Drama beneath a City Window." Others may prefer other stories: Eppridge's on drug addiction, Silk's "Olympics," Loengard's "Shakers." All are magnificent. Still, and for all that variety, I find it appropriate that the book closes with a "story" essay, one by the subtlest and tenderest of all essay makers: Leonard McCombe.

Franklin Roosevelt Has a Wild West

November 23, 1936
Photographer: Margaret Bourke-White
Designers: Henry R. Luce, Ralph Ingersoll

This is the first photo essay that *Life* ever published; indeed I believe it to be the first true photo essay ever published anywhere. More modest efforts had been attempted in European picture magazines, but no editor previously had tried to master a large subject with a comprehensive take by a single photographer, using enough pictures to tell an ambitious several-threaded story. This one appeared in Volume 1, Number 1, of the magazine. It shows a powerful talent struggling to express itself.

When she photographed the boom towns in and around Fort Peck, Montana, Bourke-White was thirty-three years old. She already had a solid reputation as an architectural photographer, and was well known to *Life*'s editors for work she had done for their sister publication *Fortune*. Her architectural photographs were made mostly with Linhof view cameras, and she surely used one for the picture of Fort Peck Dam which was put on the cover of *Life*'s first issue. Whether she used it or a smaller 3 × 5 English Soho camera for the rest of the story is not now known. What is certain is that it was a view camera of some kind. She did not use a Rolleiflex because she did not like its square format. And at that time she had not yet been introduced to 35mm cameras. So, burdened with film packs and non-candid cameras, she boldly took on what was essentially a candid story, a look behind Fort Peck to see what was going on in the shacks and honkytonks nearby.

Bourke-White was an extraordinary woman. She was strikingly beautiful in a hawklike way, with strong cheekbones, a high color, piercing blue eyes, and prematurely white hair. She had a consuming energy and was a ferocious worker. Her manner was infectious and enthusiastic, concealing an iron will. She could also be imperious. That trait, rather than getting up the backs of the people she so often ordered around to compose pictures, elicited swift cooperation. I think it was because she was so sure of herself, never even pausing to consider that she might not get her way, that she so often did.

Excluding one aerial photograph (a specialty at which Bourke-White excelled) all the other pictures in the essay are of two kinds. One is outdoor shots, some of which use people, some of which use buildings, to make their statements. The other (and the most interesting and numerous) is posed indoor shots taken with the aid of flash. There is a peculiar quality to these pictures. They have an intensity that comes out of an extreme self-consciousness. Dancers pause and stare at the camera; they are almost arranged. A girl hoists a shot glass and gazes off into the middle distance. Two drifters toast each other with drinks and, in so doing, frame a bartender. These are supposed to be candid pictures but they miss. Their effect is of another kind: the imposition of a photographic will on situations, and it may have resulted from the slow bulky equipment she was using. Whatever the reason, the presence of the photographer is very strong. It would take Bourke-White a while to learn to efface herself.

The layout, in this first essay attempt, has the direct raw power that would characterize much of the early work in *Life*. The essay opens with a then-startling sordid shot of taxi dancers and their dates for the evening. It sets the tone of the story instantly. The next sets the scene, an air view of an endless Montana plain with a shantytown in the foreground. Then the camera moves in closer for a street's-eye view of the town. Then it moves closer yet, inside the bars. The final spread is a ripsnorter, perilously close, of people crowded against a bar. This is Billings's contribution. He has laid out two nearly identical pictures so that they look like one, slanting them up boldly across the spread, giving it an immense whoop of action. These are the two strongest pictures in the Bourke-White take and certainly the most unself-conscious (it is late and noisy and although she is right behind the bar now many of the customers are no longer paying any attention to her). The wistful child sitting on the bar makes these pictures the most poignant also. Billings's use of them both was a stroke of genius. The repetition of the figures — and their slight differences — gives an added punch to each.

This essay has a flavor that is characteristic of all of *Life*'s early stories: it is extremely timely. It is actually a news story, with none of the self-containment that would characterize later and purer photo essays. The text blocks are of odd shapes or an awkwardly wide measure. The headlines fall any old place. But the overall effect of the story is tremendous. It has a structural unity that ordinary news stories told in pictures so often lack — that relentless moving in, closer and closer. The final snap was applied by Billings. He could not have learned that from anybody. It was in him.

10,000 MONTANA RELIEF WORKERS MAKE WHOOPEE ON SATURDAY NIGHT

THE frontier has returned to the cow country. But not with cows. In the shanty towns which have grown up around the great U. S. work-relief project at Fort Peck, Montana, there are neither long-horns nor lariats. But there is about everything else the West once knew with the exception of the two-gun shootings; the bad men of the shanty towns are the modern gangster type of gun-waver. The saloons are as wide open as the old Bull's Head at Abilene. The drinks are as raw as they ever were at Uncle Ben Dowell's. If the hombres aren't as tough as Billy the Kid they are

tough enough—particularly on pay day. Even the dancing has the old Cheyenne flavor. These taxi-dancers with the chuffed and dusty shoes lope around with their fares in something half way between the old barroom stomp and the lackadaisical stroll of the college boys at Roseland. They will lope all night for a nickel a number. Pay is on the rebate system. The fare buys his lady a five cent beer for a dime. She drinks the beer and the management refunds the nickel. If she can hold sixty beers she makes three dollars—and frequently she does.

THE LAW TOTES A GUN

In the Wild West town of Wheeler,* near Fort Peck, Montana, Frank Breznik (*Left*) is the law. He used to be a traveling salesman in Atlantic City. His pals are Realtor Walt Wilson and Publisher Jerry Reinertson.

FRANKLIN ROOSEVELT HAS A WILD WEST

AND you are looking at it in the photographs on these nine pages. It is about as wild and about as far west as the Wild West which Franklin's cousin Theodore saw in the Eighties. Its shack towns, of which you see one opposite. are as wide open and as rickety as git-up-and-git or Hell's Delight. The only real difference is that Theodore's frontier was the natural result of the Great Trek to the Pacific, whereas Franklin's is the natural result of $110,000,000.

The $110,000,000 is being spent on a work-relief project in Northeastern Montana. The project is an earthen dam—the world's largest —2,000 miles up the Missouri from St. Louis. The dam is intended to give work to Montana's unemployed and incidentally to promote the carriage of commerce on the Missouri. Whether or not it will promote the carriage of commerce is a question, but as a work maker it is a spectacular success. It has paid wages to as many as 10,000 veterans, parched farmers and plain unemployed parents at a time.

That it has also provided extracurricular work for a shack-town population of barkeeps, quack doctors, hash dispensers, radio mechanics, filling station operators and light-roving ladies is partly the army's fault. Army engineers, loaded with a project they didn't want and hadn't recommended, resolved to put it through on a strictly business basis. They built a decent town for their workers called Fort Peck City, fully equipped with dormitories, hospital, sanitary equipment, etc., but they provided quarters only for the workers —not for all their families. For those quarters they charged rents which left the married worker without enough margin to support a second home for his family somewhere else. Consequently, to keep his family housed and to dig himself in for the winter freeze, the married worker and his friends moved a few miles off the reservation and built the shanty towns you see here.

There are six of them, short on sanitation, long on bars and only restrained by the kind of law you see at the top of this page. Wheeler, Montana, has 3,500 inhabitants and 65 small businesses of one kind or another—mostly another. A second is hopefully named New Deal. A third is Delano Heights. A few miles away are Square Deal, Park Grove and Wilson. The Red Light suburb is Happy Hollow. Margaret Bourke-White's pictures enable you to observe at close range the labors and diversions of their inhabitants.

*SEE IF YOU CAN FIND THE MOOSE ABOVE IN THE MAIN STREET PICTURE ON THE RIGHT. (ANS: FOURTH BUILDING FROM RIGHT, FACING YOU.)

THIS IS WHEELER, MONT

OF THE SIX FRONTIER TOWNS AROUND FORT PECK IN MR. ROOSEVELT'S NEW WILD WEST.

THE COW TOWNS THAT GET . .

A relief project started the new Wild West. But you don't need a government loan to build a house there. For $2 a month you can rent a fifty foot lot in Wheeler from Joe Frazier, the barber over in Glasgow, 20 miles away. Joe had the fool luck to homestead the worthless land on which shanty towns have sprouted. You then haul in a load of grocer's boxes, tin cans, crazy doors and building paper and knock your shack together. That will set you back $40 to $75 more. You then try to live in it in weather which can hit minus 50° one way and plus 110° the other.

THE NEW WEST'S NEW HOTSPOT IS A TOWN CALLED "NEW DEAL"

THE ONLY IDLE BEDSPRINGS IN "NEW DEAL" ARE THE BROKEN ONES.

. THEIR MILK FROM KEGS

Water in the cities of the new Wild West comes from wells, many of them shallow, some condemned—and at that it may cost you a cent a gallon. Sewage disposal is by the Chic Sale system. Compulsory typhoid inoculation is non-existent. Fires are frequent—Wheeler has had 20 more or less this year. Nevertheless the workers here refuse to move to the Army's sanitary barracks. Life in barracks is too expensive; life in the shanty towns too gay. When the Army tried compulsion they wrote to Montana's Senator Wheeler for whom their metropolis was named. They won.

UNCLE SAM TAKES CARE OF THE INDIANS: THE LITTLE LADY, HERSELF.

LIFE IN THE COWLESS COW TOWNS IS LUSH BUT NOT CHEAP.

THE TIN CITY RODEOS . . .

LT. COL. T. B. LARKIN IS BOSS

COMPETITION between hot spots in the shanty towns of the 1936 Wild West is as keen as it is in New York. Ruby Smith's place (*below*) is an old favorite which has held up. Ed's Place (*opposite*) is slipping. Some say the customers are turning against Ed's murals. But Ed is faithful to them. He boasts that the painter, one Joe Breckinridge, averaged only twenty minutes a panel. Bar X (*below*) is almost as popular as Ruby's. Bar X is more dance hall than bar but that doesn't prevent the customers from drinking, or the taxi-dancers either.

BAR X

RUBY'S PLACE

This is the beer bar. The only drink you can legally sell by the glass in Montana is beer and you mustn't sell that to Indians. For the heavy liquor the customers go to another bar behind. It's merely a formality. The back bar is just as open.

ONE-FOURTH OF THE MISSOURI

This apparatus goes into one of the four diversion tunnels which will ca river around Fort Peck dam during construction, will later control rel water. With sections in place, the steel spider web will be removed. Theore

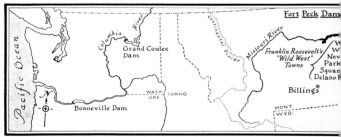

THE NEW FRONTIER TOWNS AROUND THE FORT PECK DAM PRO

. . . RUN ALL NIGHT

LIFE in Montana's No. 1 relief project is one long jamboree slightly joggled by pay day. One of its shanty towns has 16 all night whooperies. The workers are on night shift as well as day with the result that there is always someone yelling for a whiskey or calling on the little ladies of Happy Hollow. College boys mingle with bums in the crowds. Bill Stender, at the bottom of the page, is a Texas U. footballer who bounces for Ruby Smith. He hopes to get to be a football coach when he graduates but he is studying history and engineering just in case.

MAJOR CLARK KITTRELL IS No. 2

RUN THROUGH THIS STEEL "LINER"

ief workers at Fort Peck are building things like diversion tunnels. y they are building Wheeler and New Deal and the rest of the relief- towns.

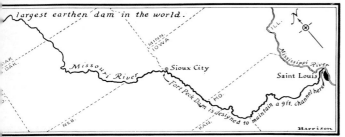

275 MILES BY ROAD FROM BILLINGS, MONTANA

ED'S PLACE

RUBY HERSELF

Ruby, second from the left is the founder of the town of Wheeler—and its rich woman. What she learned in the Klondike she has turned to good account. Bill Stender of Texas U. (the big fellow above) is keeping in condition as her bouncer.

29

MONTANA SATURD

THE pioneer mother can trek in broken-down Fords as well as in covered wagons. And she can crack her hands in the alkali water of 1936 as quickly as in the alkali water of 1849. When the Fort Peck project opened in 1933 the roads of Montana began to rattle with second-hand cars full of children, chairs, mattresses and tired women. Most of them kept right on rattling toward some other hopeless hope. Some of them parked in the shanty towns around Fort Peck. There, their women passengers got jobs like Mrs. Nelson (*right*) who washes New Deal without running water, or tried their feet at taxi-dancing like the girls on the preceding pages, or made money like Ruby Smith on page 15, or gave birth to children in zero weather in a crowded 8 by 16-foot shack like many an unnamed woman of New Deal and Wheeler. The girl at the bar (*above*) who works as a waitress ("hasher") takes her child to work with her because she can't leave her at home. She sits on the bar while her mother kids with the customers. The group on the right, it will be noticed, resembles a statue recently erected to the Pioneer Mother of the old frontier. No statues are expected at New Deal.

GHTS: FINIS

A Woman Photographs the Face of a Changing City

January 3, 1938
Photographer: Berenice Abbott
Designer: John S. Billings

One of Billings's strongest assets as a magazine editor was that he was quick to break his own rules. Steeped in news, and having assembled a staff of virtuoso photojournalists who were flooding the office with interesting stories, Billings nevertheless stepped out boldly from the conventional *Life* orbit whenever his eye was arrested by something or his history-oriented mind triggered.

Both responded when he was shown a set of photographs of New York City by Berenice Abbott. New York was changing rapidly. The mansions along Fifth Avenue were disappearing. The elevated railroad lines that threaded the city were being torn down piece by piece. New skyscrapers were shooting up all over the place. Abbott nailed down that moment of change, one foot in the brownstone past, one in the aluminum future, with a series of stunning pictures.

With respect to layout, the essay could not be simpler. The opening page is as plain as a sidewalk. Its headline is small, and in the narrow bald type that *Life* had adopted from the first as its trademark. It states the story's message bluntly. No coyness. Billings wanted the reader to know immediately what he was looking at. And if he was going to display a portfolio of static city views he wanted the reader to know right away who took them. So he inserted a headshot of the photographer, rather an odd one of a serious-faced woman wearing a wool cap. The text that explains the story is in the eye-breaking small type that *Life* used for such purposes, and is awkwardly wrapped around Abbott's face.

All that in place, Billings let the pictures tell their own story thereafter. For dignity, and to separate them, he framed them in white space. A discreet one-line caption describes each. His only further contribution is juxtaposition: the old against the new, the close against the far, the large against the small.

Abbott, of course, is a fantastic photographer. Born in Springfield, Ohio, she is part of that rich stream of midcontinental artists and writers that has poured out of American small towns and off its farms for generations. She first began working as a serious photographer in Europe, but after a few years returned to the United States. She settled in New York in 1935, and with the help of small grants from the WPA and the Museum of the City of New York, she was able to live while she addressed herself to the immense challenge of capturing a moment of transition in a huge and diverse city.

It is the city itself that she is after in these pictures; never mind its citizens. In that first shot of three city mansions, her emphasis is made clear. The only two people in it are small, black and unrecognizable. The nearer man even has his head and feet obliterated as if to further shrink him against the facades of the buildings, their architectural details brought forward by the strength of the shadows. Nothing is allowed to interfere with those three blank stone faces. Even man's busiest and most obtrusive artifact, the automobile, is still and subdued. A truck is motionless at the right, a parked car barely manages to edge its nose into the picture from the left. Everything — dark sidewalk, pointing shadows from left and right — aims the eye at three buildings.

Abbott's second picture tells her entire story in one photograph. Again men and automobiles are nothing, dark blurs at the bottom. The eye moves up through the interstices of the old El structure, a monument to the past, toward the distant towers of the future. That same incongruous mixture of time and purpose occurs next in a rush of skyscrapers viewed through the anachronistic web of rigging of a sailing vessel. Men? Yes, hundreds of them. Three are sitting on the deck, and the pier beyond is crawling with them. But one sees them only as afterthoughts. It takes some looking at the picture before they are even noticed.

The final spread again contrasts the old with the new. A gleaming white slab — with a checkerboard pattern made energetic by jigs of dark roof set against it here and there — totally overpowers the line of little old houses buried beneath it. But opposite is one such house, alive and well when faced head on. Once again Abbott has used raw sunlight to bring out the character of the house. But not too much. It is not far from noon and the sun is still high. It beats on the little house, still and serene in its empty street.

The first and last pictures in this essay, shrewdly chosen, offer many contrasts, and one finds oneself flipping back and forth to compare them. The most obvious difference is the point of view. The grand mansions are taken from low down, and from rather far away, emphasizing their size and their remoteness. The other is taken from higher up, from the level of the lower-story windows, giving a sense of intimacy. One can look into those windows. One could almost imagine oneself living there.

THE VANISHING SPLENDOR OF VICTORIAN FIFTH AVENUE IS PRESERVED BY BERENICE ABBOTT'S CAMERA

A WOMAN PHOTOGRAPHS THE FACE OF A CHANGING CITY

To Berenice Abbott (*right*) New York is "the most phenomenal human gesture ever made." For years in Paris she had photographed the faces of Europe's great. But returning to Manhattan in 1929 made her feel that faces everywhere look much the same. What people are really like, she decided, is shown by what they build. "Their houses," said Berenice Abbott, "tell more about a people than their noses. And besides, in a city as vast as New York, human beings are dwarfed by the colossal monuments of their hands." There was another angle about New York that held this Springfield, Ohio, girl with "a fantastic passion." This was the city's ceaseless change, its overnight growths, its vanishing old structures, its weird contrast of past jostling with present. Fifty years from now it would be a different city. Somebody should preserve its flavor before it was gone.

So Berenice Abbott set to work making a detached and clear-sighted document of the changing face of New York. At first she was confused by the city's frantic pace, frightened by its strange and hostile corners, baffled by lack of funds and equipment. In 1935 the WPA and the Museum of the City of New York came to her rescue. Since then she has prowled indefatigably over the city's pavements, photographing its old markets, its little shops, its vanishing elevated stations, its Victorian mansions, its waterfront slips and terraced towers. She prefers a large camera, but is not averse to miniatures. She often waits for hours till the light is right or distracting action has stopped.

Unlike the f:64 group (LIFE, April 12), she does not make a fetish of small shutter openings. When told that a picture, like the mansion above, resembles a Hopper painting (LIFE, May 3), she answers that she was doing this sort of thing before Hopper, and what artists like him are attempting is better done in photography anyhow. She does not care whether her pictures are called art or not. What she does care about is using the camera medium as honestly as possible to make for posterity a detailed document of the glory of American urban civilization.

NEW YORK OF TOMORROW WILL NOT KNOW THE DRAMATIC LIGHT PATTERNS OF THE "EL" AT HANOVER SQUARE

THE FLAVOR OF THE ITALIAN QUARTER IS CAUGHT IN THIS PICTURE OF A BLEECKER STREET CHEESE STORE

A FOUR-MASTER WITH POTATO CARGO TIES UP BEFORE THE STONE SPIRES OF LOWER MANHATTAN

IN THE *DAILY NEWS* BUILDING BERENICE ABBOTT SEES THE BREATH-TAKING VERTICALNESS THAT MAKES MANHATTAN'S SKYLINE

NEW YORK OF YESTERDAY, QUICKLY VANISHING, STILL RESIDES IN THIS QUIET BROOKLYN COLONIAL HOUSE

Displaced Germans

October 15, 1945
Photographer: Leonard McCombe
Designer: Daniel Longwell

In the summer of 1945 conditions within Germany were nearly indescribable. The country had been smashed flat by aerial and artillery bombardment, its life-support systems choked by a horde of displaced workers from other countries. Their feeding, housing, treatment of illness, and eventual return to their own homelands was preoccupying Allied occupation forces. The German himself, the loathed loser of the war, was largely ignored.

During that summer most of the biggest guns of American and British journalism were in Germany recording the chaos. Unnoticed among them was a shy young Englishman, twenty-three-year-old Leonard McCombe, who was freelancing for several British publications, photographing stories and then writing them up. McCombe was wise enough to realize that he probably should not be competing with the established superstars, who were roaring around Berlin, covering the most obvious and dramatic happenings. Moreover, even then, his eye was alert to things others did not see, his instinct drawing him to people and their dilemmas rather than to events.

One day he went down to the railroad station in the center of the city and suddenly became aware of a mordant story that was unfolding there, one that other journalists — in their blindness to the plight of ordinary Germans — were overlooking. Those ordinary Germans, having fled the Russians, having fled bombardment, having fled murderous reprisals in Poland and Czechoslovakia, were displaced persons themselves. Their plight was just as real as that of other nationals, and they were pouring by the thousands into Berlin, the country's rail center, in an effort to find their way home.

McCombe scooped the world's best photojournalists with a devastating set of pictures that were spotted by John Boyle, then representing *Life* in Germany. Boyle sent them back to New York, and they were immediately put in the magazine. Henry Luce was sufficiently impressed by the story to order that McCombe be hired, but by that time he had gone to Nuremburg to cover the war trials, and it was months before cables caught up with him, giving him that news. Meanwhile McCombe had become dissatisfied by the small recognition British publications were giving his pictures and their unwillingness to identify them with bylines. In 1946 he came to the United States and signed a working contract with *Life*. Ten years later he gave up the contract arrangement and went on the staff full-time.

What would distinguish all of McCombe's work jumps right off the page in the displaced Germans story: his instant response to the things that really preoccupy the people he is photographing. They can range from the ordinary day-to-day activities of an American working girl (page 51) to the truly hellish survival problems of the people shown here. In either case McCombe becomes one with his subject. The subject speaks directly to the reader. There is no one standing between. In Berlin that was easy. These people are so dazed, so battered by events that they are unaware of his presence.

The layout, in its foursquare appearance, is simple and straightforward, but the choice of pictures is extremely subtle. In the Billings tradition, a scene-setter opens the story: the station itself. I do not know what others Longwell had to choose from, but his choice was inspired. It tells everything, the jammed crowds, the wet, the misery, the searching, the empty track — all from the point of view of a German sitting on top of a train, waiting, perhaps for days, for it to move.

The next spread is a most ingenious bridge. It lingers long enough in the station to shift from the general to the individual: to one man's effort to get somewhere. But that man is from the middle or upper class. He wears a suit, carries a neat valise, and is used to arguing with officials. Longwell makes the brutal jump from him to the real guts of the story by moving from the station into the street for a full-page picture of a man with no feet.

Now we are where McCombe wants us to be, looking straight into the eyes and sores of the damaged flotsam that the story is really about. First a spread on conditions: on legs that won't walk further, on hunger, blindness, falling-down exhaustion. Then a spread on the effects of these hardships shown in a series of numbed faces. The horror grows, and on the last spread is made specific: rape and death. An overpowering story.

GERMANS FROM EASTERN EUROPE SWARM ON TOP OF A TRAIN IN BERLIN'S ANHALTER STATION. MANY HAVE BEEN HERE ALL NIGHT. FOREGROUND: RELEASED PRISONERS

Displaced Germans

Driven from their homes by Poles and Czechs, they pour unwelcome into Berlin

Across the eastern borders of Germany there is pouring now a vast throng of refugees. They are Germans from Eastern Europe, dispossessed and driven from their homes by the Poles and Czechs. Few have more than the clothes on their backs. Many are sick and starving. Unwanted by their own people, they come across the border at the rate of 17,000 a day, some on foot, some clinging to the tops and sides of railroad cars. Eight million had arrived in Berlin by Sept. 1 and 2,000,000 more were on the roads.

The Germans of Czechoslovakia were Hitler's pretext for Munich. The Germans of Poland and East Prussia were his pretext for World War II. For this dangerous honor they are now paying a heavy price. As refugees, they are supposed to remain in Berlin only 24 hours. Food is so scarce there that the refugees get only a couple of slices of bread and a cup of coffee. If they can prove family connections in the west, they can get into the British and American zones. But if not they shuttle back and forth between

Berlin and the reception areas of Saxony and Mecklenburg. Sometimes they are herded into open fields; sometimes they are able to hole up in villages as farm laborers. Many skulk in the ruins of Berlin without ration cards or documents. Millions of them can seriously consider the prospect of dying this winter.

The pictures on these pages, which were taken by British Photographer Leonard McCombe, are in detail terrible and shocking. But the millions of Europeans who were more terribly treated and degraded by the Nazis feel no pity or sympathy for the plight of the people who supported or permitted Hitler. These displaced Germans are being treated callously but not with the deliberate cruelty which their government once inflicted on others. They are, at least, allowed to live. The present tragic plight of these Germans is the sign of a deeper tragedy. These people allowed themselves to fall so low in the eyes of the world that the world, seeing their suffering, finds it hard to feel sorry for them.

A HURRYING TRAVELER (light-coated man in the foreground with suitcase) tries to beat the incredible congestion of the train for Halle at the Anhalter station by forcing his way up the track to the emptier cars reserved for released German prisoners on their way home from Russia. It seemed like a good idea, but it did not pay off (*see picture below*).

Most of refugees come from Poland

Most of the Germans now coming into Berlin are from the part of eastern Germany taken over by the Poles. The Potsdam agreement declared the expulsion of Germans from any country must be "orderly and humane" and lead to "equitable distribution" of the displaced people through Germany. The Czechs, who got rid of 1,200,000 Sudeten Germans before Potsdam, have since tried to comply with the declaration. The Poles, apparently anxious to nail down their claims to territory not yet officially ceded them by the Big Three, are still driving Germans out as fast as they can.

THE TRAVELER IS STOPPED by two railway guards who turn him back to crowded civilian cars. People often have to hang onto the outside of these cars for days, drop off along the roadbed from exhaustion. The 250-mile trip from Danzig to Berlin takes as much as seven days. Few trains run, because Russians have removed long stretches of track.

FOOTLESS SOLDIER, who has been released by the Russians but without crutches, is taken off the train from the east. Several other amputation cases on train with him died on the trip. As an unusual exception, this group was lodged in a Berlin hospital, because forcing it to go any farther would have been imposing a virtual sentence of death.

AFTER HUNDRED-MILE WALK, this German woman's swollen ankles have split open, exuding a festering mixture of blood and water. Near Berlin she caught a train into Stettiner station and is here seen waiting for admission into one of Berlin's wrecked and understaffed hospitals. She is suffering from starvation and general exhaustion.

RELEASED SOLDIERS from Russian prison camps are pale with hunger. One has fallen asleep. In September Russia freed 413,000 prisoners and delivered them to border.

BLIND SOLDIER and two girls from Breslau apply at Berlin *Magistrat* headquarters for instructions. The well-dressed girls had their luggage stolen by young Poles on train.

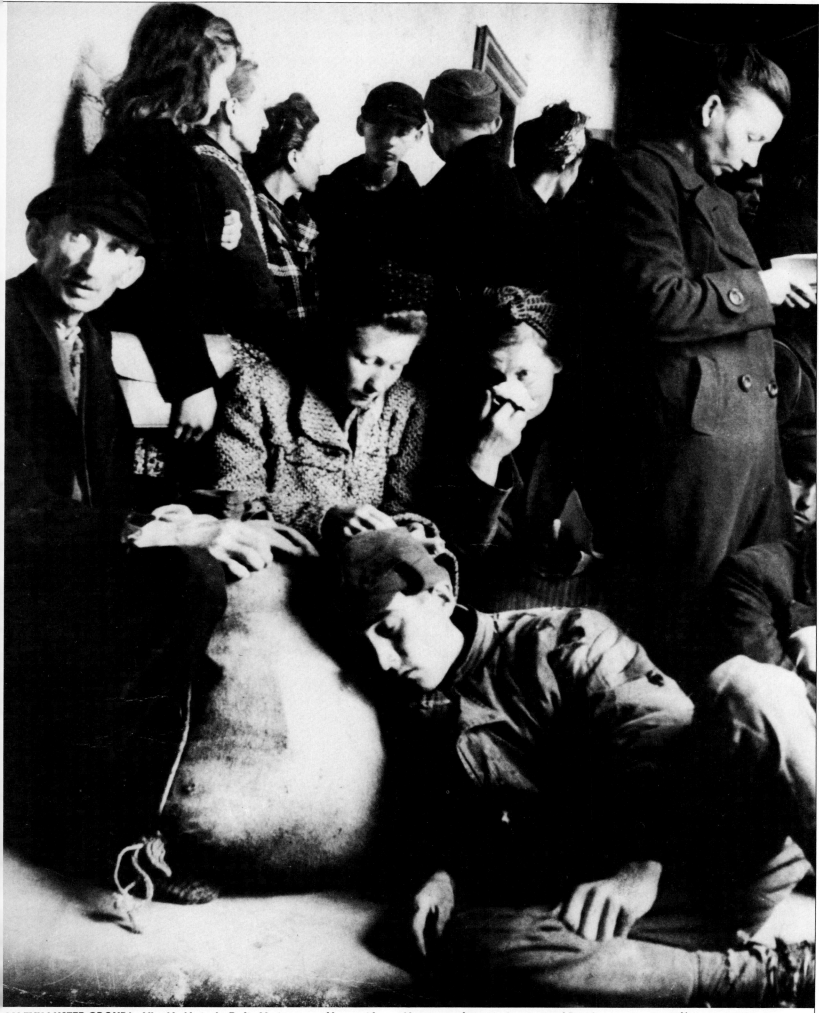

AN EXHAUSTED GROUP huddles bleakly in the Berlin *Magistrat*—an old man with his sack, two weeping women, a weary soldier. Twenty-five per cent of the refugees are able to go to relatives in American and British zones. Another 25% are domiciled in the Russian zone. Remaining 50% wander about trying to squeeze into reception centers.

ORPHANED SUDETEN GERMAN, looking aged from hunger, anxiety and dirt, was about 3 years old when Hitler made the Sudeten Germans of Czechoslovakia the pretext in 1938 for the opening moves of World War II. Since V-E Day the Czechs have set about moving all Sudeten Germans out of Czechoslovakia, confiscating their property.

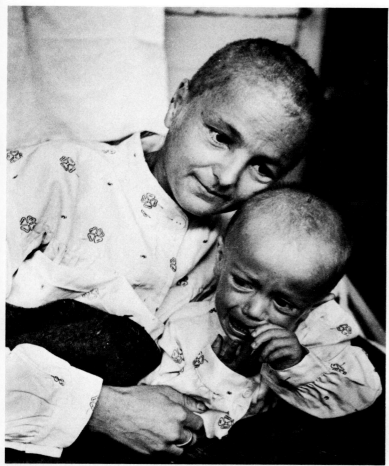

MOTHER AND CHILD faced certain death from starvation, so Berlin authorities accepted her in a bombed Berlin hospital. She had walked 180 miles from Silesia to Berlin.

SHOPKEEPER from what is now Poland carries his belongings slung over neck in a bag. He is supposed to go to transit camp for medical inspection. But he probably will not.

FAMILY FROM DANZIG, now called Gdansk as part of postwar Poland, rest on steps of railway station. Every day 100 children, lost or abandoned, are taken to orphanages.

A BERLIN GIRL comes every day to meet trains because somebody had told her that her fiance, a soldier, had been seen at a collecting station not far down the railway line.

47

GERMAN RED CROSS WORKER, bringing boiled water, is stopped for a moment by the stench from the "death carriage" of the refugee train. An old farmer calls her.

SHE BRAVES THE SMELL of dysentery and death and the dying old man, relieved by her approach, falls back. He had been a farmer in territory now taken over by Poland.

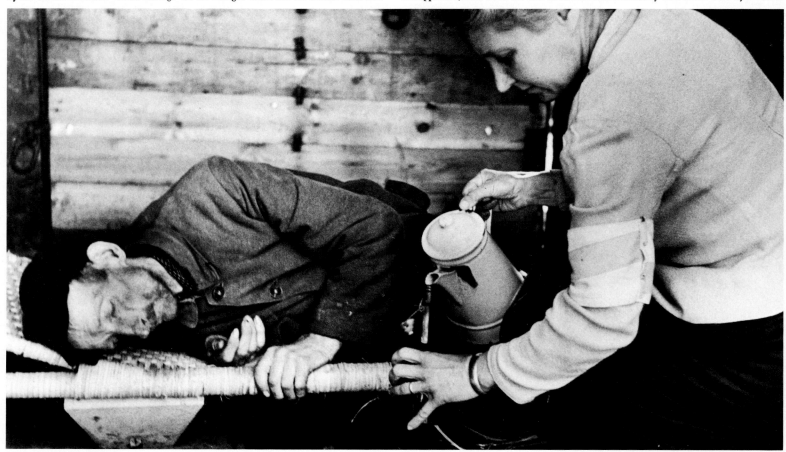

SHE POURS WATER from a coffee pot into the empty bottle of the old German farmer, who lies in the derelict cattle train, too weak even to find a comfortable position.

Boiled water is all that the Red Cross worker can give him. He is already dying—in fact, died soon after these pictures were taken, to join the three corpses already in the car.

GIRL IN HER TEENS (*center*) had been raped in train taking her out of Poland by young Polish hoodlums, who had been orphaned by the war. She is still evidently suffering from shock. The Poles, who regularly board trains to loot the German refugees, came into Berlin on the train and were not molested by either Allied or German officials.

The Private Life of Gwyned Filling

May 3, 1948
Photographer: Leonard McCombe
Designers: Bernard Quint, Joseph Thorndike

Photographers on spot assignments, particularly those in distant places, had a good deal of latitude in handling stories. The editor was too far away from the action and knew too little about what was going to happen for it to be any other way. All he knew was that the Shah of Iran was getting married. He had to leave it to the photographer to cover the event as he saw fit.

But with photo essays, lovingly scripted in the office, editors felt more in control. Here were stories they had dreamed up themselves. They had worked them out in detail, knew exactly what they wanted, where they wanted it and how. To come as close as possible to realizing their visions, editors began writing tighter and tighter scripts. For certain subjects, scientific, historical, and so on, this was necessary. For others it began to constrict the spontaneity of photographers. Essays during the 1940s began to look increasingly contrived.

That trend was abruptly reversed in 1948 with Leonard McCombe's "Gwyned Filling." If it does not startle today, it is only because McCombe's techniques were quickly picked up by others. What was then a remarkable innovation later became commonplace. But few ever surpassed McCombe in the kind of photo essay he almost literally invented.

That was a close-in, candid, stay-with-it, intimate look at one person or one situation. McCombe already had the personally involved point of view. He had proved it with his story on displaced Germans. Compare the pictures in that essay with those in Bourke-White's Fort Peck story. In the latter she is looking *at* people and things. Her presence as a photographer will not go away. McCombe, by contrast, instinctively looked out of the eyes of the people he was photographing, trying to see things as they saw them. It was that trait that tempted Wilson Hicks to assign to McCombe a story on the daily life of a career girl in New York.

This was an infinitely more difficult test than the displaced Germans had been. There, human tension was built in because of a horrible situation. McCombe did not have to go looking for it; it was all around him. Furthermore, it was spread over a hundred agonized faces and desperate personal dilemmas. Each picture peaked with its own shriek. Now he was asked to find drama in the ordinary daily round of an essentially ordinary girl. To succeed he had to accomplish two things. First, he had to learn enough about Gwyned to figure out what kind of a story he would tell. Second, he would have to get her so used to his being around her that she would ultimately begin acting naturally, so the real story could emerge.

McCombe solved both problems at once by selecting the girl himself and then almost literally gluing himself to her. He worked alone, without a researcher or assistant, listening and remembering as he photographed. At the end of the day he would write extensive notes on his take.

He arrived every morning at Gwyned's furnished room before she was up, then followed her through her day — in the street, in her office, with friends, on dates, at home with her roommate. He was on hand at three o'clock one morning when a lonely boyfriend called from San Francisco on her landlady's phone (she had none of her own). He got a memorable picture of that: Gwyned slumped sleepily over the phone, her landlady waiting, weary, cynical, forgiving. What a contrast in faces.

By that time Gwyned had become so accustomed to McCombe's presence that he was all but invisible. He photographed her at work, in the bathtub, yawning, fidgeting, fighting, crying, and he finally emerged with a set of totally unposed pictures that covered every aspect of a life that was made dramatic only by the strong feelings of the girl who was living it.

That is what brings Gwyned alive. McCombe has persuaded the reader to examine her on her terms: as an ambitious girl on the run, whose daily traumas are desperately important. Empathizing with her, the reader becomes as involved as he would if he were reading a novel. For years afterward people wanted to know what happened to Gwyned Filling. What was the effect on an obscure girl of having her life laid so bare for millions of readers, of getting her picture on *Life*'s cover? Did she succeed in the advertising business? Did she marry either of the men in the story?

McCombe's brilliant take is matched by a brilliant layout. It quickly sets the mood of Gwyned's life — hectic, brittle, revolving tensely about such matters as a nosebleed, a broken date, a quarrel with a roommate. Our first glimpse of her is a rushed one. She is caught on the street, her hair blown back, stopping momentarily to watch a fire. But her whole attitude is nervy, restless; she will rush off in another moment.

The spread that follows carries the hectic mood along — with a galloping headline and a streaming run of horizontal pictures, ended joltingly with a vertical one at lower right: her boss is late and all the rush comes to a stop. The next spread is a jagged mixture of odd moments involving people. Her life is a higgledy-piggledy series of just such one-on-one encounters. She watches people warily and feels them watching her. We see all this as she sees it, past blurred ears and eyebrows very close. She relaxes only when she gets home at night, but even there she takes her work with her.

Gradually bits of a private life surface, moments unconnected with the office, clothes, men. The strains grow, and we realize that Gwyned is paying a price for her run at success. She is now totally oblivious of McCombe, whether scratching herself or weeping on her roommate's shoulder. The intrusion is so complete, so natural, that it no longer exists. Other photographers, working this way, often got Peeping Tom effects. McCombe never did.

As it develops from spread to spread, this may seem like a simple, straightforward story. It is anything but. Gwyned's life was not organized as neatly as it is here. Things happened at awkward times and had to be rearranged, strands sorted out, a great deal of material discarded. It is this sort of essay that offers the greatest challenge to the designer. McCombe's pictures, while uniformly strong, are not individually overpowering. They draw on each other for their effect and must be fitted together with great care. In the wrong hands, "Gwyned Filling" could have been a confusing disaster.

For the curious, Gwyned did marry one of the men in the story, Charlie Straus. Her life as a career girl was a short one. Some years later she came up to McCombe in a restaurant. He did not recognize her.

GWYNED FILLING, ALONE IN A CROWD THAT HAS GATHERED TO WATCH A FIRE IN THE CITY, STANDS ON TIPTOE AND TILTS BACK HER HEAD TO GET A BETTER VIEW

THE PRIVATE LIFE OF
Gwyned Filling

THE HOPES AND FEARS OF COUNTLESS YOUNG CAREER GIRLS
ARE SUMMED UP IN HER STRUGGLE TO SUCCEED IN NEW YORK

PHOTOGRAPHS FOR LIFE BY LEONARD McCOMBE

In the spring of 1925 in St. Charles, Mo., a housewife named Mildred Filling picked up a newspaper and saw in the society column an odd first name: Gwyned. Because Mrs. Filling was about to have a child, this solved the christening problem, and it now accounts for the fact that an attractive 23-year-old girl alone among the crowds of New York would stop and turn if that odd name were spoken.

Gwyned Filling came to New York last June to begin a career. Because she wanted to feel independent she had borrowed $250 from a local bank rather than from her father, a former city official. She had a large ambition and some training, having just completed a course in advertising at the University of Missouri. With her came her college roommate, Marilyn Johnson, who had taken the same course. For

five weeks they looked unsuccessfully for jobs, during which Gwyned's $250 shriveled to $30. But finally she walked down the right street, took the right elevator and entered the offices of Newell-Emmett Co., a large advertising agency which handles the account for Chesterfield cigarets. Gwyned was hired for $35 a week, which disappears quickly in New York.

Because she had already worked her way through college and had learned to make her clothes and to eat breakfast for 15¢, Gwyned got along. With Marilyn, she found an 11x15-foot furnished room in an apartment building on 23rd Street. Although they could scarcely afford the stiff $75-a-month rent, they could find nothing cheaper. Gwyned soon made office friends, including several young men who began to take her out to dinner regularly enough to subtract

about $4 a week from her living expenses. An older couple turned over their apartment, empty on weekends, to both girls. This saves no money, but it is a release from the drab clutter of their single room.

After six months Gwyned's salary was raised to $52 a week. She commenced, under careful supervision, to write fragments of advertising copy. She also began to repay, at the rate of $21.93 a month, her borrowed $250.

Gwyned's life is interesting and often gay, but beneath the gaiety lie the problems which confront all career girls. How much of her time and nerves must she sacrifice for success? When should she marry, and will she jeopardize her chance by trying to close her eyes to everything but her career? Gwyned has no ready answer, but even as she works she knows she must find one.

51

HER DAY BEGINS WITH A FRANTIC

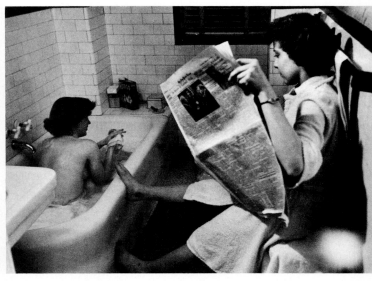

Gwyned has two alarm clocks. Both of them are broken, and thus at 7:30 she is roused by her landlady, Mrs. Bell. Even after 10 months in New York, Gwyned is still occasionally surprised to wake and find herself far from home in a small room and glances hastily across at Marilyn to make certain her friend is there.

Marilyn and Gwyned take their morning baths hurriedly according to a strict rotation schedule, each having the tub first on alternate days. The other placidly waits her turn and reads aloud inconsequential items from the St. Charles *Cosmos-Monitor*, which is mailed to them daily and remains a firm link with home.

After breakfast the girls race for the bus, which takes them eastward along 23rd Street to Fourth Avenue. Sometimes, when Gwyned is in an economical mood, either by choice or circumstance, she rises half an hour early and walks—or trots —17 blocks to the office, a distance of about a mile. The terrible aimless urgency

RACE AGAINST THE CLOCK

Breakfast is eaten hastily in a restaurant across the street. The 15¢ meal consists of two slices of toast and a cup of coffee. Gladys Hallem, the counter girl, invariably greets Gwyned with, "How are things in St. Charles, Mo. today, baby?" and then gets the girls' food quickly because she already knows what they will order.

for speed, which affects all of New York, has already taken hold of Gwyned and Marilyn. Even though another bus will be along within two minutes, the girls scramble down the rain-soaked street, splattering their shoes and stockings with water and grime, in order to make sure they will not be left behind by this one.

When she reaches the office at 9, after her frantic dash to get there on time, Gwyned must often wait patiently until her boss has time to see her. Waiting with her is George Flanagan, a copy supervisor who occasionally supplies reassurance about her work while she musters up courage to show it to her department head.

Much of Gwyned's office work is done in an endless series of major and minor conferences, at which advertising layouts are discussed, changed, accepted and rejected. When Managing Partner C. D. Newell (*above, standing*) makes one of his rare appearances in her minor orbit, she is overawed and nervous. This nervousness Gwyned counteracts by staging her own impromptu conferences (*below*) with her friend Betty Duquesne, to whom she tells her gossip of the moment. Almost any day ends with a conference with her immediate boss, Jack Cunningham (*bottom*), with whom she feels at ease and not afraid to yawn.

In Macy's baby department Gwyned eavesdrops on a customer who is inquiring about diapers, a subject dear to Gwyned's heart inasmuch as she writes copy for the Chicopee Sales Corporation, which manufactures baby products. Gwyned makes frequent trips outside the office to do research, and recently spent several hours in a casket manufacturer's salesroom to learn where Masslinn non-woven fabrics, another Chicopee product, could be put to good use. On another jaunt to a radio studio she met Actor Ray Milland, who was impressed with her homemade clothes and politely asked who her dressmaker was.

Often Gwyned is not satisfied with her day's effort and forces herself to go right on working long after she leaves the office. She hurries home, does her laundry in a coin-operated (8 pounds for 10¢) washing machine in the basement and wrestles with an advertising layout while her underwear dries in the window. Marilyn, who has a research job which requires no homework, sits on the bed nearby making bright and occasionally acid comments. During a full evening on the floor in a welter of papers, sketches and books, Gwyned is likely to smoke considerably more than her daily ration of cigarets (one pack) and to produce the following advertising copy: "As a lining at the foot of the casket, MASSLINN nonwoven fabric is softer, less expensive." She is also the author of "The Chicopee Antique Layette Show will build traffic in your department." She is in earnest about these things and her professional pride permits little humor on the subject.

Wherever she is, Gwyned is constantly in motion, scratching her head or back, twisting her ring, peeling her fingernail polish. These restless motions are extremely difficult for her to stop. When her fidgeting is called to her attention she smiles and sits uncomfortably still but soon commences to scratch again.

At rare intervals, particularly after a day of hectic travel around the city, Gwyned is overtaken by one of her most embarrassing misfortunes: nosebleeds. Here she copes with one in a restaurant, gracefully tilting back her head and inwardly running through all the salty Missouri expletives she can remember.

When she works at home the ash trays in Gwyned's vicinity are always overflowing; occasionally a cigaret, only partially snubbed out, falls and burns a brown furrow on the tabletop; orange peels and pits litter the room. In a kind of retaliation Marilyn absently gnaws pencils until she has chewed through the wood into the graphite core. Mutual irritation over these habits touches off the occasional spats between the girls. There is a sudden blaze of temper and an emotional squaring off which lasts only long enough for one or the other to realize that it is, after all, merely a question of emptying the ashtray.

In the midst of a quarrel Gwyned shouts at Marilyn with bitter but fleeting violence, which has a frightening effect in their small room. After this both are overcome by remorse and a kind of loneliness, and make peace by reading aloud from the small assortment of books they brought with them from college.

In spite of occasional disagreements Gwyned and Marilyn have a great deal in common. Five minutes after one of their quarrels they gleefully collaborate on community projects, which usually have to do with clothing. By fortunate chance the girls are of identical size, which makes it possible for them to make joint purchases and to trade dresses at will. Because their budgets allow little for clothing —Gwyned's includes only about $10 a month—they make most of what they require on a gauze-and-plaster dressmaker's dummy, shown in the process of construction above. Gwyned's wardrobe is also supplemented by gifts from her mother in Missouri, who frequently foregoes a new dress herself in order to make one for her daughter, and who often includes a present for Marilyn in her packages.

Gwyned at 23 has been in love only once, and then briefly—a high-school engagement was quietly called off when she and her fiancé changed their minds. In New York she meets a number of young men who are attracted to her. She has two office acquaintances—Carl Nichols (*above*) and Charles Straus (*p. 60*)—who are handicapped by the fact that they are in professional competition with her. Also, she has made many sacrifices to begin her career and has accordingly sur- rounded herself with a kind of protective insulation. Even when she is lonely she insists that she wants to work for at least five more years. One evening with Carl she saw a small stuffed cat in a store window. It was a charming toy. Carl bought it for her. Now she is very fond of it and keeps it in her room and idly picks it up and pets it from time to time. She remembers that evening not so much because of what Carl said or how he looked, but because it was the night she acquired the cat.

SOMETIMES HER LIFE IS LIGHT AND GAY...

George Fowler is one of Newell-Emmett's eight partners, part of whose job is to maintain cordial relations between the company and its more important clients. He and his wife have in a sense adopted Gwyned, inviting her out to their country home in New Jersey for weekends. The Fowlers see in Gwyned many of the qualities of their own daughters. Mr. Fowler is full of friendly advice, warning and advising her about how to succeed without offending others in the firm. Recently he wrote a long *Ode to Gwyned's Parents*, which he forwarded to the surprised Fillings in Missouri.

One of the brightest spots in Gwyned's New York life is her relationship with Pierre (*second from left*) and Betty Duquesne (*p. 54*), whose large walk-up apartment she occupies on weekends while they are out of town. At the Duquesnes' frequent parties Gwyned is vivacious and carefree among people she might otherwise never encounter: artists and illustrators, musicians and writers. For a few hours she is able to forget the tension of the office and the urgency of her career—there will be time to worry about it in the morning. She laughs easily and adjusts readily to new groups.

. . . AND SOMETIMES SHE CRIES

Gwyned has a deep curiosity about New Yorkers and how they behave. Walking about the city she stops when she comes upon one of the street rallies which go on daily. Here she attends a Zionist demonstration, listening with attention because anti-Semitism and Palestine are major topics among her friends.

Gwyned's favorite beau is Charles Straus, with whom she becomes more moody than with others. Charlie is shy and quiet but shows flashes of wit which Gwyned likes and is extremely capable in his copy-writing job. Often he quotes long random passages of verse and laughs at Gwyned when she tries and fails to identify them. However, his shyness sometimes irritates her. Despite her wariness of emotional entanglements at this early stage in her career, she occasionally feels a need for masculine reassurance and sympathy. Idly she touches his wrist with her finger while Charlie talks of something far away.

Gwyned's boyfriends sometimes get a sly going-over at morning gossip sessions in the office. Another subject which is brought up around the coffeepot, presided over by Gwyned's office mate Margery Paddock (left), is Gwyned's quick rise from $35 to $52 a week. "You've been here 10 months, Gwyned? Strange, it seems much less. Now, that intelligent, talented Miss Jones down the hall . . . she's been here over two years, and I wonder when they'll give her a chance to write some copy. . . ." The gossip does not much disturb Gwyned, who has long since learned to take it as an inevitable by-product of office competition.

Country Doctor

September 20, 1948

Photographer: W. Eugene Smith

Designers: Charles Tudor, Michael Phillips

Eugene Smith is considered by many to have been the greatest maker of photo essays who ever lived. His work is Shakespearean in its scope and force, and in its variety. He moves majestically from one peak to the next, producing masterpieces that are all authentically his, but that are remarkably different from one another, not only in their subject matter but in the photographic means used to create them. It says something about the ferment of talent that was bubbling at *Life* in the late 1940s that McCombe's "Gwyned Filling" and Smith's "Country Doctor" should have burst into the magazine within four months of each other.

Smith was born in Wichita, Kansas, in 1918, and got his start as a photographer by scanning the local papers to see what celebrities were passing through town. He then took pictures of them and submitted them on spec to *Life*. He joined the staff during World War II and was working as a combat photographer on Okinawa in 1945 when he was badly wounded in the face. Several operations were required to patch up his jaw and palate, and it was two years before he was able to work again. That long and painful association with surgery certainly affected his approach to the "Country Doctor" assignment. It produced a story full of homely detail, of fear, compassion, and constant encounters with pain. The pictures lack the painterly quality that would distinguish much of Smith's later work. They are just unpretentious photographs. But what photographs!

The technical similarity between this story and McCombe's "Gwyned Filling" is remarkable. Both achieved the difficult task of keeping a vivid human personality at center stage with outstanding pictures, and at the same time managing to avoid staggering it with overwhelming ones. The difference is that Smith's pictures have a somber flavor that McCombe's lack, reflecting differences in their outlook on life. For Smith life has always been tragic, full of injustice and hardship, but something which, if it is borne courageously and with dignity, brings out the nobility in man.

His Dr. Ceriani is such a man, dedicated, overworked, moving as best he can from one medical crisis to another — obscure, underpaid, aware of his own fallibility, but essentially noble. He is as concerned with the families of his patients as he is with the patients themselves. All this shows in Ceriani's face, which is a marvelous reflector of his tensions, his relief, his fatigue. The designers served Smith well by emphasizing that face in two full-page pictures strategically placed in the essay.

The photograph selected for the opener is worth a long look, for it is an extraordinary picture. At first glance it says little: a man carrying a bag. But the man is preoccupied. He walks through weeds and past the corner of an unpainted board fence. Clearly this is a poor rural community. The weight of his responsibility to that community is conveyed by his expression of worried concentration: a narrow and specific shaft of emotion, appropriate to the immediate needs of the story. But behind it, on a larger scale, loom the pain and disaster, the ultimate death that waits for us all, sensed in the lowering cloud that hangs over the doctor whose spent days are spent dealing with such things.

Overleaf, the wide range of Ceriani's duties is quickly disposed of in a burst of memorable pictures. The temptation to enlarge several of them must have been overwhelming. It is to the designers' credit that they managed to resist it, and settled instead for a great range of sensations and emotions powerfully compressed into a single spread. Then comes a self-contained story within the main story, properly isolated on its own spread and bringing the essay to a peak of anguish with two unforgettable pictures. Other vignettes follow, one with a rare (in Smith) trace of humor, the other laced with pathos. Both relieve the tension slightly, easing the reader down for a compassionate glimpse of the death of an old man and the resigned faces of those who live with him. The final spread is not so strong. It tries to get outside the clinic to the community, and succeeds only because the last picture draws us back to Ceriani himself and his concern for that community. Overall, however, the layout is masterful. It has simplified a complicated take, given each spread a life of its own, but kept the central thread.

This may seem easy after the fact. But what would-be designer, confronted with the picture of the elderly amputee staring into the camera on page 70, or with the grimacing boy on page 67, would have had the restraint to handle them as they are handled here?

After a telephone squabble with Charlie, Gwyned bursts into tears on Marilyn's shoulder. The events which lead up to one of these rare outbursts are as a rule inconsequential. Gwyned is under continual strain because she is anxious to make a success of her career. Tears might be caused merely by the shattering of a tumbler or a cigaret burn on a new dress. In this case it was the simple and harmless vagueness of Charlie Straus. For some time it had been his habit to take her out

only on weekends. Therefore she looked forward to such times. On Saturday morning he telephoned but mentioned nothing of his plans for the evening. Later another friend called her, and in annoyance she accepted his invitation to dinner. When Charlie at length telephoned again, this time with a definite plan, it was too late. Gwyned, weeping on Marilyn's shoulder, said she would never speak to him again. She spoke to him again bright and early on Monday morning in the office.

Gwyned has a friend who lives in San Francisco. When he is lonely at midnight he telephones, overlooking the three-hour transcontinental time differential. Thus at 3 a.m. old Mrs. Bell, the landlady, gets up to answer the raucous jangle and then wearily pads into Gwyned's room to say, "It's for you." Gwyned lolls drowsily over the hall table as she talks, then hangs up, puts out the light and returns to her room. Sometimes she lies awake thinking before sleep returns. She has not

solved the career girl's problem. It requires only a letter from a happily married friend to make her pause—and wonder. It takes only the sight of a tree budding in a city square to make her think of home. But she has made her choice. She is full of effervescent spirit; her fatigue falls away easily and she is enthusiastic for the career she has well started. Whether it will also end and seems a remote matter to her—what is important is that she is doing what she has always wanted to do.

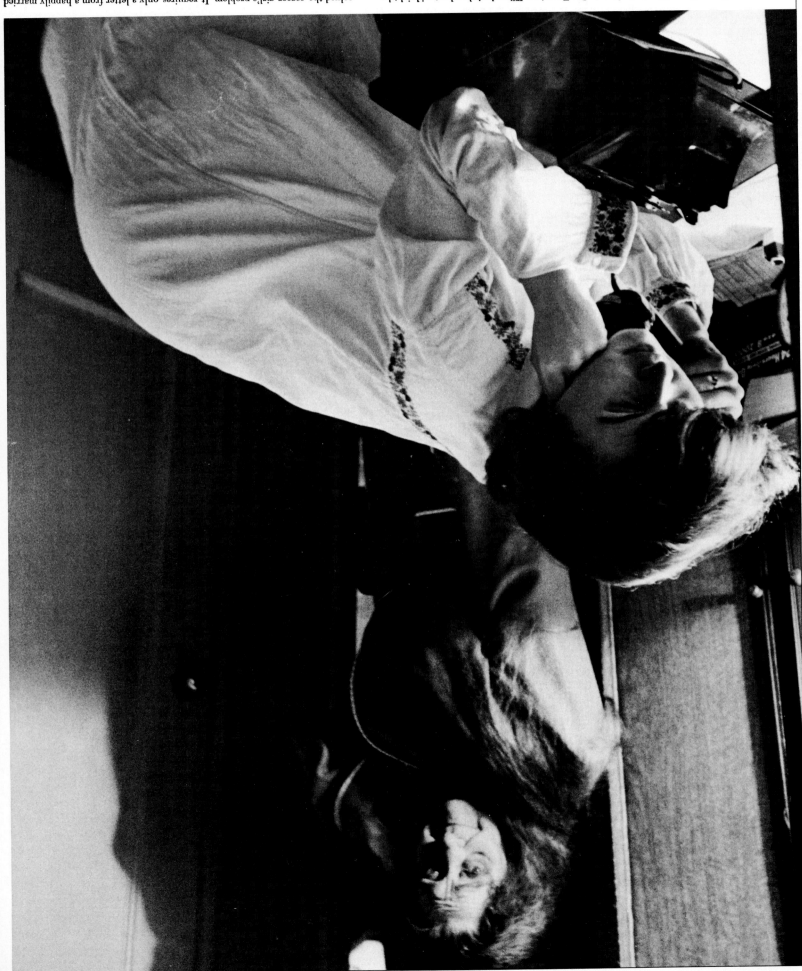

62

COUNTRY DOCTOR

THROUGH WEEDS GROWING RANK IN AN UNKEMPT DOORYARD, DR. ERNEST CERIANI OF KREMMLING MAKES HIS WAY TO CALL ON A PATIENT

HIS ENDLESS WORK HAS ITS OWN REWARDS

PHOTOGRAPHS FOR LIFE BY W. EUGENE SMITH

The town of Kremmling, Colo., 115 miles west of Denver, contains 1,000 people. The surrounding area of some 400 square miles, filled with ranches which extend high into the Rocky Mountains, contains 1,000 more. These 2,000 souls are constantly falling ill, recovering or dying, having children, being kicked by horses and cutting themselves on broken bottles. A single country doctor, known in the profession as a "g.p.," or general practitioner, takes care of them all. His name is Ernest Guy Ceriani.

Dr. Ceriani begins to work soon after 8 o'clock and often continues far into the night. He serves as physician, surgeon, obstetrician, pediatrician, psychiatrist, dentist, oculist and laboratory technician. Like most rural g.p.s he has no vacations and few days off, although unlike them he has a small hospital in which to work. Whenever he has a spare hour he spends it uneasily, worrying about a particular patient or regretting that he cannot study all of the medical journals which pour into his office. Although he is only 32 he is already slightly stooped, leaning forward as he hurries from place to place as though heading into a strong wind. His income for covering a dozen fields is less than a city doctor makes by specializing in only one. But Ceriani is compensated by the affection of his patients and neighbors, by the high place he has earned in his community and by the fact that he is his own boss. For him this is enough. The fate of thousands of communities like Kremmling, in dire need of "country doctors," depends on whether the nation's 22,000 medical students, now choosing between specialization and general practice, also think it is enough.

HE MUST SPECIALIZE

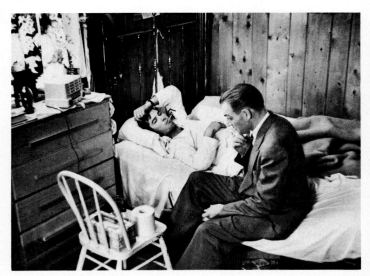

HOME CALL at 8:30 a.m. starts Ceriani's day. He prefers to treat patients during office hours at the hospital, but because this printer had a fever and symptoms of influenza Ceriani thought it would be unwise for him to get up and make the trip.

MINOR EMERGENCY disrupts Ceriani's office routine. This 60-year-old tourist, suffering from a heart disturbance aggravated by a trip through an 11,000-foot pass in the Rockies, came to the hospital to get an injection of morphine.

ANOTHER HOME CALL turns up a feverish 4-year-old suffering from acute tonsillitis. Although a large proportion of his patients are children, Dr. Ceriani is still inexperienced in pediatrics and studies it whenever he has an opportunity.

THE DAY'S FIRST OFFICE CALL is made by a tourist guide and his baby, who have come to Kremmling from an outlying ranch. Ceriani's patients are of all ages and income groups and come from doctorless areas as far as 50 miles away.

IN A DOZEN FIELDS

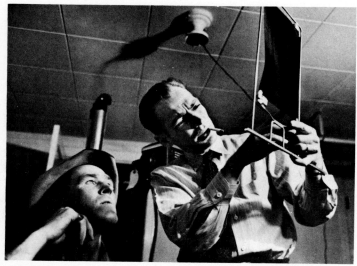

X-RAY PICTURE is explained to a rancher by Ceriani, who developed the negative himself. In addition to the X-ray machine, the hospital contains about $10,000 worth of equipment, including a $1,500 autoclave and an oxygen tent.

BROKEN RIBS, the result of an accident in which a horse rolled on this patient, are bound with adhesive tape by Ceriani. Many of his hardy patients walk in with injuries which would make city dwellers call at once for an ambulance.

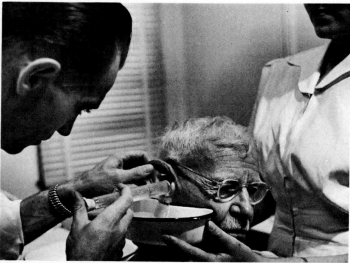

PROBLEMS OF AGE—in this case a slight deafness complicated by deposits of ear wax—are daily brought to the doctor. Here, in an operation chiefly important for its effect on the patient's morale, Ceriani removes the wax with a syringe.

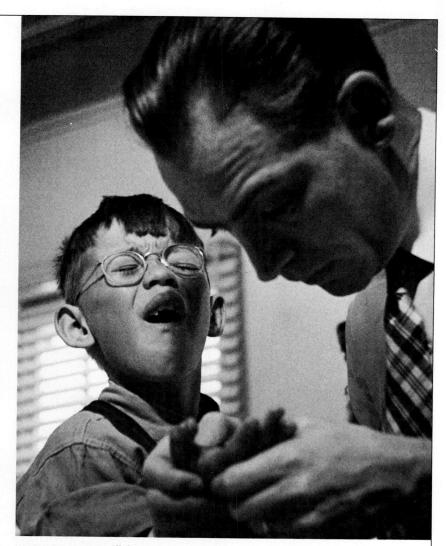

WOES OF YOUTH fill Ceriani's office with noise. Above: he examines stitches in the lacerated hand of a squalling 7-year-old. Below: he uses a rubber tube to remove the mucous which clogs the throat of an infant he has just delivered.

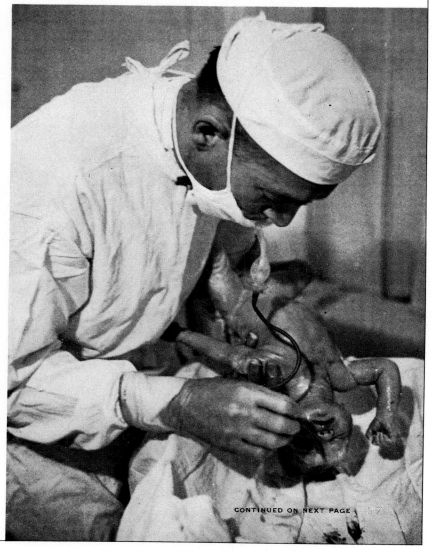

67

CONTINUED ON NEXT PAGE

AN ACCIDENT INTERRUPTS HIS LEISURE

Dr. Ceriani's moments of relaxation are rare and brief. Last month, taking a chance that he would not be missed for three hours, he asked two employes of the Denver and Rio Grande to take him out on a railroad gasoline car to Gore Canyon. There he fished alone in the rapids of the Colorado, working expertly over the white water for almost 30 minutes. Suddenly he saw the car coming back up the canyon far ahead of time, and automatically he commenced to dismantle his fishing rod. Ceriani had no feeling of resentment at the quick end of his excursion; he merely stood still waiting for the car to reach him, wondering what had happened and hoping that it was not serious. When the car arrived Chancy Van

Pelt, the town marshal, hopped off and said, "Little girl at the Wheatly ranch got kicked in the head by a horse. Can you come now?"

Lee Marie Wheatly, aged 2½, was already in the hospital when Ceriani arrived. While her parents watched he looked for signs of a skull fracture, stitched up a great gash in her forehead and saw that her left eyeball was collapsed. Then he advised the Wheatlys to take their child to a specialist in Denver for consultation on removal of the eye. When they left Ceriani was haggard and profoundly tired. He did not remember that he had been fishing at all until, on his way out of the emergency room, he saw his rod and creel lying in the corner where he had thrown them.

AT 4:15 two friends start to give fisherman Ceriani a ride to Gore Canyon in a railroad motor car.

AT 5:00 Ceriani begins his day's fishing in the boiling, trout-filled rapids of Colorado River.

AT 5:30 Kremmling's town marshal has come after Ceriani and they start back to take care of an emergency case.

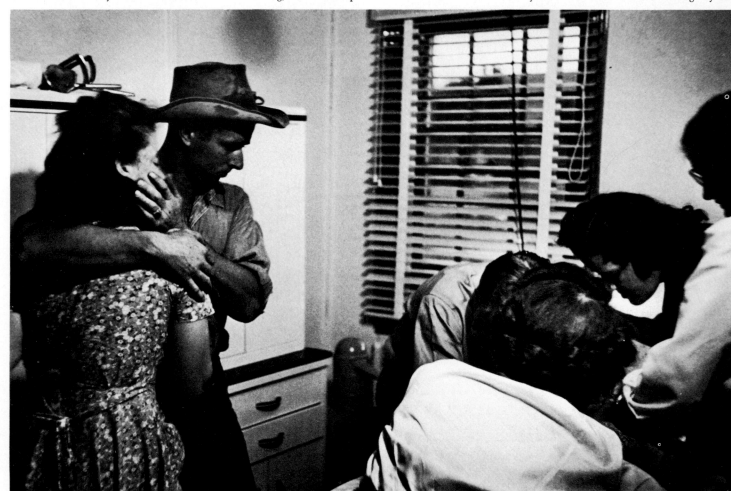

THE CHILD'S PARENTS watch in anguish (*left*) while Ceriani examines their daughter. The hospital's two nurses, one of whom is on duty in the hospital at all hours, had tried to check the flow of blood from her forehead and had given her a dose of phenobarbital while Ceriani was on his way back from fishing trip.

HAVING DONE HIS BEST for the child, Ceriani is worn out and tense as he completes the emergency treatment. He has stitched the wound in her forehead so that she will have only a slight scar, but already knows that nothing can be done to save her eye and tries to think of a way to soften the news for her parents.

HE SETS A BADLY DISLOCATED ELBOW

Young Robert Wiggs had a dislocated left elbow. He had been to a rodeo in nearby Granby, had a few beers and tried to ride a wild horse. When he was brought by his friends to the hospital, he was in great pain and swearing loudly. "Don't tell my mother," he said.

Dr. Ceriani X-rayed the arm. Then, because it was necessary to give Wiggs ether, he questioned him about the beer he had drunk. Wiggs said, "Only a few," and the operation proceeded. The boy's friends and a nurse held him while Ceriani set the joint and made a cast for it (*opposite page*).

As the effects of the ether began to fade, Wiggs began groggily to repeat, "Don't tell my mother." At this Ceriani glanced across the table. There stood Mrs. Wiggs, who had been notified of the accident and had rushed to the hospital in time to hold her son's hand during the last of the operation. Ceriani grinned at her, trying to convey two ideas. One was that her son would be all right. The second was that Ceriani himself was a man who might not long ago have had a few beers and tried to ride a wild horse, and therefore did not think this affair was one of the utmost gravity.

CERIANI HELPS CARRY THE PAINFULLY INJURED BOY INTO THE HOSPITAL

HE PULLS AT THE BOY'S ARM TO BRING THE ELBOW JOINT BACK INTO PLACE

...AND AMPUTATES A GANGRENOUS LEG

Old Thomas Mitchell had a gangrenous left foot. He was 85, and when he was brought to the basement emergency room three months ago it seemed unlikely that he would live long. But he survived, and when Dr. Ceriani came to tend him he would say, "I want to see the mayor. When is the mayor coming?" as though such a visit would clear up the trouble.

For a long time Dr. Ceriani postponed the inevitable amputation, afraid that the old man could not survive it. Twice he told the nurses, "Tomorrow I will do it," but when tomorrow arrived Mitchell had grown weaker.

Finally the old man rallied and Ceriani hastily made his preparations. With great gentleness he carried his patient (*opposite page*) up to the operating room, gave him a spinal anesthetic and cut off his left leg below the knee. The old man, conscious but with his vision blocked by a screen, was not aware of what was being done and did not discover that his leg was gone until long after. He continued to say, "My foot hurts," while Dr. Ceriani, busy now with other cases, sighed in relief. Last week the old man was much improved and asking with increased spriteliness to see the mayor.

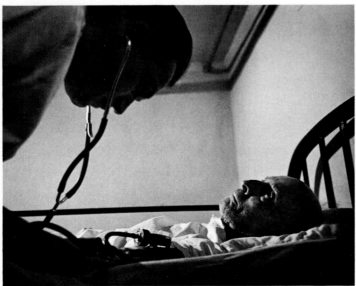

BEFORE THE AMPUTATION CERIANI CHECKS MITCHELL'S BLOOD PRESSURE

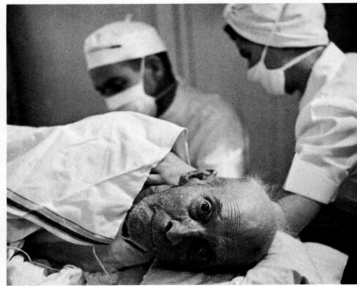

IN THE OPERATING ROOM THE OLD MAN RECEIVES A SPINAL ANESTHETIC

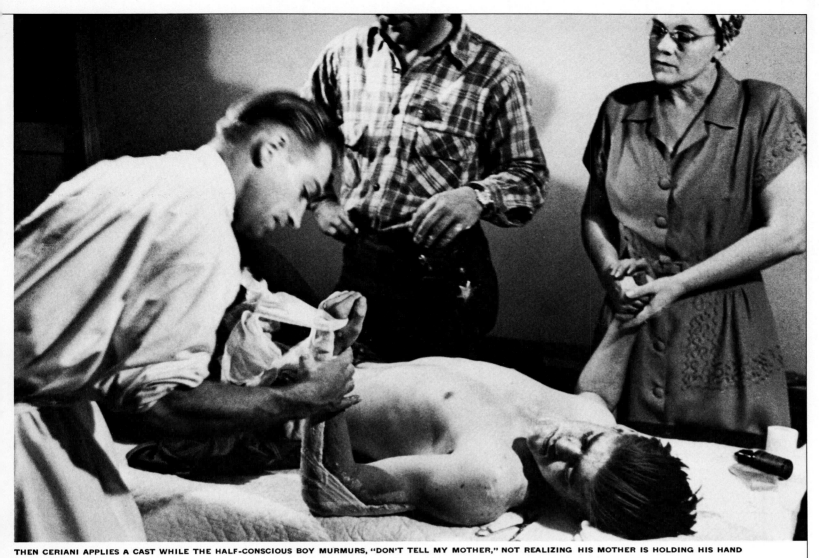

THEN CERIANI APPLIES A CAST WHILE THE HALF-CONSCIOUS BOY MURMURS, "DON'T TELL MY MOTHER," NOT REALIZING HIS MOTHER IS HOLDING HIS HAND

BECAUSE THE HOSPITAL HAS NO ELEVATOR, CERIANI PICKS UP HIS PATIENT IN THE BASEMENT WARD TO CARRY HIM UPSTAIRS TO THE OPERATING ROOM

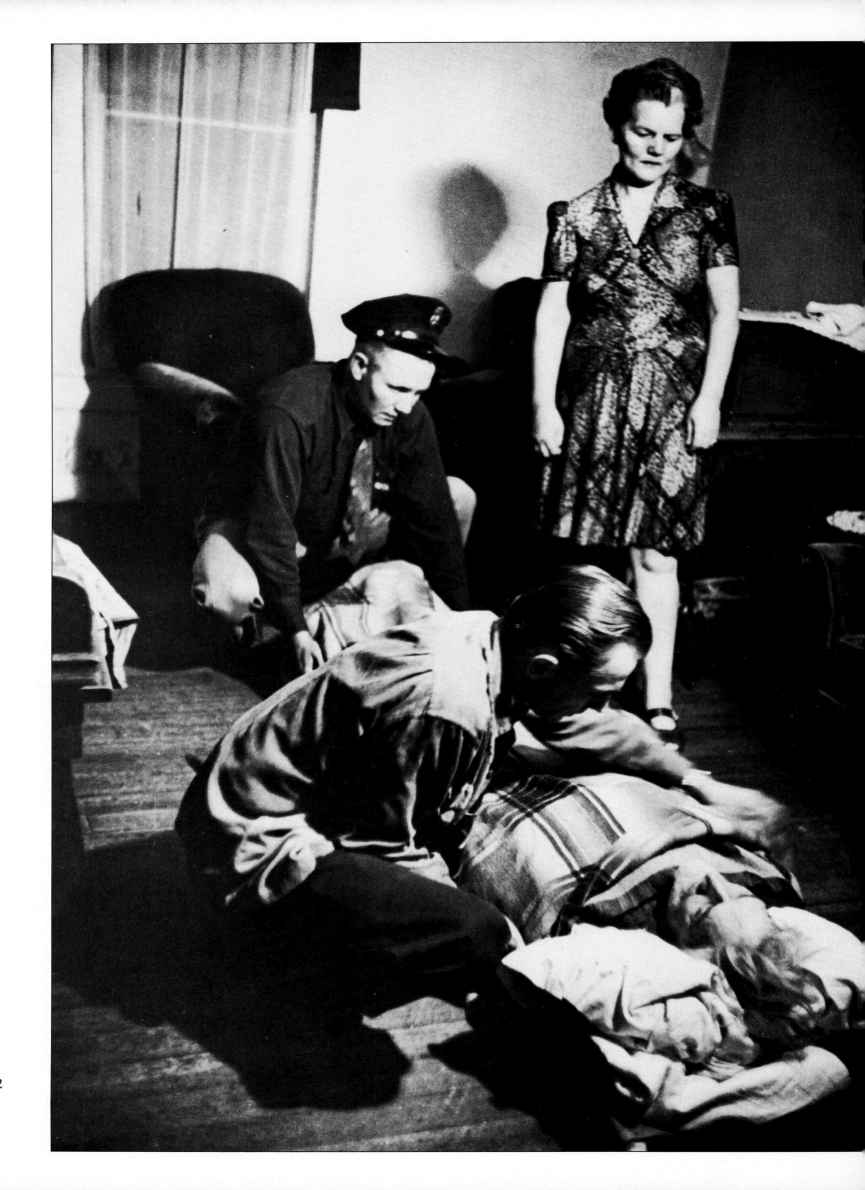

IN THE KITCHEN, WHILE THE WOMEN WHISPER, CERIANI TELEPHONES THE PRIEST TO TELL HIM THAT THE OLD MAN WILL NOT LIVE THROUGH THE NIGHT

AN OLD MAN DIES AT NIGHT

A few minutes before midnight the people in Joe Jesmer's house called Dr. Ceriani to tell him that Joe was very sick. Ceriani put on a cloth jacket, went over there quickly and found 82-year-old Joe dying after a heart attack. He was still conscious, but in his pain and bewilderment he felt that he was somehow trapped and needed rescuing. He continually said, "Please, please get me out of here."

Ceriani and Chancy Van Pelt got Joe onto a stretcher (*opposite page*), while Helen Watson, a roomer in Joe's house stood watching quietly and without tears. Ceriani called the priest, asking him to come to the hospital. Chancy and he carried Joe out to the ambulance and drove off. There was nothing Ceriani could do except make Joe comfortable and watch him die. At about 2:30 it happened. He left the hospital then and went home, finding his wife asleep and his own house as quiet as all the rest in town.

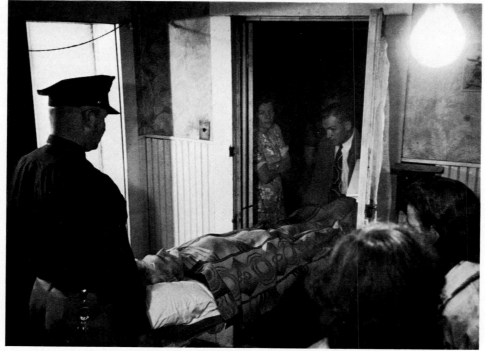

AT MIDNIGHT JOE JESMER'S WOMENFOLK STAND SILENTLY AROUND THE DOOR TO SEE HIM TAKEN AWAY

■ **IN THE PARLOR** Ceriani tucks a blanket around the dying man before taking him out into the night.

THE HOMELY WOODEN BUILDINGS AND WIDE TREELESS STREETS OF KREMMLING STAND ON A 7,000-FOOT PLATEAU BENEATH THE TOWERING ROCKY MOUNTAINS

COMMUNITY ABSORBS MOST OF HIS TIME

Kremmling lies on a 1½-mile-high plateau on the edge of the Rockies. Tourists and transcontinental travelers find the country beautiful, as does Ceriani, who also finds it advisable in bad weather to take chains, blankets, an ax and a can of beans with him on trips to ranches in the hinterland. The town itself consists of about 150 small buildings, including the hospital (*below*), and a few old log cabins. Mrs. Ceriani, who came from rural Colorado, was already familiar with this environment and adjusted easily to it. She faithfully reminds him to send out his bills—which are far lower than those of an urban physician—and has long since grown used to emergencies at all hours and to the sudden collapse of her plans to see a movie or play bridge. She has learned to accept all the problems of her husband's career except one Even after four years of marriage, she is still unable to reconcile herself to the fact that his time is not his own. She and her two young sons must see him at unpredictable intervals, on special occasions (*left*) or simply fall asleep waiting for him to finish his work.

THE DOCTOR AND FAMILY watch a parade in Kremmling. Ceriani holds 11-month old Gary, while wife Bernetha steadies 3-year-old Philip on the rail.

THE HOSPITAL, one block away from Ceriani's house, is a neat white wooden building with three separate wards which can accommodate a total of 14 patients.

74

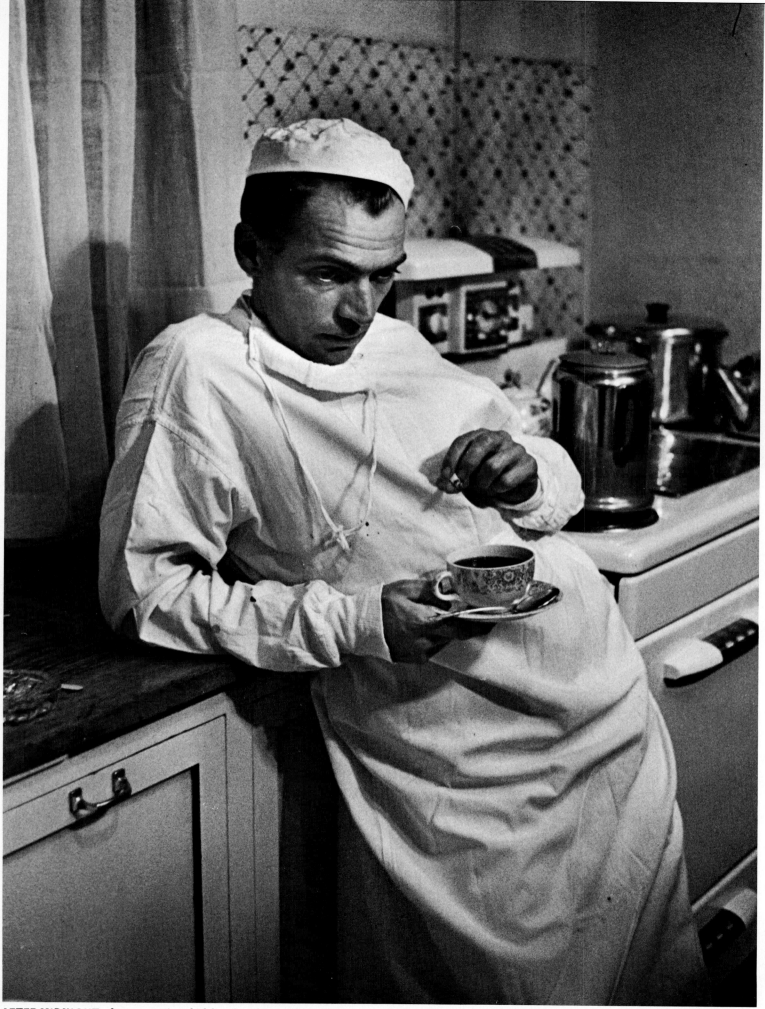

AFTER MIDNIGHT, after an operation which lasted until 2 a.m., Ceriani has a cup of coffee and cigaret in the hospital kitchen before starting home. The nurses constantly admonish him to relax and rest, but because they are well aware that he cannot, they keep a potful of fresh coffee simmering for him at all hours.

A Last Look at Peiping

January 3, 1949
Photographer: Henri Cartier-Bresson
Designer: Charles Tudor

Cartier-Bresson is an anomaly in the history of the photo essay because his best takes did not always turn out best in the magazine. That is not entirely his fault. As one of the most dazzlingly talented of all photojournalists, he was sometimes capable of eruptions of superlative pictures that simply swamped the ability of *Life*'s editors to exploit them properly. An example is the story shown here, the first he ever shot for *Life*.

Not exactly "for" *Life*. He shot it for himself, but *Life* heard about it and bought it. In 1948 Chiang Kai-shek's control of China was slipping away under the advance of the Chinese Communists. Cartier-Bresson was there, in Peiping. In fact he was the last Western photographer to leave. Here was an unparalleled opportunity to document the dying moments of an old and exotic and intricate way of life before it vanished forever. He took full advantage of it with an avalanche of pictures that hit Peggy Sargent's desk late one afternoon just as she was about to depart for *Life*'s annual Christmas party. "Don't worry about that tonight," she was told. "Do it tomorrow."

"Tomorrow" turned out to be several days of eyeball-straining labor. Cartier-Bresson's take consisted of a hundred rolls — 3,600 pictures — on a bewildering variety of subjects, their quality average exceptionally high. Furthermore, traveling with them was his own reputation. He was already internationally known. He was also a perfectionist, a man who strove for "decisive moments" in all his pictures, a man who objected to having any of them cropped because his own framing when he took them was the way he wanted them to be — tampering would hurt them.

People are central to Cartier-Bresson's work. In the constantly changing movements and expressions that reflect the moment-to-moment unfolding of human lives — in private feelings, in encounters with others, in the intense preoccupation with small daily activities — it is there that he looks for pictures, striving to catch life at its moments of aesthetic and emotional peak. He has caught such peaks over and over again in pictures notable for an incomparable elegance of composition.

Cartier-Bresson was glad to work for *Life*, and over a decade produced a series of memorable picture stories. But his approach to them was basically antithetical to *Life*'s. Preoccupied as he is with decisive moments, he is a one-picture man at heart. He singles out, isolates, and enthrones gems, whereas the essay maker tries to bring the gems together, to establish links between them, *not* to enshrine them as separate works of art. That is why his "Peiping" take proved so hard for Peggy Sargent to edit. Not only was it hard for her to find his "peak moments" among strips of pictures of a single subject that were all marvelous but that peaked in different ways, but it was also hard for her to resist marking too many. When Cartier-Bresson came to New York later and complimented her on her editing, she was enormously relieved.

"Peiping" was also hard to lay out. The editors, conscious of its news-scoop value, chose to run it as the lead story in the news section of the magazine. They also felt obliged to print as many pictures as they could, out of respect for the story's uniqueness and historical importance. Twenty-six were used. Not many, considering the dimensions of the entire take; too many for the space allotted them. They jostle and crowd each other, struggling to express themselves, competing with one another for attention. Many of them are far too small. Here, in essence, is a salon show compressed into a single magazine article. It is a feast, but a frustrating one, each course so rich that it interferes with the enjoyment of the others.

By strict photo-essay standards, "Peiping" is not an unqualified success since it does not do justice to the pictures chosen for reproduction. But as a photojournalistic coup it scores resoundingly. The essay's very clutter reflects the unimaginable chaos of a crowded and alien society at a time of desperation. Perhaps that was the central point that had to be gotten across. Perhaps, also, that was the best way to handle a story in which too many pictures were too powerful.

Therein lies a thorny dilemma for editors. Cartier-Bresson extricates himself from it neatly. He would say: "If you wish to make essays out of my pictures, that is up to you. But do not ask me to be judged finally by what you do, or even by the pictures you choose." *Life* did not always choose ones that measured up to his own standards. He was notably gracious about that at the time. He could afford to be because he regards magazines as evanescent things. The blue-white diamonds in a photo essay he can salvage and use again in other ways. They can become part of his permanent testimony as a photographer. Those of less than gem quality will be forgotten.

But when it comes to republishing his essays in something more permanent like a book, he feels differently. He is reminded of the less-than-notable pictures they contain and feels, in his own words, "very distressed." In 1953 *Life* ran a charming essay by him on the daily goings-on in a Roman city square. As an essay, it is superior to "Peiping." It is tighter, more skillfully presented, seamless, utterly beguiling. Journalistically it is a brilliant tour de force. Photographically it is not up to his best work. He refused to permit its inclusion in this book. By his standards he was right.

A LAST LOOK AT PEIPING

**PHOTOGRAPHS FOR LIFE BY
HENRI CARTIER-BRESSON**

By the Yellow Calendar of China, 1948 was a Year of the Rat, and the month of December came in the Eleventh Moon. By any calendar they use, both East and West will probably long remember that in this time—when ice was decking the lakes which mirror the gold roofs of the old Ming palaces—Communist armies drove Peiping's defenders behind the city's high gray walls, and surrounded China's ancient and incomparable northern capital.

As complete isolation drew near, LIFE asked the famous French photographer Henri Cartier-Bresson to fly from Burma to Peiping for a last look at a city which is known the world over for its gracious way of life. He spent 10 days there, working when dust storms (*right*) darkened the December skies and when the sheen of frost made clear days brighter. He got away on Dec. 14, on one of the last civilian planes to leave the last airfield open for normal use. In the middle of war he brought out a warming record of a city and a people whose deep equanimity is still a light in dark times, a nostalgic reminder of a China which has lived through many conquests. The Peiping he saw had known the legions of the barbarian Genghis Khan, the architectural triumphs of the Ming Dynasty (LIFE, April 29, 1946) and the extravagant decay of the Manchus in the long reign of a mighty woman, Empress Dowager Tzu Hsi.

Peiping was not a city of heroes; the people expected the Communists would take the city and they preferred that to seeing it damaged by battle. They were not especially craven: everywhere the desire for peace, no matter what the price, was doing almost as much as the Communists to destroy Chiang Kai-shek's China. The people, who put great faith in lore, remembered last week that the Yellow Calendar says, "If it is fine on the day of Tung Chih (Dec. 22) and the sun is bright, in the next year the people will sing peaceful songs." All across north China the day of Tung Chih was fine and bright.

THE FORBIDDEN CITY, a 15th Century group of golden-roofed imperial palaces, finally opened to public in 1924, is nearly obscured by a dust storm. Passing scholar protects nose and mouth with mask.

ON A FAIR MORNING A PEIPING TEAHOUSE IS FILLED WITH THOUGHTFUL MEN WHO BRING THEIR BIRDS AND CRICKETS AND NIBBLE WATERMELON SEEDS

BIRD-WARMER, a covered cage in old man's hand, shields pet on strolls.

WHITE PIGEONS delight an owner. Tail whistles give a musical flight.

GRAY THRUSH goes along for ride as a Peiping newsboy peddles papers.

BIRD MERCHANT offers for sale geese, small thrush perched on twig.

BOXERS, who relax by exercising and never hit anybody, are a common sight in palace courtyards. Here a class practices beside the Temple of Imperial Ancestors. The supple scholar at left demonstrates defense called "All Directions."

OLD FRIENDS meet in Peiping street and visit while clasping hands. The elderly Chinese at the left is a seller of patent medicine who peddles his panaceas from a cloth which is spread out before him on the street, but since he has age, he has respect and dignity.

CITY FINDS SERENITY IN BIRDS AND BOXING

Every Chinese aspires to long life, happiness and—at least until Marx began defying Confucian views—nobility of the mind and spirit. These virtues found their finest expression in the salubrious northern air of Peiping, in the shadows of palaces and temples and China's greatest universities, where the scholar class rose to an intellectual nobility which outlived the emperors. The scholars' traits, often adopted by other men, came to include a deep serenity that still characterizes the daily life of Peiping. It is common to see long-gowned professors flying kites or riding bicycles decorated with bright whirligigs. Professors and clerks practice Chinese boxing, an unbelligerent mixture of queer ballet and shadowboxing which relaxes mind and body. But Peiping's serenity is best seen in the gentlemanly habit of carrying pet birds and singing crickets as companions. Cartier-Bresson wrote about a teahouse. "The fumes of centuries gone float on the rays of the winter sun. One man flies a bird on a string as he would a kite or toy. Another comes in with his bird covered against the cold. One stirs his cricket with a horsehair and the cricket sings. Now the room is full of lip noises of tea sipping and of bird songs and cricket chirps and smiles."

CHIN QUILT and fur ear muffs help this aged ricksha rider to bear the icy winds of December.

LONG-GOWNED SCHOLARS, traditionally most esteemed of China's people, regard Peiping as shrine of their culture. These two are browsing at a book market.

MERCHANT Huang Jui, a famous antique dealer who is nearly 70, will stay in his beloved Peiping. But he is worried about his bronzes.

SKATERS ride bicycles onto the palace lake near the Bell and Drum towers (*background*). Lake froze just before Cartier-Bresson left.

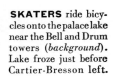

BLIND FORTUNE TELLER rings his brass gong as he wanders through one of Peiping's many narrow *hutungs* (lanes) in his search of sooth-seeking clients.

THE DAY'S WAR NEWS reaches many Peiping citizens when they pause, while strolling, to read the public bulletin boards erected by local newspapers.

A PALACE SWEEPER stops work to warm his hands as the dawn silhouettes tiled roofs of Forbidden City. Small tile figures on eaves ward off spell of evil stars.

81

DEFENDERS on Mongolian ponies guard arch-bordered route to Peiping's south airfield. Reds seized field two days after Cartier-Bresson took this picture.

MOTHERS search for faces they know in parade of soldiers suddenly conscripted to defend the city. However no one expected a really bloody battle for Peiping.

CITY POLICE, white helmets reflecting sunlight that pierces the haze over palaces of the Forbidden City, participate in a defense rally as Communist armies surround and isolate the ancient city.

CONSOLATION from soldier is all one mother finds in search for her son. Like many of those resting (*background*) in a palace courtyard, he was conscripted before his family found out anything about it.

83

HISTORY DOES NOT INTERRUPT A WAY OF LIFE

Photographer Cartier-Bresson wrote at Peiping, "Looking at these gentlemen in long robes, I feel that they will hear that the war is over a long time after it has ended. The course of history does not seem to interrupt a way of life." In the theaters there was still Chinese opera, discordant drama that resists the most elemental lessons of harmony but prospers. On the streets there were still the jugglers who perform and pass the skullcap, and peep-show men who sell a look at tiny tableaux in small bottles. Curio dealers still calmly took their wares to clients' homes, citizens still sought out Peiping delicacies in dark old restaurants, and brides went to weddings in red sedan chairs while great drums pounded. Big funerals, noisy and bright, not solemn—"brilliant offerings to death," Cartier-Bresson called them—still filled the streets with pageantry. Sons watched their ancestors' coffins lowered away as always (*opposite*), but the picture showed very little of death and very much of the durability of custom. Death, like conquest, was incidental in a civilization that keeps on living.

PEEP SHOWS are in tiny bottles in Peiping. Bottle showman holds his profits tightly in his right hand.

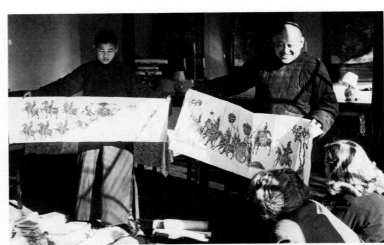

CURIO DEALERS still court their customers by taking their scrolls (*above*) and other wares to show in private homes and large hotels. Without tourists business has been bad.

MONGOL FOOD, a Peiping delicacy, is cooked on "firepot" by Chinese army colonel and his girl friend.

WEDDING DRUMS, gold-rimmed and played by musicians in green gowns, spread their deep rumbling spell over the city even when soldiers (*background*) fill the streets.

FUNERAL procession, as brilliant as a carnival, includes paid mourners who honor a dead matriarch.

SERVANTS' EFFIGIES (*right*), made of paper, will be burned at grave (*opposite*) to assure the deceased matriarch of good help in heaven. The children at left are relatives.

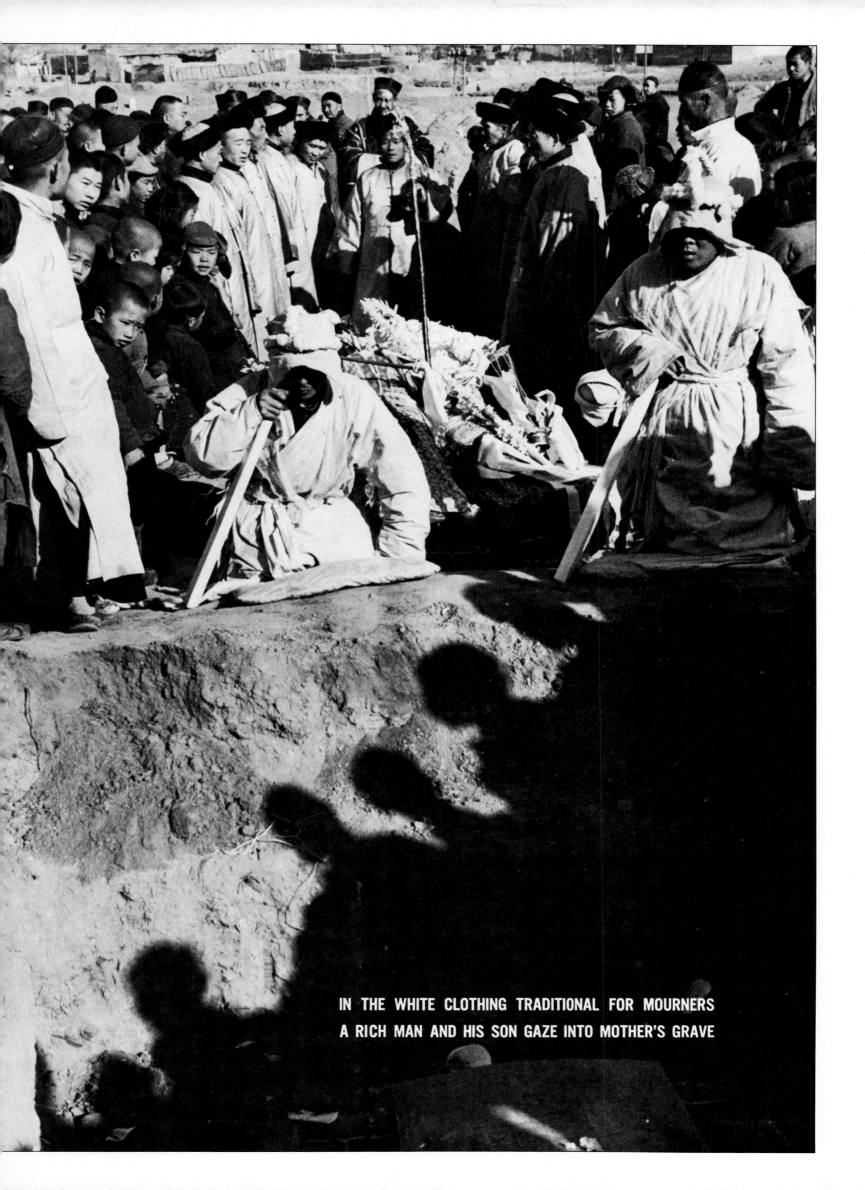

IN THE WHITE CLOTHING TRADITIONAL FOR MOURNERS
A RICH MAN AND HIS SON GAZE INTO MOTHER'S GRAVE

85

Fight Trainer

February 12, 1951
Photographer: Eliot Elisofon
Designers: Charles Tudor, Bernard Quint

Eliot Elisofon used to tell this story about himself: determined as a very young man to become a *Life* photographer, he locked himself in a room for two weeks with every issue of the magazine he could get his hands on. He analyzed all the news leads and photo essays, studying not only the techniques by which the most successful had achieved their ends, but also the photographic thinking that had made them succeed. In other words, not only the how but the what. He grasped from the start that the two were quite different, something that not every photojournalist learned. They might be good technicians, they might be extraordinary ones, but unless they had a highly developed sense of the what, they would not make good photo essays. Elisofon's cram course apparently worked. *Life* liked his pictures and hired him.

Whether the story is exaggerated or not, it says something about Elisofon. He was a learner. Having learned something, he became an instant expert on the subject. Brash, ambitious, restless, extremely talkative, he had his nose into almost everything throughout his life — which ended unexpectedly as a result of a massive stroke in his New York apartment in 1973. He also had an uncanny talent for parlaying one thing into something else. A single example: Sent to remote parts of Africa on photo-essay assignments, he began collecting primitive African art. In time (and largely at *Life*'s expense, because the principal cost of the stuff in those days was not buying it but getting there and finding it), he amassed a collection of museum quality that is now indeed in a museum in Washington. He then began photographing his collection, producing hundreds of dazzling pictures. These led to the publication of books, which made him an authority. That put him on the lecture circuit, and eventually turned him into a museum curator at Harvard.

He was an unusual and remarkably versatile man. During his career at *Life* he was given assignments on almost every conceivable subject. This one, on a prize-fight trainer, were it not for Elisofon's reputation as a quick study, could have been labeled one of Wilson Hicks's "oddball" assignments, for Elisofon's knowledge of boxing was zero when he started. But with the help of a good script and some strong researcher assistance on the scene, he emerged talking authoritatively about boxing, and with a story that would have warmed Billings's heart because it was so informative.

This essay is typical of many that appeared in *Life* in the 1940s and early 1950s. It is tightly scripted, consisting, actually, of nothing but point pictures and how-to sequences. There is even one of Billings's patented let's-know-everything-about-dark-glasses items: a picture of the supplies a trainer must have at ringside during a fight. What lifts it out of the ordinary is Elisofon's skill at making something out of ordinary situations.

The fight-training business is a grubby one and it takes place in a grubby environment, Stillman's Gym in New York. The essay's hero, Charlie Goldman, is a rough little man, but a nice one, who just happens to be a genius at what he does. Elisofon got hold of those elements very quickly, and shot a grubby essay — one whose pictures have deliberately cluttered backgrounds and awkwardly flailing figures, but from which Charlie Goldman does indeed emerge as a training genius and a thoroughly decent man surviving in a dirty business.

The story opens on a one-two punch, a double scene-setter: Charlie outside Stillman's Gym and inside it. There follows a spread that swiftly stakes out the corners of his small world: his room, his hangout, card playing with friends, his occasional dates, and, of course, one shot of him at work training a fighter. This is a model of what an informational spread should be. It tells a great deal with no loss of time, and in remarkably interesting pictures. They are deceptive. Although they were set up with great care by Elisofon to include exactly what he wanted, they do not seem contrived. Instead, they have an offhand and intimate quality that instantly lifts them out of the routine. The one of Charlie in his room and the one of him playing cards are both such fine photographs that it takes a second look to remind that they are point pictures. Either could have been used much larger in a different kind of layout.

The flood of information continues on the next page, but is purveyed differently, with contrasting lighting, wide-angle lenses, and with slow shutter speed to give a close-in effect of fast-moving action. On the opposite page Elisofon returns to a standard lens and conventional lighting in order to make his points clearly. These contrasts in technique had to be recognized and exploited by the designers. Mixing them would have been fatal. The story then builds to an actual fight by one of Charlie's comers, a tough youngster named — as it happened — Rocky Marciano. Billings would have applauded the use of one photograph by a Providence sports photographer on the ground that it was a sensational picture that fitted the need of the story perfectly. As he would have put it: "It could not have not been used."

The aspiring photojournalist could take a leaf from Elisofon's own book and devote a good deal of time to studying this essay. It is a work of art, so subtly contrived that it succeeds, as any work of art should, in making the reader forget how it speaks in his preoccupation with what it says.

AFTER TRAINING SESSION Charlie Goldman leaves gym with his black kit bag. He trains his nine fighters on a rigid schedule, works six hours a day in gyms and an average of two nights a week at fights.

FIGHT

Charlie Goldman

When boxing fans notice Charlie Goldman they see a gnomelike little man in a white sweater, who jumps up into the ring at the bell, patches up a fighter's face, claps an ice bag on his temple, mutters instructions for the next round as he rubs the fighter's belly. Charlie Goldman is a trainer, and in the prizefighting trade he is known as a "winning trainer." In a boxer's corner in a close bout he can be the difference between winning or losing. But Charlie's big job is done in less public places smelling of stale air and liniment, places like Stillman's Gym (*left*), where he trains and tutors nine fighters that he

WATCHING HIS BOYS, Charlie Goldman keeps an impassive eye on Heavyweight Rocky Marciano as he cuts loose a vicious right at Middleweight Walter Cartier, a stable mate, in a gym sparring session.

TRAINER

is a shrewd teacher of boxers and a great corner man

PHOTOGRAPHED FOR LIFE BY ELIOT ELISOFON

handles full time for seven different managers.

Forty years ago Charlie Goldman was one of the country's best bantamweights. He once went 42 rounds in a Brooklyn saloon (the place was raided before the fight was finished) and twice fought the champion. Today his beady eyes peer owlishly through heavy horn-rimmed glasses, and he is half bald. But little else about Charlie has changed since his fighting days. His body is still bantam-size. He still wears his Baltimore heater (derby) and affects no jewelry except a gold ring his father gave him long ago. "People who wear jewelry get stuck up," he says.

In the old days of boxing a fighter's manager took care of training, teaching, seconding their men. Today most managers leave these jobs to trainers, and there are only a handful of really good ones in the business. Charlie Goldman has a simple philosophy for teaching fighters. "It don't do no good to tell them," he insists. "You got to show them." With endless patience, without ever raising his voice or changing inflection, he keeps harping on such ABCs as keeping the wrists stiff while punching the heavy bag. During the heat of fight Charlie is imperturbable. "Lots of corner men yell at you," says Sammy

Giuliana, one of his young welterweights, "but not Charlie. 'You're doing good,' he says, 'just go for the stomach. Hit him in the stomach.' Charlie, he's a great corner man. He inspired me. That's what he did, inspired me!"

To fighters Charlie is teacher, disciplinarian, mascot, friend—and the closest thing to a Mr. Chips the profession ever had. Every week Charlie is offered new fighter-prospects, and he gives each one a trial before turning him down. "They are my stock in trade," he says. "Training promising kids is like putting a quarter in one pocket and taking a dollar out of the other."

AT THE GYM Charlie puts one of his lightweights, Libby Manzo, through an exercise once used by Champions Benny Leonard and Jack Britton. Dancing energetically from side to side, Manzo bounces rubber ball. This bores Stillman habitués but helps sharpen Manzo's footwork, coordination between hand and eye.

IN HIS ROOM, over fireplace, Charlie has pictures of old Heavyweight Jake Kilrain and himself in 1909 (*top*, *left*). At left are strung Christmas cards. "One nice thing about this business," he says, "everybody sends you cards. I got cards from priests, ministers, even a cop in Los Angeles who once gave me directions."

He works in a small world

CHARLIE LEAVES HIS BOARDINGHOUSE FOR WORK

"If they ever find out how old you are," Charlie's friends tell him, "they'll put you in the old men's home." That gets a chuckle out of him. At 63 he has a formula for staying young. He sticks with young people: "They jump around," he says. "You play pinochle with old guys, and one fellow has rheumatism and another has a stiff back and the other guy reads obituaries."

Charlie works in a small world of gyms and promotion offices, of fighters, ex-pugs, managers, gamblers and small-bore characters who talk—usually out of the side of their mouths—of almost nothing but fights and dames. A bachelor, he lives alone in a second-floor room (*opposite page*) at Mrs. Browne's boardinghouse on West 91st Street. The room, decorated with

fighter pictures, including a full-page one of himself from a 1909 *Police Gazette*, is also a workshop where Charlie prepares his own liniment of egg whites, turpentine and vinegar. Charlie's work has not made him rich. He never takes any money from a young boy who averages only $50 for a preliminary bout. With more established men, he is paid a daily fee and a share of the purse. But even in a good year, he does not make more than $4,000.

On off nights, when he is not handling a fighter at one of the local arenas or traipsing off for an out-of-town bout in Detroit, Charlie is rascal enough to go out with girls. He likes to call them his adopted nieces. "I usually take them to the fights," he explains. "I get free passes."

IN THE EARLY WINTER MORNING CHARLIE ESCORTS HEAVYWEIGHT WALTER HAFER TO CENTRAL PARK FOR ROADWORK. FIGHTER RUNS AROUND RESERVOIR

HANGOUT for Charlie is Matchmaker Weill's office on Broadway.

WINNING GIN HAND is flashed on Pete Mello, who runs the Catholic Youth Organization gym. Kibitzing are two of Charlie's boys, Cartier and Jim Gambino.

"ADOPTED NIECE" gets a full-course Chinese dinner at Ruby Foo's.

is thrown at Charlie by Sammy Guilian in this drill to teach the boxer combinations of punches

RIGHT UPPERCUT catches Charlie's glove, which he wears padded part to palms and holds out as target

"PEPPER" is applied by Walter Cartier when, with Charlie watching at close of skipping session, he turns the rope twice for every jump. In a gym the fighters do everything in three-minute spurts.

LEFT JAB flicks out with the right ready to shoot or be tucked under his chin to ward off a counterpunch

POWER is developed by working on the big bag. Here Charlie watches to make certain that Cartier tightens up on muscles when he hits. The light bag is for loosening up the muscles and sharpening eyes.

LEFT UPPERCUT gets good leverage. "You can fight without a right but not without a left," says Charlie

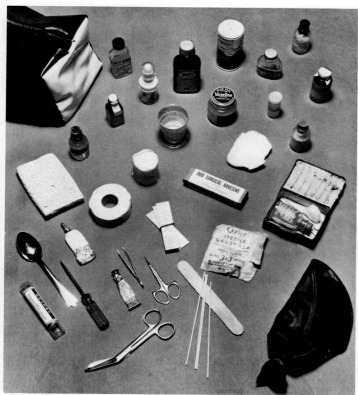

TRAINER'S IMPLEMENTS include these 32 items. Bag Charlie carries them in, gift from fighter, is initialed Dr. C. G.—not as a gag but as mark of respect.

His tricks pay off

As a judge of raw talent, Charlie Goldman has a 100% record. Of the hundreds of prospects he has given the test (*below*) and turned down, not one has ever gone beyond a four-rounder. He looks for one thing—a punch. "It's the short cut to the money," he says. A punch is a thing fighters have to be born with. The rest Charlie can teach them. He works his fighters harder than most trainers, putting on the gloves himself to teach correct technique (*opposite page*), hammering at fundamentals of stance and leverage, demanding boresome repetition so that good habits become instinctive, trying to develop the almost-lost art of feinting. He uses a prosaic assortment of props (*right*) and a homely set of adages. "The punch you throw," he says, "will take care of itself. It's the next one you gotta have ready."

The results are a matter of record. One of his star fighters, Middleweight Walter Cartier, had lost five of 23 fights before Charlie took him over. Since then Cartier has developed a left and won 16 straight fights. Although Charlie has handled four champions in the past—Featherweight Joey Archibald, Lightweight Lou Ambers, Welterweight Marty Servo and Middleweight Al McCoy—he has never hit the biggest jackpot of all, the heavyweight championship. But now he has dead aim on it (*next page*).

WOULD-BE FIGHTER at Catholic Youth Organization gym asks Charlie to test his stuff. After taking a few punches, Charlie advised, "Give up fighting."

NEWSPAPER UNDER ARM reminds Chico Vejar to keep his elbows close to his body as he shadowboxes before mirror. Leverage is lost when elbows are wide.

TOWEL OVER SHOULDERS, ends held in the hands, helps a fighter shorten his punches. Doing it here is Jimmy Gambino, 19-year-old unbeaten heavyweight.

ROPE ON ANKLES hobbles Sammy Guiliani, prevents him from getting feet too far apart. It was useful in changing Guiliani from southpaw to a right-hander.

OLD ROCKY commits sins of leading with right and being off balance and wide open in a 1949 fight.

NEW ROCKY is on balance as he gets lesson from Charlie on how to use punishing right to stomach.

Charlie's boy wins close one

Charlie's prize handiwork is Rocky Marciano, 25, a leading contender for the heavyweight title. He is no fancy Dan, just a rugged, willing, "uphill" fighter who can bail himself out of trouble with one punch. He has knocked out 29 of his 33 opponents and never been beaten. Last week as he got ready to fight Keene Simmons in Providence, Rocky was cool and unruffled as Charlie taped his hands. "He goes in for a fight like I go in for a glass of beer," says Charlie. But Rocky got hurt early and Charlie worked feverishly to stop the flow of blood from his left eye. He told Rocky to slip away from punches and try to avoid trouble. By the fifth round Rocky had his breath and his punch back again (*below*). In the eighth, with Simmons helpless, the referee stopped the fight. "I wasn't worried," said Charlie. "Rocky's a bulldog."

AT ROCKY'S WEDDING last month Charlie arrived late, saw 475 guests and exclaimed, "Gawd, they told me this was going to be a quiet little affair." Then, as Rocky beamed, he got kissed by the bride.

BLOOD FLOWS from Rocky's left eye after Simmons rocks him in second round with a hard right.

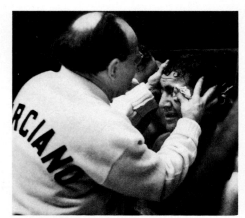

FIRST AID is administered by Charlie, who uses adrenalin chloride, squeezes cut together with gauze.

THE PUNCH for which Rocky is famous smashes Simmons' face in fifth round and helps turn the tide of last week's fight. This photograph was taken by J. David Lamontagne of the *Providence Journal*.

VICTORY SMILES are exchanged by Marciano and Charlie after getting back to dressing room after Simmons fight. Rocky is now in line for a fight with Joe Louis. If he wins that one, he will probably get a shot at Ezzard Charles, the champion, and Charlie's big dream—a crack at the heavyweight title—may come true.

Winter in Maine

February 26, 1951
Photographer: Kosti Ruohomaa
Designer: Bernard Quint

A dour countryman to his marrow, Kosti Ruohomaa did not fit the *Life* photographer mold at all. He was a rawboned, lanky man with a lifetime of exposure to the elements engraved on a deeply seamed face. Laconic, black-humored, he lacked the brashness, the energy, the desire to promote himself, the drive for glitter and success that propelled many of the better-known *Life* staffers. In fact, he never did become a staffer. He worked only spasmodically for *Life*, getting occasional assignments, always going his own way.

Ruohomaa grew up in Rockland, Maine, on a blueberry farm owned by his father. His parents were Finnish immigrants, and his mother never learned to speak English. She wore peasant clothes and preferred to pad around the house in bare feet. The house itself had a solid, not-quite-American look, having been built by Kosti's father. Kosti went to school locally, did farm chores until he was grown, then went off to art school. His artistic career carried him only as far as working on animated cartoons in the Disney studio in Hollywood. He gave up art, returned to the East in 1942 and again became a farmer. Along the way he had picked up some skills in photography and finally decided he would become a professional. His first paid assignment was a story on a small boy going to a rural school in winter. It was shot for *Life*, and one of its pictures wound up on the cover. From then on he was able to get work as he wanted it, but his wants were modest, and his output was always small.

The quality, however, was very high. He shot a beautiful photo essay, "Maine Winter," in 1945. Having hit on a good thing, he shot another on the same subject in 1951, this time concentrating on night shots or back-lit arrangements that give a dark brooding impression: the view of the world that an owl might have, sitting with fluffed-up feathers at twilight in a spruce tree. This second Maine essay speaks even more strongly than the first of the iron rigidity of that frozen land, of the cold and stillness that settle over its lonely ponds and silent village streets when the temperature heads toward zero, when not a breath of air stirs and boots squeak in the snow.

The layout has its awkward moments. First, being all mood, it should have started on a double page instead of opposite a four-color advertisement for floor waxes — clearly there were mock-up problems that week.

Another difficulty was that the designer had to accommodate not only the conventional headlines, text block, and captions, but also quotations from poets that the editor had decided should go with the pictures. The solution, on page one, was to select a wide picture that left space above for most of the type material, and space below for the quotation. Down there, the credit line for the quotation, an added design irritant, could be discreetly buried and would not tangle with the headlines and captions at the top of the page. The result might have been better if the type material at the top had been centered and the small picture of Kosti's father's barn left out. But it is a beautiful photograph — its effectiveness unfortunately lost through being reproduced so small — and I can hear someone at the final layout session saying "We can't lose that one. Let's stick it up in the corner."

At any rate, that is where it landed. My guess is that this story was originally laid out with a double-page opener that was forced by the ad mock-up to be shrunk to one page. In the pages that follow, all textual intrusion is minimized to allow five powerful pictures to speak for themselves. They do it splendidly, with just enough variety in bleeding to keep the eye moving along. The best photograph in the essay — and perhaps as good a picture of a train pulling into a snowy Maine village as has ever been made — is bled all around. There is nothing there to distract the eye except the modest label that identifies the station.

Ruohomaa's pictures of people were almost exclusively of his Maine neighbors: farmers, lobstermen, seiners, and other country types with whom he felt at home. Many of them are fine pictures, but they are really only footnotes to his true preoccupation: Maine itself. It is there, in a hard cold country, come to by immigrants from another hard cold country, that he found his greatest expression in a small output of truly exceptional photographs. Ruohomaa was a heavy drinker, and he died in 1961, exhausted and virtually paralyzed, at the age of only forty-seven.

Winter in Maine

ITS FROZEN NIGHTS EVOKE POETS' PRAISES

PHOTOGRAPHED FOR LIFE BY KOSTI RUOHOMAA

The people of Maine say proudly that they have only two seasons: July and winter. Their down-East winters are harsh, filled with snow and driving sleet and bitter winds. But the frozen beauty of its nights has inspired poets to passages of homely eloquence, an eloquence that has been caught in these photographs which are as cold as a Maine country road.

After Milking

Chickawaukie Pond

*Last night, coming in from the barn, I stood awhile
in the moonlight looking down towards the pond
in winter solitude. . . . Nothing could have seemed
more frozen to stone, more a part of universal silence.*

*All about me, too, seemed still, field and faraway stand
of pine lying frozen in the motionless air
to the same moonlit absence of all sound. . . .*

"NORTHERN FARM" BY HENRY BESTON. COPYRIGHT 1948, BY PERMISSION OF RINEHART & CO.

The branches of the trees make lace
Along the drifted snow beneath,
There is no friendliness in the place,
Except in twelve small squares of light
Set in a house's midnight side. . . .

Maine's northern counties can count on eight feet of snow before winter is over. Most of the state gets by with four feet. The city streets on a snowy night are empty, but along the highways, where a brittle crust forms on the drifts, there are plenty of customers for the all-night diner. Down-Easters brag about winter, but by March they'd just as soon try something else.

Diner near Waldoboro

Park Street in Rockland

In some sections of Maine there are more than 200 freezing days a year, and the thermometer has dropped down to 36° below zero. Throughout the winter lakes and ponds are frozen over, and chill arctic currents sweep along the coastline. Not until the early days of April does a film of water finally appear on the surface of the ponds and the sun begin to thaw the frozen earth.

Where, from their frozen urns, mute springs
Pour out the river's gradual tide,
Shrilly the skater's iron rings,
And voices fill the woodland side. . . .
Chill airs and wintry winds! my ear
Has grown familiar with your song;
I hear it in the opening year,
I listen, and it cheers me long.

"WOODS IN WINTER" BY HENRY WADSWORTH LONGFELLOW

Pond at Benner Hill

Pemaquid Light

103

Spanish Village

April 9, 1951
Photographer: W. Eugene Smith
Designer: Bernard Quint

This essay moves far away from Smith's "Country Doctor" to inhabit an icy pinnacle of perfection all its own. The photojournalist's warm and running concern with one person is replaced by the painter's cool preoccupation with single compositions of awesome power. They are made by an eye that strips down its subjects to reveal the intense sparks of life glowing at their cores. Smith's technique is devastatingly appropriate to its subject: strong chiaroscuro effects to reflect the true look of things in a remote tableland village where the sun is as sharp and bright as an ax and the shadows inky; an emphasis on textures — dirt, dust, stones, chaff, plaster, and black cloth; a sense of chronic hunger everywhere — the only villager who is not thin is the priest. The three husky policemen, of course, are not villagers. They draw their sustenance from afar, from Franco.

"Spanish Village" is perhaps the most famous of all *Life*'s photographic essays. I am so familiar with it that it is hard for me now to imagine its pictures being rearranged in any other way, hard to remember that they came together in this particular form after a great deal of arguing, of preliminary sorting and discarding, after many other arrangements were tried and abandoned.

The final organization seems simple, but it is a maze of subtlety. Of its seventeen pictures, no two are the same size, no two line up horizontally or vertically. The purpose of this — aided by a generous use of white space — is to isolate each picture slightly so that the reader is encouraged to look at it as an individual work of art before he goes on to consider it in relation to other pictures in the story. That device could be murderous to a photo essay if it got out of hand. It would explode spreads, ravage the eye, impose its arty self. That it does none of those things here is a measure of its skill. Everything fits together miraculously in a bewildering but unnoticed blend of full bleeds, partial bleeds, and white surrounds. Margins grow, shrink, and disappear effortlessly.

But fitting things together is just a starter. There must be some internal coherence to the arrangement. There is, first, a philosophical coherence based on faith. The story starts with the birth of religious experience, with the first communion of a seven-year-old girl, and ends in death, with prayers over an old man's corpse. Between are found: a spread showing people moving about within the confines of the village's alleys — with two dark figures headed inexorably toward each other from opposite pages, the giver of real food and the giver of spiritual food — then a spread devoted to labor, with people lifting, tugging, throwing, screaming, their thin energies directed every which way in a kind of semi-starved desperation; next a spread on the quieter moments that villagers spend doing things together behind walls, but even there under the eye of the detested national police.

The story ends on one of the most stunning photographs that Smith or any other photographer has ever taken. The eye lingers over each of the six faces in turn, and then on the hands, and only belatedly discovers that there is a seventh face — and another hand.

ON THE OUTSKIRTS

At midmorning the sun beats down on clustered stone houses. In the distance is belfry of Deleitosa's church.

Spanish Village

T LIVES IN ANCIENT POVERTY AND FAITH

The village of Deleitosa, a place of about 2,300 peasant people, sits on the high, dry, western Spanish tableland called Estremadura, about halfway between Madrid and the border of Portugal. Its name means "delightful," which it no longer is, and its origins are obscure, though they may go back a thousand years to Spain's Moorish period. In any event it is very old and LIFE Photographer Eugene Smith, wandering off the main road into the village, found that its ways had advanced little since medieval times.

Many Deleitosans have never seen a railroad because the nearest one is 25 miles away. The Madrid-Sevilla highway passes Deleitosa seven miles to the north, so almost the only automobiles it sees are a dilapidated sedan and an old station wagon, for hire at prices few villagers can afford. Mail comes in by burro. The nearest telephone is 12½ miles away in another town. Deleitosa's water system still consists of the sort of aqueducts and open wells from which villagers have drawn their water for centuries. Except for the local doctor's portable tin bathtub there is no trace of any modern sanitation, and the streets smell strongly of the villagers' donkeys and pigs.

There are a few signs of the encroachment of the 20th Century in Deleitosa. In the city hall, which is run by political subordinates of the provincial governor, one typewriter clatters. A handful of villagers, including the mayor, own their own small radio sets. About half of the 800 homes of the village are dimly lighted after dark by weak electric-light bulbs which dangle from ancient ceilings. And a small movie theater, which shows some American films, sits among the sprinkling of little shops near the main square. But the village scene is dominated now as always by the high, brown structure of the 16th Century church, the center of society in Catholic Deleitosa. And the lives of the villagers are dominated as always by the bare and brutal problems of subsistence. For Deleitosa, barren of history, unfavored by nature, reduced by wars, lives in poverty—a poverty shared by nearly all and relieved only by the seasonal work of the soil, and the faith that sustains most Deleitosans from the hour of First Communion (*opposite page*) until the simple funeral that marks one's end.

PHOTOGRAPHED FOR LIFE BY W. EUGENE SMITH

FIRST COMMUNION DRESS

renza Curiel, 7, is a sight for her young neighbors as e waits for her mother to lock door, take her to church.

"EL MEDICO"

Dr. José Martin makes rounds with lantern to light patients' homes. He does minor surgery, sending serious cases to city of Cáceres, and treats much typhus.

SMALL BOY'S WORK

The youngest son in the Curiel family, 5-year-old Lutero, sweeps up manure from the street outside his home. It is carefully hoarded as fertilizer, will be used on the eight small fields the family owns or rents a few miles out of town.

"SEÑOR CURA"

Out on a walk, the village priest, Don Manuel, 69, passes barred window and curtained door of a home. He has seldom meddled in politics—the village was bloodily split during the civil war—but sticks to ministry. Villagers like that.

◄—**YOUNG WOMAN'S WORK**

Lutero Curiel's big sister Bernardina, 18, kicks open door of community oven, which the village provides for public use. At least once a week she bakes 24 loaves for the family of eight. The flour comes from family grain, ground locally.

DIVIDING THE GROUND

At harvesttime many of the villagers bring unthreshed wheat from their outlying fields to a large public field next to town. Here they stake out 5-by-12-yard plots where they spread the full stalks, thresh grain as forefathers did.

HAGGLING OVER LOTS

Sometimes luck gives one family stony ground for threshing, another smooth. This brings arguments since the smooth ground makes for easier threshing—a process begun by driving burros over stalks with a drag that loosens kernels.

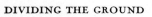

SEEDING TIME

Beans planted, the villager presses hard on his flattened plow as it scrapes the dry soil back into furrows. A neighbor woman leads donkeys, one borrowed.

PLOWBOY FOR HIRE

Genaro Curiel, 17, son of man planting beans (*above*), carries his crude wooden plow as he heads for work at a wage of 12 pesetas (30¢) and one meal a day.

WINNOWING GRAIN

With the straw already broken away, wheat kernels are swept into a pile and one of the women threshers tosses them up so the breeze can carry off the chaff.

111

GUARDIA CIVIL

These stern men, enforcers of national law, are Franco's rural police. They patrol countryside, are feared by people in villages, which also have local police.

VILLAGE SCHOOL

Girls are taught in separate classes from the boys. Four rooms and four lay teachers handle all pupils, as many as 300 in winter, between the ages of 6 and 14.

◀ **FAMILY DINNER**

The Curiels eat thick bean and potato soup from common pot on dirt floor of their kitchen. The father, mother and four children all share the one bedroom.

A CHRISTENING

While his godfather holds him over a font, the priest Don Manuel dries the head of month-old Buenaventura Jimenez Morena after his baptism at village church.

THE THREAD MAKER

A peasant woman moistens the fibers of locally grown flax as she joins them in a long strand which is spun tight by the spindle (*right*), then wrapped around it.

113

HIS WIFE, DAUGHTER, GRANDDAUGHTER AND FRIENDS
HAVE THEIR LAST EARTHLY VISIT WITH A VILLAGER

A Portfolio of Distinguished Britons

January 14, 1952
Photographer: Alfred Eisenstaedt
Designer: Bernard Quint

A short, muscular man with a mahogany face, Alfred Eisenstaedt is one of the legends of photojournalism. It was his skill at this new form of reportage that brought him to the attention of *Life*'s editors even before the magazine was launched. He was one of its four original staff photographers, the others being Margaret Bourke-White, Tom McAvoy, and Peter Stackpole. He was the only one of the four who was still on the staff when *Life* closed its doors. The first two had died and Stackpole had retired. But "Eisie," as he is universally known, kept right on. Today, at eighty, he is still busy with a stream of assignments.

Eisie was raised in Berlin, was given a camera on his thirteenth birthday, and has been taking pictures ever since. He was drafted into the German Army in World War I and survived the near-loss of both his legs from a shell burst. After the war he sold buttons and belts for a living, but slowly began selling photographs too, to newspapers. In 1929 he decided to risk it all on photography, and a protean talent began to emerge. Eisenstaedt is the second of journalism's masters of candid news photography, the rightful heir to Erich Salomon. Where Salomon appeared as by magic, snatching pictures off-guard of the great and near-great all over Europe, so did Eisie. He caught Marlene Dietrich *before* she became famous in *The Blue Angel*. He caught Goebbels, Hitler, Mussolini, Eden, Churchill, and later Eisenhower, Truman, and John Kennedy. He was one of the greatest news photographers who ever lived, shooting a thousand or more assignments for *Life*, making one memorable photograph after another. But he was more. He was also a superb technician and, when given the leisure to work over his pictures, a maker of outstanding photo essays, many of the later ones in color.

"Distinguished Britons" is a peculiar story in not being typical of Eisenstaedt's work. That is, it does not have the swirl of fast-caught action, the sense of being at the center of world events, the snatches of grief or joy, the moments of privacy or tenderness that have elevated many of his pictures. Instead we are treated to a series of sober portraits.

It is only when those portraits are carefully studied that it begins to become clear what a tour de force this essay is. Although its pictures are rich enough in their execution and appear self-conscious enough in their composition to qualify as studio portraits, they are actually candid photographs, taken in natural light and without any studio props whatsoever. In addition, they were all made in only eleven days. Only Eisie could have done that. When he has to, he can work at phenomenal speed. His eye is extraordinary and his control over his equipment (always a Leica) has long been wholly instinctive. If what he wants appears, he can get it. If it doesn't, he isn't beyond shouting, as he once did to the Japanese General Tojo on his way to execution: "Hey, Tojo, look at me." Tojo did.

Shouting at these eminent Englishmen would not have worked. Nevertheless, in an unparalleled burst of creativity, he did manage to get remarkable portraits of eighteen of them (one, of Sir Augustus John, went on *Life*'s cover that week), and to do it with an astonishing range of effects, each appropriate to the man.

The object here was not to trick up the story but to make it respectful to its central subject, which is really the British character. Each of these men, in his own fashion, speaks of British reserve. Here is a gallery of cool, measured looks, tight-lipped, guarded, amused, edging on the aloof, some inward-looking and world-weary, full of long familiarity with power or fame, full of the long knowledge that there is nothing new under the sun, some quizzical, some hard and practical, some stern with the weight of public responsibility — all British.

The little touches, where more than a face is shown, are masterly: the roll of plans, the ruler, the outstretched arm and the angled leg of the architect, all of which make a kind of blueprint out of him; the out-of-focus bit of paper being waved impatiently to match the impatient expression of the man of affairs; the brittle hand of a brittle peer whose ancient blood may at last be warming itself on nerves alone; the enormous collar that will soon swallow its owner as he shrinks into old age.

The layout matches its subject admirably. It moves with the stately pace of a member of London's Athenaeum Club, with long captions that urge the reader into second, third, and fourth looks at the portraits as facts about them are learned. Unlike the uneven layout technique of "Spanish Village," everything here is as symmetrical as a Palladian facade — as it should be. The match-ups are calculated. Two intellectuals with haunting eyes dominate the first spread. The second manages to compose six portraits of markedly different men by matching off poses and sizes: a pair of three-quarter-view head shots against four half-length figures whose clothing further matches: gray above, black below. Next, a change of pace is achieved by using only two pictures that again complement each other in their composition and their dependence on background. Then a return to another busy spread of shrewdly balanced choices, and an exit, dreaming — with the best picture in the take. Once again the difference is made by a multitude of unnoticed small details, from the handsome type used for the caption headlines to the decorative flourish of the cursive lettering introduced on the opening spread and reminiscent of the lettering on an engraved formal invitation. All these little touches have maximized the impact of a marvelous set of pictures with a marvelous layout.

118

A Portfolio of

Distinguished Britons

by Alfred Eisenstaedt

From the drizzle of drab news that has blown from Great Britain these past few years, the world has sometimes gained the impression of a tired and dispirited nation whose greatness was draining away. The drizzle has clouded but hardly altered a prime fact about Britain's regenerative powers: that she still possesses and is still producing a great many people of eminence in a great many fields. This is assurance that while Britain is condemned to more austerity, she is by no means condemned to mediocrity. This winter, in a 10-day round of calls, LIFE Photographer Alfred Eisenstaedt visited a representative group of British men of stature. His aim was to show his subjects candidly, as their character might be revealed to anyone encountering them at work or at home. His study of Painter Augustus John is on the cover, and on these pages LIFE presents a portfolio of 17 others on whom he called.

GEORGE MACAULAY TREVELYAN

The possessor of the fierce visage on the opposite page is one of the more impressive sights of Cambridge University: an erect old man who strides its grounds, hatless and coatless no matter what the weather, flashing dark looks and flaunting a cigaret from a holder. Behind his look of ferocity is a kindly nature and one of the most tremendous minds to mature in Britain in this century. At 75 Dr. G. M. Trevelyan, lately retired as Master of Trinity College at Cambridge, is probably his country's most eminent historian and its most readable one. His *English Social History*, published during the war first in the U.S. and then in England, has sold 473,000 copies and is the greatest phenomenon in its field since his great-uncle Thomas Babington Macaulay's *History of England* came out a century ago. An outspoken, impatient man, Dr. Trevelyan is a tireless hiker and a jealous lover of the green loveliness of his land, who warns his country that unless its beauties are preserved against the defacements of modern life, "the future of our race will be brutish and shorn of spiritual value."

THE VERY REVEREND MARTIN CYRIL D'ARCY, S.J.

If Catholic thought exerts an influence out of all proportion to Catholicism's numbers in the intellectual life of Protestant England, Father D'Arcy (*right*), who is 63, can take a good deal of credit for it. As Master of Campion Hall at Oxford University during the '30s, this priest from Bath was the center and mentor of a large and lively circle of young artists and writers, including Evelyn Waugh and Lord Cherwell, who have since made their marks in many fields. From 1945 to 1950 he was Provincial of the Jesuits' Society in England, constantly traveling between scattered Catholic communities but finding time to write such scholarly inquiries as *The Mind and Heart of Love*. These and his disciples have spread his fame. Nowadays he works in a cluttered room in London's Farm Street Church, the Jesuit headquarters, where Eisenstaedt photographed him. Father D'Arcy impressed his visitor as "the ideal priest from a photographer's standpoint: he looks lean and ascetic, yet there is kindness written all over his unworldly face."

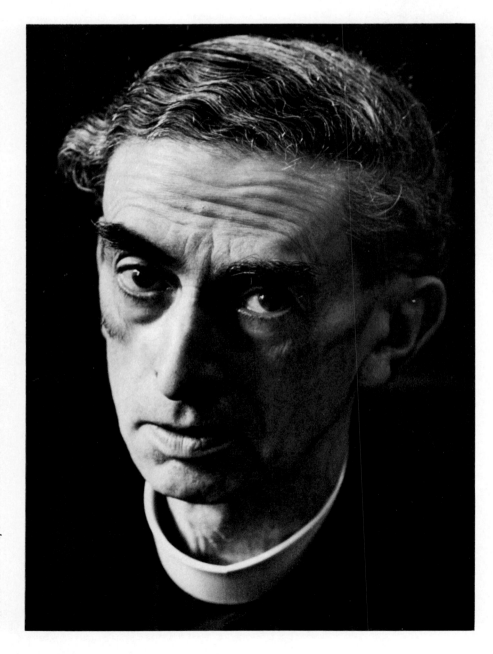

119

SIR DAVID MAXWELL FYFE

This brilliant Scottish barrister (*right*) wears such a heavy mask of dignity that cruel wits (and the London *Sketch*) have jingled of him that "*The nearest thing to death in life, Is David Patrick Maxwell Fyfe.*" The burly Home Secretary and Minister for Welsh Affairs in the new Conservative government is not all that sober-sided. As the deputy chief prosecutor at the Nürnberg trials he spent his free evenings writing a serial fairy tale for his young daughter Miranda, and one of his parties there, complete with pipers and Highland toasts, melted Andrei Vishinsky into making thunderous pro-British speeches. At 34 Fyfe was the youngest King's Counsel in 300 years; now at 51, married to Actor Rex Harrison's sister, he is an M.P. from Liverpool and a Conservative Party big wheel. Eisenstaedt saw him for exactly 4½ minutes, found him "extremely polite."

VISCOUNT CAMROSE

In the gritty South Wales mining town of Merthyr Tydfil, back in 1893, a 14-year-old boy submitted an essay in a contest run by the local *Times*. He was the youngest entrant, and across his winning essay the editor wrote, "This competitor should enter journalism." The competitor did. His name was William Ewert Berry and he became the first Viscount Camrose (*above*), millionaire chairman of the dignified London *Daily Telegraph*, confidant and sometime critic of Winston Churchill, and one of the shrewdest British press lords. His brother Gomer, Lord Kemsley, once his partner in a vast empire, runs the country's largest publishing chain. Eisenstaedt saw Camrose, 72, in his office and roof garden overlooking Fleet Street, and found him "enormously tall and awe-inspiring, very much the boss, forbidding and intimidating . . . he could be a Tammany boss."

SIR WILLIAM EDWARD ROOTES

Dictating a letter in his Devonshire House office, 57-year-old Sir William, the motormaker (*right*) is the picture of the dynamic and incisive man of affairs. From a rural bicycle and auto agency started by their father, who is still living, Sir William and his brother, Sir Reginald Claud Rootes, built a huge British motor firm. As chairman of Rootes group, which makes the Humber, the Hillman and the Sunbeam Talbot, Sir William has a passion for detail and a flair for fast action: when war neared he switched from cars to airplanes and made one out of every seven British bombers during the war. An international supersalesman, he spends much of his time on the road studying foreign markets for such hot products as his sleek little Hillman Minx. He is now in the U.S. as head of his country's Dollar Exports Council, formed to boost sales in the dollar area.

Sir Alexander Fleming

It was in 1928 that Fleming (*left*), examining a culture plate which had been left uncovered on his desk, noticed a strange mold which was dissolving a colony of staphylococci. The mold was penicillin, first of the family of new antibiotic agents out of which grew both an important drug industry and Fleming's reputation as Great Britain's most famous bacteriologist. Thirteen years after his accidental discovery Sir Howard Florey and Dr. Ernst Chain completed the research that made penicillin available in quantity in time for World War II, and in 1945 the three of them shared the Nobel Prize. Eisenstaedt photographed Sir Alexander in the same small, upstairs room at St. Mary's Hospital in London where he discovered penicillin and where the 70-year-old scientist is continuing his research on how the antibiotics, chiefly penicillin, do their germ-killing work.

Bertrand Russell

"When I saw him," said Eisenstaedt, "I decided to do nothing but portrait heads of him: I said, 'Except for you, I haven't found anybody who sits as still as a monument.' Lord Russell said, 'The best occupation of a crocodile is to rest.'" The craggy, 79-year-old, thrice-married philosopher (*above*) has not come to rest yet, although he no longer gets involved in uproars over free love (as he did in England in 1933) or jailed for antiwar articles (as he was in London in 1918) or barred from colleges for his agnostic beliefs (as he was in the U.S. in 1940). Since winning the 1950 Nobel Prize for Literature Lord Russell has toured Australia, made a lecture tour of America (which he thinks may be his last) and gone on giving advice to a heedless world. His latest book, *New Hopes for a Changing World*, based on a series of BBC lectures, will be published in the U.S. next week.

Viscount Moore

Heir to an old Irish peerage, Charles Garrett Ponsonby Moore, 41, is the apotheosis of a peculiarly British 20th Century type, the cultured, titled socialite who is also a brilliant, hard-working businessman. He began his career as an advertising salesman, interrupted it to fight in France, and is now managing director of the influential *Financial Times*, a director of the *Economist* and chief stockholder in trade journals for doctors and bankers. He is known as one of the brightest brains in London's City, the empire's finance center. An enthusiast of classical music and opera, Lord Moore struck Eisenstaedt as "what a poor man thinks a lord should be—most charming, elegant and looking rather languid. When he carried my bag down from his wonderful apartment in Bentinck Street, I thought, you couldn't give him anything heavy to carry—he might fall down."

SIR HUGH CASSON

In the New Year's Honors List this outstanding young architect (*above*) attained his knighthood at 41, a reward for his services as head of the design group that created the gay and adventurous look of the Festival of Britain (LIFE, Aug. 20). The slender, witty son of an Indian civil servant, Hugh Casson went to Cambridge and then starved in bohemian Chelsea. He got his architectural start when his father let him spend a £1,500 legacy on the speculative building of an imaginative country house—which brought him orders for half a dozen like it. He camouflaged airdromes during the war, and, after a surprise telephone call from the Festival of Britain director in 1948, spent two years straw-bossing an eager team of architects. The result was to give the best modern architectural ideas an airing that should stimulate building in Britain for years to come.

SIR EDWARD BRIDGES

The devoted, self-effacing careerists of the Civil Service are the British Empire's truly indispensable men. As Permanent Secretary to the Treasury, Sir Edward Bridges (*opposite page*), 59, not only heads this army in dark suits but epitomizes it. A serious, iron-gray figure, Sir Edward, Eton-and-Oxford educated son of Poet Laureate Robert Bridges, dresses and works and thinks in the stiff-collared tradition of his profession. He gets to his office overlooking the Admiralty at 9 a.m., often works until midnight, sometimes sleeps in the Whitehall bomb shelter where he had a room during the war. On weekends, before his life got too crowded, he used to paint and play the clarinet in his home in Surrey. Eisenstaedt photographed him in his office, where there is an old print of Pembroke on the wall, a red dispatch box and Sir Edward's topper on the table.

JOYCE CARY

With the transatlantic publication of such novels as *Mister Jo*
son, *Herself Surprised* and *The Horse's Mouth*, Joyce Cary (*lef*
63, is belatedly becoming known in America as a major mode
novelist. Recognition had come belatedly to him in England t
and it was largely Cary's own fault: an old Africa hand, a veter
of the Cameroons fighting and magistrate in the remote Nigeri
district of Borgu, he turned to writing when the African heat bro
his health but was too dissatisfied with his work to let anything
published before he was 43. He was born in Donegal to an aris
cratic family from Devonshire. The sociable Cary (pictured in
turtle-neck sweater, his working garb) now lives in a red-brick V
torian pile locally known as a "North Oxford monstrosity," and
ten dines with philosopher friends from the university he attend

CHRISTOPHER FRY

"In my plays," says the 44-year-old playwright-poet (*above*),
want to look at life—at the commonplaces of existence—as if v
had just turned a corner and run into it for the first time." With t
triumph of *The Lady's Not for Burning* in London's West End
1949 Christopher Fry, who never made more than £8 a week in h
life, turned a corner and ran into 20 times that much money—ar
fame to boot. On the strength of it the Frys, who had made do in
16-shilling-a-week cottage near Oxford, took a London house. B
nignly influenced by T. S. Eliot as well as by Shakespeare, Fry
verse plays revive a long-lost art form, the lines falling upon heare
like lyrics in a strange new tongue. So far four of his plays, the newe
A Sleep of Prisoners, have been seen in the U.S. and next month La
rence Olivier's production of *Venus Observed* opens on Broadwa

SIR HENRY DALE

Nearly half a century ago Henry Dale (*left*) quit an obscure £15
a year university lectureship and became one of the pioneer r
search scientists in British industry. His early studies of ergot e
tracts for the Wellcome Laboratories led to important discoveri
about the nature and function of histamine in human physiolog
—and to the 1936 Nobel Prize which he shared with Dr. Otto Loew
As president of the Royal Society [of science] during World War I
and as chairman of the scientific advisory committee to the war ca
inet, he had great influence on the accelerated pace of science r
search in his country. It was he who decided to speed the deve
opment of practical applications of nuclear fission, and to conce
trate the British atomic research staff in the U.S. At 76 he is a bi
broad, energetic man, still one of his country's leading physiologist

David Low

In 1919 a book of caricatures brought a gleam to the eye of Novelist Arnold Bennett, who forthwith dispatched a note to the London *Star*, which forthwith lifted the artist from the relative obscurity of Australia. Now regarded as the world's top political cartoonist, David Low (*right*) is a merry-eyed little man, half skeptic and half idealist, who sees himself as "a nuisance dedicated to sanity." His nuisance value was well appreciated by Lord Beaverbrook, who kept him on his Tory *Evening Standard* 23 years; they disagreed about nearly everything save their freedom to disagree publicly. Two years ago out of political sympathy Low switched to Labor's *Daily Herald*. In a secluded Hampstead studio he wields his mighty pen —a lance tilted at premiers, dictators, Colonel Blimps and other inflated characters, but never dipped in the poison of viciousness.

Dr. Edgar Douglas Adrian

"He looks to me," said Eisenstaedt, "like a nice old Mr. Rockefeller." The gentle, retiring Professor Adrian (*above*), an eminent physiologist, is a successor of Sir Henry Dale as president of the Royal Society and to Dr. Trevelyan as Master of Trinity at Cambridge. He is excessively shy and climbed out a window to escape reporters on the day his 1932 Nobel Prize was announced. He is famed for dramatic research on the workings of the brain and nervous system: in 1929, with a long needle piercing a muscle of his arm, he recorded muscle movements that sounded like machine-gun fire when amplified. He was the first man to photograph the brain at work, by transforming its electrical impulses into light rays. An expert sailor and retired mountain climber, Professor Adrian, 62, is now doing research at Cambridge on the physiology of the sense of smell.

Sir John Douglas Cockcroft

The director (*right*) of the Atomic Energy Research Establishment at Harwell, a pleasant Yorkshireman who is also a first-rate administrator, is Britain's foremost nuclear physicist. Last year he got an overdue Nobel Prize, which came 19 years after he and Dr. E. T. S. Walton, who shared it, had completed the first disintegration of the nucleus of lithium, a milestone in the transmutation of matter. Sir John's staff at Harwell, working on a budget that is small change compared to American outlays, may not have produced a bomb but has exported more industrial and medical isotopes than the U.S. And Harwell recently inaugurated the world's first atomic hot water heating plant. Sir John's own pleasant home, with a fine collection of classical records, is so close to the piles that its rooms recently were found to be a bit radioactive, but not enough so that he had to move.

GILBERT MURRAY

Among England's populous ranks of classical scholars the name and fame of Professor Murray, who turned 86 in his Oxford home last week, are unsurpassed. His translations of the Greek dramatists, begun in 1902, have become standard in the language. But his reputation does not rest on classical studies alone. When he was invested with the Order of Merit in 1941, the London *Times* observed that he "might equally have earned it by his success in transmitting the light of Hellas to a generation that is forgetting the Greek tongue— or by the noble failure of his long works for peace." For since the days of the League of Nations he has been in the thick of the fight between civilization and barbarism. He is an eloquent advocate of the U.N., of the Marshall Plan and of what he terms "a united civilization determined not to perish through continual strife but to relight those lamps which went out, one by one, in 1914." Eisenstaedt found the splendid old man wearing mittens—taken off for the photograph—when he called on him at Oxford and came away with the impression of "a man with a great feeling for other people—a very great man and very humble."

A New Way to Look at the U.S.

April 14, 1952
Photographer: Margaret Bourke-White
Designer: Bernard Quint

One of the first photographs ever taken of Margaret Bourke-White shows her as a very young woman perched on a perilous outcrop atop New York's Chrysler Building. She had the mountain climber's affinity for high places, partly because she was naturally venturesome, partly to find new ways of looking at things. During World War II, as a combat photographer, she persuaded Air Force generals in North Africa to let her fly on bombing missions. From those experiences, plus later flights over Germany at the end of the war, she rapidly became an extremely able aerial photographer. She designed her own cameras, or, I should say, modified them by putting handles on them so that she could hang out of the open doors of small planes or helicopters. Once she had herself suspended by a cable from the bottom of a helicopter. Another time the helicopter she was in suffered an engine failure, fell into the sea, and turned over. She and the pilot were nearly drowned. She lived at the cutting edge of her profession, and drove herself mercilessly.

When talk began about doing a major photo essay on the United States as seen from the air, it was almost a foregone conclusion that Peggy would get the assignment. She barely finished it, having managed to conceal that she was already so badly crippled by Parkinson's disease that she could scarcely work. This was first picked up by John Dille, *Life*'s man in Tokyo during the Korean war. When she went out to photograph the war, Dille went with her, and discovered that the elemental force that had always swept everything before it was no longer there. She had to be helped in and out of jeeps. Her hands had trouble with her camera controls. She came home a sick woman, but managed to convince *Life*'s editors that she was still able to work.

She wasn't. All she had left was her eye. She had herself flown all over the United States, composing pictures, but she had to have a young *Life* reporter with her to focus her cameras and make the stop adjustments that she was no longer capable of making herself. He set up every picture according to exact instructions from her. He held the camera. She looked through it. When the subject was framed to her satisfaction she told him to trip the shutter.

This was her last big assignment for *Life*. She went downhill rapidly after completing it, and finally submitted to an operation that she hoped would arrest her disease. It was only partially successful. Alfred Eisenstaedt shot a harrowing story on her efforts to come back, the exercises she did with demonic concentration, the contortions of a once-beautiful face that could no longer make its muscles behave. She lived on for several years of increasing helplessness, and died in 1971.

Her last essay is a fine one. As is so often the case, it does not seem as original or as spectacular today as it did in 1952, because aerial photography is now a commonplace, and much of the population now flies about in planes. Back then this was not so, and the patterns and strange angles that Bourke-White got were a sensation.

The essay presents few layout problems, the principal one being that of using as many photographs as possible without hurting their effect by making them too small. This was solved on two spreads by emphasizing the verticality of some of the compositions, allowing them to be made quite narrow. On another spread the common denominator of water manages a strong joint statement from four pictures that might have suffered otherwise.

OVER THE TEXAS STAR on the San Jacinto Monument near Houston, helicopter-borne camera looks sharply down 570-foot shaft to steps and parking space below. Tower marks spot where Sam Houston defeated General Santa Anna in 1836.

A NEW WAY TO LOOK AT THE U.S.

Camera and helicopter give an exalted view of the land

PHOTOGRAPHED FOR LIFE BY MARGARET BOURKE-WHITE

The helicopter can hang suspended in the air like a bumblebee at a blossom. It dodges and hovers where ordinary planes and even birds cannot. It can become an almost stationary platform in the sky—and it was as a photographic platform that LIFE's Margaret Bourke-White has used it during the past few months. The pictures she took from the "whirlibirds," shown on these 12 pages, give LIFE's readers a new and exalted view of the U.S. They place familiar scenes and objects in a perspective that men have been able to imagine but few have really seen.

To shoot her story Miss Bourke-White first sought technical advice from Navy helicopter experts. Then, traveling over the country for several months, she rode with crop dusters, traffic patrols and pipeline inspectors, sometimes flying low to catch men at work and play, sometimes coming dangerously close to monuments and bridges, and sometimes hovering high in an almost Olympian inspection of the land and sea beneath.

IN THE FACE OF LIBERTY in New York Harbor the camera picks out the fringes of sightseers who look out windows in her crown a Miss Liberty-arm-length away. In the background is the Jersey shore.

A LANDMARK. Chicago's famous Wrigley Building, looks like candy castle from a helicopter above spire. Building is split in two parts and a railroad track runs between them. Behind them is Chicago River, with Michigan Avenue bridge.

132

BUS TERMINAL makes busy pattern in New York. Cars enter the cross-Hudson Lincoln Tunnel from West 39th Street (*right*) and West 40th Street (*lower left*). Tunnel exit is at upper right. Ramps lead to terminal and parking space on roof.

133

GRAIN ELEVATOR, operated by the Norris Grain Co. on the southeast side of Chicago, unloads corn from lake boat in a Calumet River slip (*right foreground*). In the freight yards (*background*) snow-covered gondola cars are loaded with coal.

GRAPE HARVEST is gathered in a vine yard near Fresno, Calif. as a crew travel along on a trailer collecting boxes of fru

that pickers have left along rows. Sometimes low-flying helicopters are used after a rain to dry grapes with their down-wash.

SULPHUR VAT at Newgulf, Texas makes a ridge between rows of loading freight cars. These vats, the biggest piles of sulphur in the world, are formed by pouring molten sulphur between aluminum walls, removing the walls when it hardens.

BEACH HOLIDAY dots the sands of Coney Island with New Yorkers out for sunshine. Slanting off to right from boardwalk is the big Steeplechase Pier. In foreground are the tower and wire guides of the amusement park parachute jump.

BEACH ACCIDENT, the near drowning of a Coney Island bather named Mary Eschner, draws knot of people. Reviving victim lies in center, attended by lifeguards. Some bathers (*foreground*) wave at helicopter as they run from water.

ISLAND CLUB, the New Rochelle Yacht Club, sits offshore in Long Island Sound, is reached by boats which dock at upper right. At right center of island is swimming pool with diver poised on board.

OCEAN QUEEN, the 1,031-foot long Cunarder *Queen Elizabeth*, is nosed out of the Hudson River channel by a team of chuffing tugboats and headed toward her dock at New York City's 50th Street.

AIRCRAFT CARRIER, the U.S.S. *Boxer*, her crew lined up on flight deck, steams to dock in San Diego after six months off Korea. Main groups of planes are Panthers (*foreground*), Skyraiders and Corsairs.

ILLINOIS LOCK makes its own whirlpool at Lockport, on the Illinois Waterway. One of seven in the waterway system, this 600-foot-long lock raises the canal about 40 feet to the level of Lake Michigan.

GOLDEN GATE BRIDGE, looking toward San Francisco, is photographed through one of its 746-foot towers, tallest in world. To make picture helicopter hovered dangerously close to tower and its cables.

CALIFORNIA WATERSKIERS zip along behind their speedboats as they race over one-mile course in Marine Stadium at Long Beach, an artificial aquatic base about a mile and a half from the ocean.

139

BEACH RIDERS guide their horses along the shore at high tide at Ocean Beach, near Fort Funston, Calif., as the long, low Pacific rollers make mountainlike patterns of the surf.

140

The Prairie

December 15, 1952
Photographer: Howard Sochurek
Designer: Bernard Quint

Some years before he became the managing editor of *Life* George Hunt served a short hitch as chief of *Life*'s Chicago Bureau. He had never been in the Midwest before and was confronted for the first time by the vastness and flatness of the American prairie. It overwhelmed him. "You've got to get that down in pictures," he said to Howard Sochurek, a young photographer assigned to the bureau. This essay is the result.

It was not an easy one to do. All Sochurek had to go by was a wide wave of Hunt's arm and a wild gleam in Hunt's eye, and the repeated words: "It's BIG; it's FLAT." Other than that there was nothing, no theme, no research, no script. Without a great deal of hard thinking and great technical virtuosity, but mostly without an unimaginable amount of hard work, there would have been no story. People tend to think of photojournalists as aesthetic magicians who wander about and perform almost effortless miracles by having the genius to recognize and shoot inspired pictures. It goes without saying that the ability to recognize good material is built into even marginally talented photographers. What does not show in most "inspired" pictures, and will never be properly appreciated by anybody who is not a working photojournalist or who has not labored alongside one on a sprawling assignment, is the sheer drudgery that makes the inspiration possible. More than any other photo essay in this book, "The Prairie" shows how an intrinsically dull story can be brought to life by intelligence and hard work.

There are, in fact, two kinds of stories. In one kind things are happening; it is up to the photographer to catch them. In the other nothing is happening; there it is up to the photographer to conjure up something — to think pictorially day after day, searching for themes, trying to make something of all the static nothing that is spread around him. Sochurek's "Prairie" is such a story, and it took all his skill to pull it off. He drove for thousands of miles back and forth across Kansas and its neighboring states, looking at things, thinking, occasionally shooting a few pictures. Gradually it came over him that his story line lay in the growing size and mechanization and increased prosperity that American wheat farmers had been experiencing ever since the Dust Bowl days. Megafarming was in bloom, with its huge holdings, its heavy capitalizations, its ponderous equipment, its airplanes. And yet its practitioners were still Midwest dirt farmers — just grown big.

With his theme in place Sochurek had to realize it. He did it with a series of pictures of bewildering technical virtuosity. It is doubtful if any *Life* photographer, with the possible exception of Gjon Mili or Ralph Morse, has a greater arsenal of techniques than Sochurek. Here are inside shots, outside shots, day shots, night shots, fast candid shots, carefully posed shots, high camera angles, low ones. There are wide-angle and telephoto effects, back-lit and front-lit pictures, point pictures, moody ones that exploit sunlight or dust, and a heartstring-tugger to end the story. Each relies on some photographic device to enhance its visual effect. Each is the result of thinking. This is not to say that other photographers do not function this way; Sochurek just does it more. An idea for an interesting picture will begin to bubble in his head. He will worry at it until he can find a reason for making it. Then he will go looking for it until he finds it. That kind of photojournalism is backbreaking. I know, because I have traveled on stories with Sochurek. He is a bear of a man who never seems to get tired, never seems to get cold, never seems to be in a hurry. All he does is work. He works with a shattering slowness, a paralyzing deliberation. I remember going out with him one day in the dead of winter to a cemetery in a small town in Illinois to photograph the grave of a soldier killed in Korea: a single point picture in a large essay we were doing. Howard spent about three hours there. He shot fifty or sixty pictures of that grave, composing each with the greatest care, his camera on a tripod, trying with all his skill to turn a routine picture into something worth looking at.

There lies Sochurek's strength. He is not a subtle photographer, but he is an enormously patient and resourceful one. And he is thinking all the time. That way, he makes the designer's job easier because, in addition to thinking about individual pictures, he also never stops thinking about the story as a whole. Bernard Quint, who laid out this one, has said that the trouble with many photographers who work on essays is that they think only of individual pictures. Sometimes they arrive back at the office with nothing *but* individual pictures — with nothing to hold them together. Quint had a fairly easy time here. An opener that said FLAT was there, ready-made. So was a night shot that said BIG FARMING IS A BIG-RISK BUSINESS in a picture of a hail-insurance agency, livened by a device that Sochurek has used over and over again: silhouetted figures. Next come all the wheels and machines, the intimations of space and wealth and distance that make up the heart of the story, and then the reminder that farmers are still farmers, with pictures of a barn dance and a church service. The ender was also there, waiting for Quint to put it in its proper place. Sochurek had been carrying the idea for that one around in his head for weeks, but he had to find it. Finally he did. He composed a picture of touching smallness and abandonment and failure, a fine contrast to all the clanking success that precedes it, framing a dead bush in the door, emphasizing the weeds drifting across the porch and into the room. The doll was hidden in the shadows at the right, so he moved it. But he left the bottle of nose drops right where it was on the windowsill.

THE PRAIRIE

Its loneliness and its awesome immensity shape a distinctive way of American life

PHOTOGRAPHED FOR LIFE BY HOWARD SOCHUREK

As he methodically trudges along with his dog, this man—a lonely figure in the immensity around him—is at home in his world without walls. Under him lie thousands of acres of flatland, above rises a vaulted ceiling, beyond stretches an elusive rim where all life seems to vanish. These are his dimensions and they are the dimensions of the part of the country in which he lives—the American prairie.

As a geographical region the prairie is defined by the extent of its own spacious elements. It is a tremendous open corridor running from Oklahoma north through Kansas, Nebraska and the Dakotas, across the Canadian border. On the west it is flanked by the Black Hills and the Rocky Mountains, and on the east its boundary forms where the horizons shrink and the land ceases to be big.

The winds of modernity have tempered the hard life which the homesteaders led when they came to plow up the buffalo grass. The long fingers of the rail lines and the black-tops have brought the people together, and prosperity from wheat, cattle and from the riches under the soil has given them daily comfort and time for travel. But with all the surface changes, the essential character of life on the prairie has not changed. It is still a living shaped by the prairie's vastness, and in no other part of the world is there a way of life comparable to it.

DWINDLING TOWN, Richfield, Kan., had 1,500 inhabitants in 1886 (*top*). In 1913, the Santa Fe bypassed Richfield and today (*bottom*) it has only 100 people.

BIG DISTANCES COMPEL FARMERS TO COMMUTE

Space leaves its mark on the prairie towns and on the prairie people. There are towns that were prospering communities years ago, but when the railroad lines were cut through, they were bypassed, and now they are silent and forgotten. Today there are towns dying along the highways too, because the modern roads lure the motorists on at high speeds to the larger centers. The centers themselves are few and far apart, so the prairie people must drive long distances for the most usual necessities— to pick up the mail, see a movie or take a music lesson.

But in recent years many farmers have moved to towns to enjoy the facilities. Now they commute to their farms. Some commute daily—by car or plane—and some weekly. Some "batch it" during planting and harvesting, living on the land in a trailer or a cook shack. Others, called "suitcasers," have city jobs but farm wheat part time. The "suitcaser" on the opposite page runs a farm implement business in Spearville, Kan., owns a 160-acre section of wheat land 72 miles from his home and another 240 miles away in Colorado. His yearly commuting mileage: 60,000.

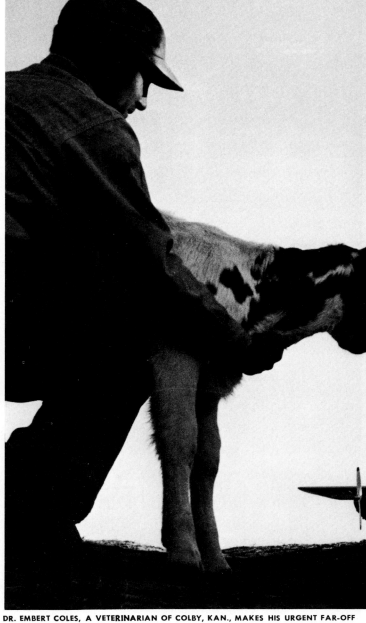

DR. EMBERT COLES, A VETERINARIAN OF COLBY, KAN., MAKES HIS URGENT FAR-OFF

AT HIS FARMHOUSE Ruben Crist, a Kansas cattle and wheat operator, sits beside a picture window, looking out over part of his huge acreage. He farms 12,500 acres, 7,500 in wheat and 5,000 in pasture.

AT HIS TOWN HOME in Garden City, 28 miles from farm, Crist sits by window looking out on

As he methodically trudges along with his dog, this man—a lonely figure in the immensity around him—is at home in his world without walls. Under him lie thousands of acres of flatland, above rises a vaulted ceiling, beyond stretches an elusive rim where all life seems to vanish. These are his dimensions and they are the dimensions of the part of the country in which he lives—the American prairie.

As a geographical region the prairie is defined by the extent of its own spacious elements. It is a tremendous open corridor running from Oklahoma north through Kansas, Nebraska and the Dakotas, across the Canadian border. On the west it is flanked by the Rocky Mountains, and on the east its boundary forms where the horizons shrink and the land ceases to be big.

The winds of modernity have tempered the hard life which the homesteaders led when they came to plow up the buffalo grass. The long fingers of the rail lines and the black-tops have brought the people together, and prosperity from wheat, cattle and from the riches under the soil has given them daily comfort and time for travel. But with all the surface changes, the essential character of life on the prairie has not changed. It is still a living shaped by the prairie's vastness, and in no other part of the world is there a way of life comparable to it.

A CONTINUAL WARNING of the danger of hail is flashed by the jagged neon sign of an insurance office in Cimarron, Kan. Inside, F. C. Walker, president of the company (*right*), discusses a policy with a prospective customer. Hailstorms

strike with such force that the pellets, sometimes the size of baseballs, can mash a farmer's entire wheat crop into the ground. Last year, the worst on record for hail destruction, hailstorms in Kansas alone destroyed two million acres of wheat.

WHEELS AND WINGS of one 5,000-acre wheat farmer, Fred Dikeman of Syracuse, Kan. (*second from the right*), add up to a remarkable variety of equipment. The plane is a Beech Bonanza. Dikeman also has two more tractors and five more trucks. With him are his three sons who now operate the farm.

TWIN TRACTORS, hitched together in tandem so one man can drive both, is a common prairie device that doubles pulling power and work one man can do.

WEIGHTED WHEELS give better traction to Ellisworth Sherman's tractors. A wheat grower, he farms 10,000 Kansas acres, has 18 tractors, 13 combines.

WHEELS ARE ITS BASIC TOOLS

On the prairie the wheat farms and the cattle ranches are huge. A 1,000-acre operation is considered small; a big one is 50,000 acres. Farmers invest hundreds of thousands of dollars in wheeled equipment—fleets of tractors, trucks and combines. On his 5,000-acre farm one Kansas operator has 185 tires in use. The equipment is the biggest made but is still not big enough. To save labor farmers continually devise means to increase the pulling load of the tractor—a vehicle which in cultivating one section of wheatland (640 acres) during one season travels 3,300 miles.

With their machinery the farmers can wrest more and more out of the land, but nature often intervenes to frustrate them. The blizzards, the brutal droughts, the fearfully sudden cyclones, the crushing hailstorms—all make man's effort to master the prairie a gamble on the predictability of its land and sky.

CHURNING UP DUST, BIG PRAIRIE DISK PLOWS CUT OUT A 40-FOOT SWATH THROUGH SOIL OF A COLORADO FARM

AT HIS FARMHOUSE Ruben Crist, a Kansas cattle and wheat operator, sits beside a picture window. looking out over part of his huge acreage. He farms 12,500 acres, 7,500 in wheat and 5,000 in pasture. **AT HIS TOWN HOME** in Garden City, 28 miles from farm, Crist sits by window looking out on

DR. EMBERT COLES, A VETERINARIAN OF COLBY, KAN., MAKES HIS URGENT FAR-OFF

BIG DISTANCES COMPEL FARMERS TO COMMUTE

Space leaves its mark on the prairie towns and on the prairie people. There are towns that were prospering communities years ago, but when the railroad lines were cut through, they were bypassed, and now they are silent and forgotten. Today there are towns dying along the highways too, because the modern roads lure the motorists on at high speeds to the larger centers. The centers themselves are few and far apart, so the prairie people must drive long distances for the most usual necessities— to pick up the mail, see a movie or take a music lesson.

But in recent years many farmers have moved to towns to enjoy the facilities. Now they commute to their farms. Some commute daily—by car or plane—and some weekly. Some "batch it" during planting and harvesting, living on the land in a trailer or a cook shack. Others, called "suitcasers," have city jobs but farm wheat part time. The "suitcaser" on the opposite page runs a farm implement business in Spearville, Kan., owns a 160-acre section of wheat land 72 miles from his home and another 240 miles away in Colorado. His yearly commuting mileage: 60,000.

DWINDLING TOWN, Richfield, Kan., had 1,500 inhabitants in 1886 (*top*). In 1913, the Santa Fe bypassed Richfield and today (*bottom*) it has only 100 people.

CALLS IN A RENTED PLANE. LAST YEAR HIS WORK TOOK HIM 3,000 MILES IN THE AIR, 39,000 BY AUTOMOBILE

"SUITCASER" DENNIS DUESING HEADS FOR THE CITY

house of another farmer who works acreage in Colorado, 100 miles away. Crist's house has 12 rooms.

TRIP TO TOWN for a violin lesson is made in the family car, a Lincoln, by Jean Ann Ware, 13-year-old daughter of a wheat farmer. Her mother drives Jean 21 miles to Garden City every Saturday morning.

ANNOUNCEMENT of a party to be held at Pawnee Acre, Kan. community center stands by roadside.

BEFORE PARTY Pawnee Acre members spruce up the building while a baby sleeps through the noise.

IN DIGHTON, KAN. FLYING FARMERS WIND UP A "FLY-IN" WITH A SQUARE DANCE. AFTERWARD THEY ROLLED OUT COTS

THE PEOPLE FORM IN ISLANDS

The rhythm of the square dance, the recitation of the youngster, a box supper for the parents of the school children—these are some of the things that dispel the loneliness of the prairie. Many years ago a man's neighbor was a remote and distant figure. Now the prairie people come from miles around to go calling or to go into town for the simplest forms of social life.

Some of them—the plane owners—are organized into the Flying Farmers who put on cross-country flying tours and hold social gatherings. And here and there, at a crossroad or on a rise in the land, stands a solitary community building, perhaps an old Army barracks.

AND SLEEPING BAGS AND SLEPT IN THE DANCE HALL

OF SOCIAL LIFE

Though there is a radio at home and movies in town, this center is kept going because the town is far off and the 30 or 40 families who support the center find that most of the social pleasures they really want can be found in the suppers, the literaries, the dances and plays, and the card parties that go on inside of it.

EARLY ARRIVAL for the Pawnee Acre box supper sits outside the community center waiting for other guests while the headlights of an arriving automobile curl into the driveway from the lonely prairie road.

A RECITATION by schoolboy is given close attention while his teacher stands ready to prompt him. Before evening was over, Pawnee Acre guests had sat through a school play, taken part in an auction.

AFTER SUNDAY SERVICE A BRIEF BUSTLE OF ACTIVITY DISTURBS THE USUAL SOLITUDE AROUND THE 45-YEAR-OLD LYDIA METHODIST CHURCH STANDING IN THE KANSAS FLATLAND

HERE MAN MEETS HIS MAKER

PERTINENT STATISTICS ARE KEPT ON THE CHURCH WALL

As modern machines have taken over the burden of work across the prairie, the big farms have become bigger and the small farms fewer. The change has left in its wake a trail of old empty farmhouses which, inhabited once by the small farmers, have been swallowed up and consolidated in the advance of bigness.

For the people who remain on it, the prairie holds a deep and abiding sentiment that shows itself in the simple details of a graveyard alone in the middle of the land or of the warm unity found in a prairie family. It is an attachment that is generated, perhaps, by the immensity of the surroundings, which can enrich a man, whether he speaks of it or not, with a profound yet reserved understanding with his God.

There are many religious sects on the prairie. As with the social life much of the worshiping is done in the town churches. But here and there out on the squared-off sections of prairie space, stand the lonely angled shapes of the old country churches. The congregations continue to keep them freshly painted and patched and to worship in them. On Sunday mornings at 10 o'clock the same families take their seats on the wooden benches in the Methodist church in Lydia, Kan. (*above*). For an hour they hold Sunday school. Then, on the arrival of the preacher who drives out 22 miles from Leoti, they have their service—pious but undemonstrative and quietly unaccented like the expanses of land that stretch off on all sides.

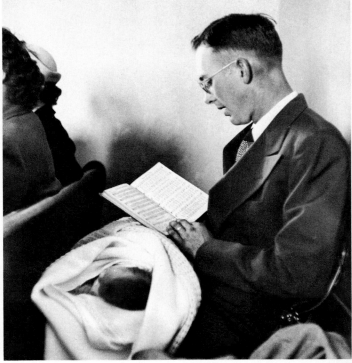

OLD PARISHIONER, Mrs. John Grusing, teaches Sunday school. She came to the prairie in 1908 seeking room to raise her five children, later had eight more.

YOUNG PARISHIONER, Charles Rewertz, joins in singing *Faith of Our Fathers* during service. Like others with sleeping babies in laps, he has to remain seated.

152

A DESERTED HOUSE YIELDS TO THE PRAIRIE, WHOSE WEEDS COME CREEPING IN OVER THE OLD BOARDS ➡

Three Mormon Towns

September 6, 1954
Photographers: Dorothea Lange and Ansel Adams
Designers: Charles Tudor and Bernard Quint

One of the most unusual photo suggestions ever to come Life's way was one by Dorothea Lange and Ansel Adams that they be allowed to collaborate on an essay on three obscure Mormon towns. Here was a subject that no Life editor would even have thought of, let alone tried to script. That it would be done by two people whose photographic styles had almost nothing in common made it even stranger.

Actually, the suggestion was not nearly so quirky as might seem. To begin with, Lange and Adams were already legendary figures in American photography, Lange as a documenter of America's rural poor during the Great Depression, Adams as the best landscape photographer that this country has ever produced. The prospect of combining those enormous talents was intriguing. Further, Lange and Adams knew each other intimately. They had long admired each other's work and felt at home in the West, and they shared a passion for craggy surfaces: Lange for faces lined by toil and exposure, Adams for the original rock itself.

The story that resulted is more Lange than Adams — something that was not exactly Adams's fault. His reputation rests on landscapes taken by 8 × 10 view cameras with very small apertures, in which details of texture and tonal balance are preserved with an almost microscopic care. Adams has, in fact, formalized his theories about photography in a series of books. Basic to his approach is an understanding of, and an ability to control, the various shades of gray that make up the spectrum of a black-and-white photograph. This presupposes great care in printing. Indeed, the ultimate Adams photograph is printed by him. High-speed reproduction of his pictures on Life's presses does not begin to do justice to them.

Lange, on the other hand, had a grainy style that was made for the weathered faces she found in the three Mormon settlements. Starting life as a portrait photographer, she gave up that career in the 1930s to join the Farm Security Administration. Much of the rest of her life was devoted to photographing migrant workers and other dispossessed or ground-down people. She had an instinctive affinity for country folk, particularly those living on the edge of subsistence. One of her most famous photographs, "Migrant Mother," shows a young woman with a grim, beaten face, her two shabby children collapsed against her. She and her husband are itinerant pea-pickers, and he has just had to sell the tires off their car because the pea crop has frozen and the state has cut off relief. Now she stares into space, wondering what to do next. Lange's picture of that woman was so powerful that when it was published the Relief Administration reestablished state aid.

The essay that these disparate talents produced is a fascinating one. Adams contributed the setting: a mountain range, a street, an abandoned house, some clouds and a church. In the essay these are made large, providing anchors around which Lange's photographs are fitted almost like ornamental human borders. These smaller pictures are the most effective: an old hand on an old hat, another on a child's head, the working end of a shovel, an armful of pickle jars, a small girl looking out a window and falling into poses as beautiful as a ballerina's. To repeat, Life could not do justice to Adams's pictures, and that may be one reason why only seven of them were used, compared to twenty-seven of Lange's, whose down-to-earth gritty quality was not hurt in the slightest by Life's printing. But the main reason for the disparity surely has to be subject matter. One large picture can set a scene, but it takes many faces to bring it to life.

In any event, the proportion seems right. A difficult meld has been made seamlessly, starting with an opener that, for once in Life, introduces a story indirectly. No Mormon town is shown, no Mormon face. Instead we get a mountain and an old felt hat. Misguided? On the contrary! Consider what the designers had to say on that first page: "Reader, two photographers are going to speak to you about a dream held by religious pioneers striking out into a bitter land, and about some of the directions that dream has taken since. It would be a mistake to distract you with any of the details of that dream before we set in your eye the backdrop against which it is laid (the Utah mountain landscape which one of us has photographed) or the kind of person you will find there (symbolized by the old hat that the other of us has photographed)."

A tricky story often has to have a tricky introduction. If it explains itself faster in Life than I can explain it here (and it does), it can be considered to have succeeded.

The main design problem, after the opener, is to make sure that the differences in the three different towns are clearly established. That is done effortlessly, both in layout and by picture selection. The dying town contains a few static shots; some weathered boards, an empty house, an old man and an old woman who seem as motionless as everything else there. The living town, Gunlock, is full of energy. It dances with little pictures and with the activities of its guarantee for the future: its children. The third town, the one in transition, gets its flavor from a mixture of the old and the new: a face from the past set against a scrim of neon signs and a drive-in movie. That could have ended the story, but when the page is turned there is an extra dividend: a portrait so full of dignity and serenity, speaking so eloquently of a long hard life lived close to God, that it recapitulates the entire essay. Only when one has thoroughly soaked up what falls between, does one appreciate the brilliant selection of this essay's opener and its ender.

The soaring battlements of Zion National Park

Three Mormon Towns

HERE CAN BE FOUND THE LAND OF ZION'S PAST AND PRESENT

Photographed for LIFE

by DOROTHEA LANGE and ANSEL ADAMS

Last year Miss Lange, whose documentary photographs are famous, and Mr. Adams, who is one of America's greatest scenic photographers, told LIFE of their desire to find and portray three towns which together might suggest the whole diversity and depth of Mormon life. LIFE commissioned the project and now presents the story which they assembled with Writer Daniel Dixon.

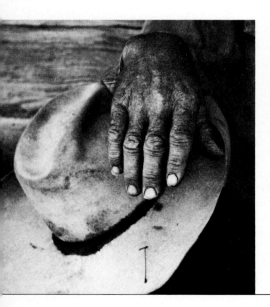

Weathered hands in a hard land

*T*HIS is the place," said Brigham Young, but at first the brethren were not sure: this was bleak country to call the promised land. They had come 1,400 miles from a past of prejudice and oppression and now their leader had delivered them as he knew he must, for only in the heart of an ungenerous wilderness would they be safe from enemies who twice before had driven them from cities of their faith.

But Brother Brigham could see more than isolation in this land; his eyes, like the prophet Joseph's, burned with images of the future. He saw the desert yield up the walls and roofs of another great city, the seat of an empire, the throne of the kingdom of God on earth. By then the most sceptical of the Saints could sense that there was a nobility in the vast horizons and the wind that smelled of juniper and thunderstorms and the soaring rock temples carved by eternity from the same rock that would blunt plows. This was a place which brought them close to God.

So in 1847 to a land both splendid and forbidding came a people visionary and practical. Ten years after that day when the first wagons groaned to a halt, Brother Brigham's vision of empire was taking shape: the Saints had pushed their little colonies north into Idaho, west to California, south to the rim of the Grand Canyon. Near Zion Park in southern Utah stand the villages of St. George, Gunlock and Toquerville and in them live the grandchildren of pioneers who came from London slums and tidy New England farms to the land they called Zion. These towns differ from each other and from their past; in them are three different expressions of what the Mormon people have become since, a century ago, they ventured into the wilderness on a great adventure of courage and faith.

155

A man's beginnings stay with him

Main Street without end

*Toquerville is old
and quiet but its
children have gone away*

This house was built by the women in the early days while the men
were out fighting Indians. That's why the stones are so small.

Now the house is empty. Through shards
of glass the passer-by glimpses another house.

156

SOME of the towns of Zion have scarcely changed since the pioneers platted the broad streets and lined them with Lombardy poplars and with sturdy houses built of adobe or the rough stone of the region. One of these unchanging towns is Toquerville. It does not have a bank or a movie house, a motel or a cafe. It has a post office and two small grocery stores but no neon sign. Its people are old. Their children and grandchildren have gone away—to live in Salt Lake City, Las Vegas, Los Angeles. Those who remain no longer fight the wilderness and have retired to memories and their church.

Age alone has not kept Toquerville a place apart. Although the Saints are a friendly people, theirs is a lofty, lonely faith. They believe that they are God's Chosen People, keepers of His revealed word, destined to lead all His children into Heaven at the Latter Day. Trucks and tourists and the great highway which bisects their town are not so important to them as their strong and enduring vision of Zion. Sheltered by the stately trees the pioneers planted and sustained by small, productive gardens, the people of Toquerville live quietly in a world the rest of the world nearly forgets.

In the backyard the visitor finds an odd, sagging fence dividing the past from a fertile garden and again the other house amid poplars.

It was her people first lived in the stone house out front. They are now dead.

Four young riders in summer

Gunlock is young
and beginning
to meet the future

NINE miles of jolting dirt road lead
from the highway to the hamlet of Gunlock, a flash of green
in a narrow valley. Twenty-two families live here
on 247 irrigated acres. The lands are watered from a gentle
stream which can rise within hours to flood stage,
washing out ditches and roads and leaving the fields
covered with gravel and boulders.

Life in Gunlock is most often pleasant and simple,
full of friends and horses and children. Mail comes
three times a week. The general store sells horseshoes,
fly swatters, overalls, soda pop, a few groceries.
Outside the store, at the edge of an irrigation ditch,
stands the town's only gas pump. There is an old adobe
schoolhouse and a new church, which the people built
with their own hands, as they built the barns and houses
which lead up to the church on either side of the road.

It is not altogether an easy life in Gunlock.
The people have large families which their farms
are often too small and their cattle too few to support.
Some of the men now go daily to St. George, 22 miles away,
and work for wages. As the United States swirled over
and assimilated the empire of Zion over a half century ago,
so now the world outside is reaching toward Gunlock,
which in a few years will no longer be what it has always
been, an isolated hamlet at the edge of the wilderness.

Pause to talk cattle prices

158

Main Street full of children

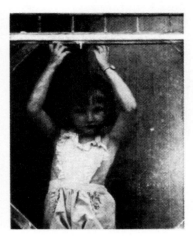

Abundance from the garden

A winter's provender

The future's shy grace

159

Gunlock enjoys the Lord's Day

Waiting to go in

Flowers for the church

Sunday best

Time to leave

The immanence of God

160

The young elders of Gunlock

Recessional

Temple built by the faithful

The gathering of the family

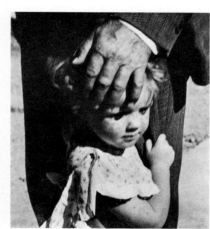

The hand of love

Worldly way station on Route 91

St. George has

*I*N 1861 Brother Brigham dispatched 300 families
to found St. George and raise cotton.
The cotton never grew but the settlement survived.
"Once," someone says, "no good Mormon would give a Gentile
a bed to sleep in; now they make a business of it."
And so they do; for Route 91 linking Salt Lake City
and Los Angeles courses through town like a river of gold

Merchant, churchman, owner of the town's first motel

The new era beckons . . .

. . . to the restless

The tourists take over Main Street

taken up worldly ways

and most of St. George's 4,500 people earn their living catering to passing strangers. They run gas stations, cafes and 23 motels. But while they seem to have given up the past for the present and abandoned the plow for the gas pump their struggle is unchanged. They seek, like their grandfathers, to wrest a living from the desert, and in their way they, too, are pioneers.

. . . to the enterprising

. . . and the weary

"My father was born in England. He was the first man to plow a furrow for an irrigated crop in the Salt Lake Valley. I was the fifth child of his third wife and had 20 brothers and sisters."

To her, viewing the strange new ways of St. George, this is still, as Brigham Young said, The Place.

164

Irish Country People

March 21, 1955
Photographer: Dorothea Lange
Designer: Bernard Quint

Whether Dorothea Lange and Ansel Adams fortified each other in their joint essay on Mormon towns or whether they got in each other's way can be argued. My own opinion is that, with the help of good design, they pulled it off. Nevertheless, it is with a feeling close to joy that one turns the page to find a story that is all Lange, that returns to the principle that the purest essays are those seen through a single eye.

And what an essay this is. It is full of the smiles and indulgences that only a long career of looking with concern into the faces of the poor could justify.

Lange's life was never easy. As the most eloquent documentary photographer in the Farm Security Administration, she became the quasi-official spokesman for all the distressed and dispossessed of the great American Dust Bowl, of migrant labor camps, of unemployment lines and soup kitchens. All that misery lay heavily on her, and the international reputation her photography earned her was not always enough to redress the burden. She suffered for her fellowmen. Furthermore her own health was intermittently poor. That explains the great lift to the spirit that this story produces. She went to Ireland in a happy mood, felt healthy and at home there, and shot a superlative essay.

She had no illusions about Irish poverty. It is as real as it was in Oklahoma in the 1930s and it is far more durable, having lasted for centuries. But it must have buoyed her spirits immensely to learn that people in Ireland were not destroyed by poverty. In a land of small expectations, small successes loom large. To endure is a kind of success. The countryman of western Ireland may have to work very hard for very little, but he is not stunned by a sense of failure, as the American itinerant worker was in the 1930s. On the contrary, Irish country lives have meaning and hope: a good sale at the market, the priesthood for a worthy son, a bit of money from a child in the States, and always the comfort of a world that can be depended on because it changes so little from decade to decade.

One can almost see Dorothea Lange settling into western Ireland with a broad grin, enjoying the mud and the drizzle and the slow country talk and the quiet hours in pubs and the small excitements of market day. What a relief, after looking for so long at the numb and bewildered side of a poverty that has given up, to find a side that is functioning and cheerful, that greets hard work and privation with its own broad grin. Of all the pictures in this book I think my favorite is of Patrick Flanagan and his two sheep, not only because it is such a gorgeous picture but because I *know* how Dorothea Lange must have felt when she took it.

I last saw Dorothea Lange in 1964. Although she looked ill and frail, she said nothing about herself. Predictably, she was full of a scheme to help others — forgotten or impoverished photographers. I am ashamed to say that I was too busy to stop what I was doing in order to help her. She died a year later, of cancer.

Photographed for LIFE by DOROTHEA LANGE

Irish Country People

SERENELY THEY LIVE IN AGE-OLD PATTERNS

THE forefathers of the Irish around the world who are celebrating St. Patrick's Day looked very much like the smiling lad above from County Clare in western Ireland. He is of the seed stock, the rural people of the towns and countryside who for 100 years and more have been exporting Irishmen. His home is near Ennis, in poorish farming country although boiled potatoes come as mealy and mellow there as elsewhere in Ireland. Here as always the families worship, work stubborn land, bend to bitter winds together, and are quietly content. His people live to the ancient Irish ways and a visitor finds them, as the following pages show, humorous, direct and generous—good ancestors to have.

ON WATCH over a kreel in the bend of Market Street, Ennis is a cheerful boy of 15 or so who must do his share of the work.

A wild and rugged country tests

FARM FAMILY works together.
As John O'Halloran (no relation to Bridie)
carts hay, his wife and daughter Anne (*right*)
carry milk from cows in the barn.
Two sons also help him work the 80 acres.
A second daughter is in school
and two more, seeking their fortunes
still farther west, have emigrated to America.

168

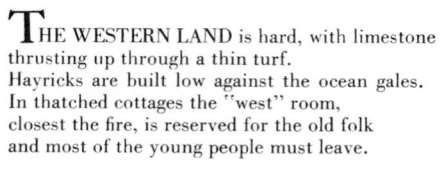

THE WESTERN LAND is hard, with limestone
thrusting up through a thin turf.
Hayricks are built low against the ocean gales.
In thatched cottages the "west" room,
closest the fire, is reserved for the old folk
and most of the young people must leave.

SCHOOLGIRL, red-headed Bridie O'Halloran, 10,
learns her lessons in Gaelic and mixes it
with English in everyday talk. She is quick,
bright but shy with strangers,
answering all questions in whispers
with many a respectful "sir" and "ma'am."

a man's best

SON AND MOTHER work 30 meager acres
in Clare. Although not the eldest, Michael (*above*)
has stayed on the farm with his mother,
Mrs. Nora Kennally, 55 (*right*),
a widow since "himself died two years ago."
Three other sons and two daughters
are in the Kennally family, but they have married
or have left home for jobs elsewhere.

WANDERING MINSTRELS, the Dunn boys of Limerick, the taller of them blind, fiddle and strum at the country markets and fairs through the west. Here, as they strike up a tune, two solemn "kidgers," Sean and Mick McInerney who come from Lisahn, listen intently.

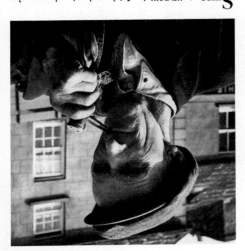

ON CATTLE DAY in Ennistymon market, Church Street, named for the Church of Ireland church which stands at top, is jammed. Pigs have the place to themselves once a month and there are weekly markets in oats, cabbages and potatoes and in burning turf and bogdale.

THE CATTLEMEN (*left*) carry hazel rods to make the beasts mind, and wear "Wellingtons," rubber boots named after the high leather boots worn by the Duke of Wellington's troops. A group stands about Hinchy's, a fine pub now run by a third-generation Hinchy.

STILL A "BOY" by Irish reckoning because he is unmarried and landless, Paddy Reynolds who "works around" the farms, comes often to Ennistymon market, 16 miles west of Ennis. Here, having driven in the cattle, he listens judiciously while his employer bargains.

The work is rewarded on market day

A JOVIAL MAN with a great fondness for having his picture taken is Patrick Flanagan who shares a 70-acre farm with his brother in County Galway near Tubber on the Clare border. He was selling sheep on the Tubber green when he saw the camera and with a chortle grabbed up a couple for a group portrait. The only thing to plague the happy-go-lucky life of Flanagan is myxomatosis, the rabbit-killing disease that has spread from Europe to Eire. Now that there are fewer rabbits in the fields, the foxes have taken to eating lamb.

Townspeople

A WARM WELCOME waits within an Ennis pub.
The town's 6,000 people, beset by the rains,
are never too far from a tap.
Stout at 16¢ an English pint is favorite
in the town's 52 pubs, including one run by
Mary Griffin (*right*), shown with daughter Lillian.

SHOPKEEPER Bridget Wylde makes her living
selling small things—chocolate bars,
a box of matches, a quarter ounce of snuff in store
founded by her father some 65 years ago.
The Irish seldom shop for price but stick to stores
that suffer bills never wholly paid off.

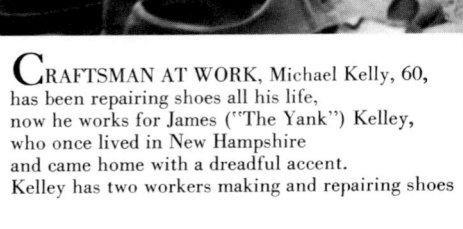

CRAFTSMAN AT WORK, Michael Kelly, 60,
has been repairing shoes all his life,
now he works for James ("The Yank") Kelley,
who once lived in New Hampshire
and came home with a dreadful accent.
Kelley has two workers making and repairing shoes

172

Tʜᴇ PRIEST, Father Carthage, a Franciscan, strides along O'Connell Street, Ennis, by the rear of the Old Ground Hotel. The priest has special honor at Irish hearthsides and mothers pray that at least one of their sons will one day be received in the holy orders.

WOMAN IN BLACK, Ellen Shannon, one of the poor called "shawlies" because they wear shawls, pauses for a chat in an Ennis street carrying her pitcher of milk. A widow, she works for a country family, has a son at home and another working in England.

in a vasty shop he bought when he came home. Now he says he is going back come spring for he can't stand Ireland's winter cold. However, since he is doing well in his business, many people in Ennis, a town that loves wagering and computing odds, are willing to bet he won't.

OF A SUNDAY AFTERNOON the young men of Ennis turn out for the hurling, a shin-shattering, head-splitting Irish version of field hockey popular in all Ireland but especially in Clare where this year hopes are high for winning the national league championship.

HANDS LINKED almost in symbol of the close family relationship of the country Irish, small boys in a big crowd hold tight to their grandfather's hands at a horse show. At their elders' side in church, at games, in work and at the market the boys are shaped to Irish ways.

The quiet life rich in faith and a bit of fun

OF A SUNDAY MORNING the people of Mount Callan, dressed in their best and clutching umbrellas against the inevitable rain walk over a country byroad to Cloonanaha, a spot in the middle of the farmland containing a school, a church and nothing more.

ISLAND OF THE DEVOUT, holding fast to the sturdy Catholicism that over 300 years stubbornly resisted the persecution of Elizabeth, Cromwell and the rest, the Irish are good Mass-goers. At overcrowded St. Mary's it is the men who must kneel or stand saying their beads in the rain while the women are inside, drier but hardly warmer. The church offers only one Mass on Sundays, celebrated by a priest who comes from Inagh, six miles away, and it is always crowded by people full of the faith that is forever the mark of the Irish.

Drama beneath a City Window

March 10, 1958
Photographer: W. Eugene Smith
Designer: Bernard Quint

This essay is actually a postscript to Smith's career as a *Life* photographer. That had ended nearly four years earlier as a result of increasingly bitter differences over the handling of his stories. One bone of contention was printing. He had learned early in life what many other photographers have learned: that the print is at least as important as the negative — some would say twice as important. When he first came to New York he lived in a small apartment with his mother. At the start she did his printing for him in a tiny darkroom they had set up in the apartment. Later he did his own. As a war photographer for *Life* he was forced to send his film back to be processed by the *Life* lab, but when he recovered from his war injuries sufficiently to begin working again, he resumed printing. It was soon clear that he was a master at it, along with Nina Leen, Andreas Feininger, Gjon Mili, John Loengard, and Cornell Capa. He liked his prints rich and dark, so dark that when he submitted a set he had printed for "Country Doctor," Charles Tudor said that the *Life* presses would not be able to handle them. Over Smith's objection they were redone, lighter. The most striking visual difference between "Country Doctor" and "Spanish Village" is not a difference in photographic style or subject matter. It is because the former was printed by *Life* and the latter by Smith.

He began spending more and more time in his darkroom, partly to escape from a real world that he was having increasing difficulty in coping with, partly in an endless search for perfect pictures. Sometimes he would make twenty or thirty prints of a single negative before he was satisfied. In addition to their being very dense, this took so much time that *Life*, despairing of ever getting delivery of some of the stories assigned him, considered ways of getting around the problem. Before a solution was found another fight erupted in 1954 over a major essay he had photographed of Albert Schweitzer in Africa. This was a huge and chaotic story with scores of outstanding pictures but a poorly realized central theme. The layout sessions were long and harrowing, not helped by Smith's insistence that every arrangement that was arrived at was a failure and that his ideas, all involving much more space, were the only ones that would rescue the story. He was finally told by Thompson that the time for arguing was over and that a magazine had to be put to press. The end product was a flawed masterpiece, a mélange of wonderful pictures that never really came together. So, in some measure Smith was right. Unfortunately he did not have the designer's skills to back up his dissatisfaction with what *Life* was doing, and he was deeply dissatisfied with the story that was published. He and *Life* parted company.

Three years later he rented a studio in a dingy part of Manhattan. I remember going there with him and a couple of friends from *Life* one evening. We sat around, talking, having drinks, and listening to music from a classical radio station that Smith kept turned to around the clock. Smith was on hand part of the time. Most of the time he was behind a closed door, printing pictures. That went on throughout the night, and I learned from him then, and from other encounters with him at about that time, that night and day and meals and an ordinary schedule had simply vanished from his mind. He ate when he felt like it, slept when he felt like it, worked the rest of the time. The pictures in this essay were taken during that period, almost absentmindedly over a number of months as he looked out of his window at what was going on in the street below. It is a kind of Everything-Goes-On-In-The-Piazza, but shot with a dark eye. The prints are masterful. In their richness and beauty they make an essay of a subject that otherwise might have been almost too flimsy.

The window-frame view solidifies it, that and the consistent downward angle of most of the photographs, and — wait a moment, there is more, this *is* a photo essay — that equally consistent richness in the printing, a sense of mystery in the pictures, of unplayed-out stories, each with an underpinning of sadness. There are the young lovers at the florist's, whose future together, Smith hints, may be a shaky one; the model, a pinpoint of voluptuousness, headed on who knows what shabby errand in a slate-colored world; the child in her communion dress, as fresh as a flower petal and as sure to wither. Even the two scenic shots are in keeping with the rest. They are pictures of the world taken by a man in a cave. There is light and life out there, but he is far from it.

All this is realized in an exceptionally sensitive and elegant layout. The opening scene-setter, a banality by this time, is livened with a hopping little two-step of pictures raggedly arranged at the bottom. Next comes a trio of unresolved vignettes, then a marvelous spread of snow and slush tones, followed by a facing pair of "cave" pictures and the flowerlike child for an ender. The pictures keep getting bigger and bigger, and their cumulative effect grows.

Smith has had a tangled and difficult life. He has had two unsuccessful marriages. Health problems have plagued him, later money problems. Both combined nearly to crush him in 1977. But he was able to return from Japan, where he had been living for a number of years, to a post on the faculty of the University of Arizona, which has also agreed to become the repository of his photographic collection.

Drama beneath
a City Window

Photographed for LIFE by W. EUGENE SMITH

Seeking a workshop where he could be free of distraction, Photographer W. Eugene Smith last year rented a dingy, third-floor loft on lower Sixth Avenue in Manhattan. But he soon found that his quarters held a great distraction and a rare photographic challenge. As he watched from the window, he grew absorbed by the shifting moods, the ebb and flow of movement in the street below. From that moment on, by day and by night and with mounting excitement, he kept recording the ceaselessly changing view and produced the masterly photographs on these pages.

The window, to him, was a proscenium arch and the teeming street a bustling stage. The passers-by sometimes turned into symbols —of man intimidated (below) of man fighting back (bottom). There were dramas fleetingly seen and moments of sudden loveliness as this segment of a city street became a world in miniature.

*I*n the cars crowding a pedestrian (above), Smith saw man threatened by machines; in a jaywalker's gyrations (below) man's nervy defiance.

*A*long the street below the loft window passes an unceasing flow
of human traffic. Sixth Avenue there is in the heart of the city's
wholesale flower district and each day begins, near dawn, with the bustle
of deliveries. At 9 and in the noon hour and toward 5 the sidewalks
are crowded and noisy. In between, the passers-by are fewer and
more leisurely. It is then, most often, that Smith catches glimpses of
little dramas whose beginnings and endings he can only surmise. A sense of
argument, revealed in the tilting heads, the imploring gesture, hovers
over a boy and girl (above) poised before a florist's shop at Eastertime.
Smith could only wonder what words went with the boy's gesture.
A mock-solemn quarrel over buying a corsage? Or a difference
that was, for the moment, more serious? The two moved on, taking the
answer with them. Often the passers-by provide brief vignettes: the pride
of a man (right) seeing his chic companion into a convertible;
the arresting contrast of the lone woman (far right), possibly a garment
district model, at once sensual and businesslike on the wide asphalt avenue.

*U*nexpectedly an afternoon snowfall brought to the street a different pace, pattern, atmosphere. The dusting of snow gave the usually grimy and depressing corner (above) new aspects of beauty. At the intersection of 28th Street, commerce went on (below), but the tempo was cautious, the avenue's sharp noises muffled. For Smith, "There was a dreamlike quality—the slow rhythm of the people walking, the remoteness of the traffic, the soft fall of the snow." The sidewalk (right), with its random trampling of footprints and the solitary stroller huddled beneath her umbrella, took on the look of a carefully conceived impressionist painting. Traffic transformed the snow into patterns (bottom right) that were precise and bold and that, set against the whitened tops of a delivery cart, gave a mundane moment a quality of artful charm.

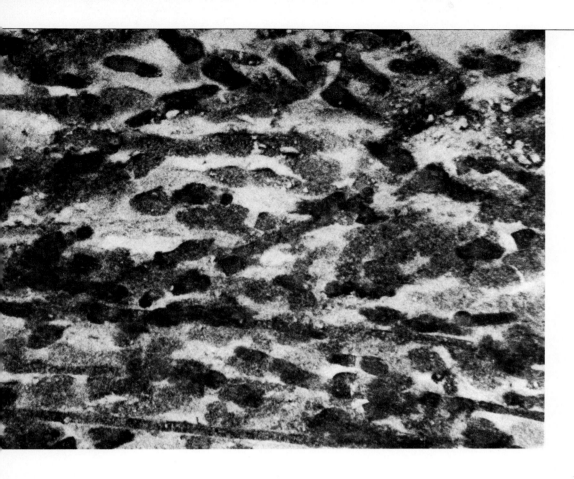

O n the horizon from Smith's window loom the city's great skyscrapers. Interrupting his work late one night, Smith saw the New York Life Insurance Building towering behind a smaller building across the avenue where one single light burned—a reassuring and companionable sign of life in the still, pre-dawn hours.

He accidentally broke his window, painted black by a former tenant. Through it the sharp and soaring arrogance of the Empire State Building was aptly framed by thin, jagged shards of glass.

*B*ursting from the florist's in what was probably her Communion dress, the girl seemed a Dresden figurine come alive. Amid city's tired things—ashcan, hydrant, battered flower stands—she became a creature of lovely fantasy. "For the moment," Smith remembers, "she took over the scene. Everyone turned to look at her." Then she was gone.

184

In a Dutiful Family Trials with Mother

July 13, 1959
Photographer: Cornell Capa
Designer: Charles Tudor

Some of the best things that ever appeared in *Life* were examinations of large topics of general interest. These were produced in serial form, and sometimes ran to as many as half a dozen installments. They combined the work of teams of photographers, leaned heavily on color, and often contained large infusions of original artwork. The burden of organizing those ambitious series fell largely on Charles Tudor, which explains why so little of his work as a designer appears in this volume, for those series were not photo essays in the strict sense. Nevertheless, when *Life* decided to tackle the subject of old age, one of the installments in that series was a true photo essay, shot by one man, Cornell Capa. Being part of a larger, continuing news story, it ran in the news section in the front of the magazine, which is how Tudor came to lay it out.

Capa's contribution was a self-contained unit in the series, a close look at the problems of one old woman forced to live with her son and daughter-in-law. It is a memorable story, with all the ingredients that the greatest essays have: intimate involvement with its principals, strong emotion, a powerful story line that cuts close to the experience of the reader, and unforgettable photographs.

Cornell Capa spent his early years in the *Life* darkroom, eclipsed by an older brother, Robert, famous for his electrifying coverage of the Spanish Civil War, of World War II, and finally Vietnam, where he was killed by a land mine. His spectacular exploits, spectacular photographs, and melodramatic life-style almost totally submerged the quieter, gentler Cornell, who, in my opinion, is at least as good a photographer as Robert. He is far more sensitive, a lineal descendant of Leonard McCombe, with McCombe's concerned way of insinuating himself into the small but consuming problems of ordinary people. But he and McCombe are far from being identical.

Nearly all photojournalists have a killer instinct hidden somewhere in them. In many it is brutally apparent; they will do almost anything to get a photograph. In men like McCombe it is faint, but it is there. He was not above gently but persistently feeding fire to a disagreement that his career girl, Gwyned Filling, was having with her boyfriend one evening, provoking a storm of tears in her and producing an emotion-packed picture that he felt his story needed. In doing that he was meddling with a life at a moment of crisis, but, photographically, he was right. Gwyned, weeping, ran for a full page.

In Capa I have never been able to find a trace of photographic ruthlessness. He relies instead on an inborn sensitivity to whatever lightning is in the air, and on the reflexive skills of a Cartier-Bresson to capture it. He also differs from McCombe in having a sense of humor. Capa is a witty man. Where appropriate, sly shafts fly through his pictures. In his essay on England's Westminster School, for example, wit flickers like sunlight.

Old age, however, is not a funny subject, and Capa approached the tragedy of Annie Mahaffey with tenderness, but also with respect for the real fury that kept blazing up in it. It is a fantastic story, shot from so close in that it has moments that are almost unbearable. On center stage throughout is old Annie, self-pitying, cantankerous, feeble, hopelessly trapped in a situation she cannot stand but must endure. Played off against her is her daughter-in-law, just as trapped but more resilient simply for being young and healthy. There is not a weak photograph in this story; Tudor was too wise and experienced to admit one. There are four that are absolutely stupendous, and Tudor made the most of each. One counterposes a stooped, wrinkled, half-mad-looking Annie against the unblemished profile of one of her grandchildren. Tudor gave it a little over a page. The second encapsulates the entire story in one photograph: the daughter-in-law and a friend socializing cozily over a cup of coffee while Annie sits alone in the background, doubly excluded — inadvertently by them, and deliberately and stubbornly by herself. Tudor let that one run for a double spread. He also gave what amounts to double-spread treatment to a pair of pictures that work as one. There he dug into the past for a device that had been used by John Billings in his famous slanted-bar spread in *Life*'s first photo essay: two photographs taken seconds apart, telling almost the same story, each enhancing the other by the small differences between them. Here the right-hand one is the real overwhelmer, with the watchful but determinedly silent eye of the harassed daughter-in-law saying everything there is to say about the endless burden to her of having Annie in the house. That is her picture. The last one is Annie's again. We come to the end of the story and find her beaten, head down, with no hope for anything.

Having been used as a news story, this essay has the direct meat-and-potatoes style of layout that always characterized the news section of *Life*. But it suffers in no way from that. It is so strong, and the enormous scale of the best pictures so potent, that a fussier treatment might actually have hurt it.

There is an element in the essay that may not be noticed immediately but that supplies an added dimension. Not once is the daughter-in-law's face presented in sharp focus. She exists as a kind of patient soft-edged presence against which Annie rages in vain; it is as if Annie herself never sees her clearly. She is a pillow for useless punching, a shadow that does not hear complaints. We find ourselves thinking that if Annie's clouded old eye would only clear a little, she would perceive the daughter-in-law as less of an adversary than she seems.

Was this subtle device deliberate on Capa's part? Did he take only pictures of this kind? Or was Tudor inspired to select only them? I was curious enough to go back and study Capa's contact sheets. The credit goes to Capa.

187

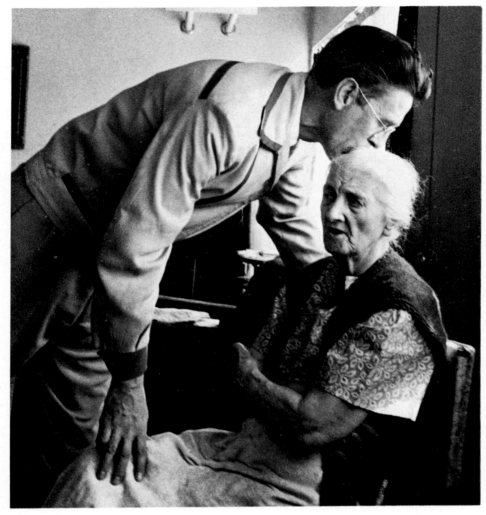

"George, he's the best of them, but he's between two women."

Kiss from son, leaving for job as night foreman at paint factory, is taken for granted by his mother. He spends much of daytime helping around the house.

IN A DUTIFUL FAMILY TRIALS WITH MOTHER

In the pinched, wise face of 80-year-old Annie Mahaffey and in her querulous words, "They're all going to miss me when I'm dead," lie all the anguish of an aged person trapped in a sad, familiar drama of old age. The drama has also enmeshed the young—her son George, her daughter-in-law Mary, their seven children—as it has most of the three million other U.S. families who have aged parents in their homes.

Annie Mahaffey lives in George's six-room house in Philadelphia—loving the family and loved by it, resenting it and being often resented. A widow since 1940, Annie had taken George and Mary into her house when they were married 16 years ago. Soon their growing family forced them into larger quarters, finally into a housing development where Annie lived in a separate apartment. After two years—the only two years George and Mary have had to themselves—the development was razed. Annie could not look after herself any more. "She had nobody else to live with, and not enough money," explains George, who is a quiet, hard-working man of 42. So George and Mary took her back in with them.

Annie virtually never leaves the house for fear of falling sick away from home. Her days are spent in just two rooms—her own retreat upstairs and the family's tiny downstairs living area which is divided by a short partition into a parlor, dining alcove and kitchen. Strategically placed at the end of the partition is Annie's easy chair. She finds endless pretexts—the mail, the milkman, the telephone calls that seldom come—to sit there hour after hour where there is no danger of being left out or ignored. Here, she can keep track of the active household. "I watch and listen," says Annie—whose comments are quoted with these pictures—as she sits at her post (*next page*).

Photographed for LIFE by Cornell Capa

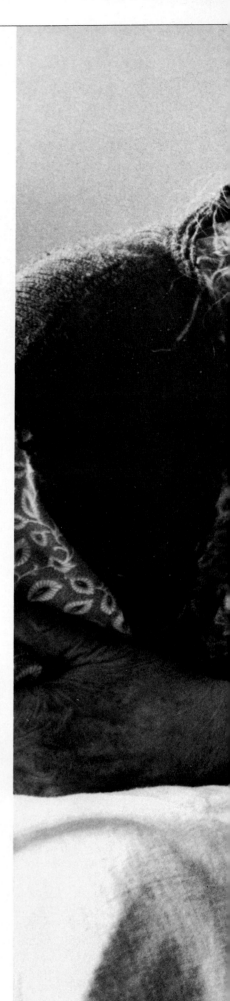

"They're all going to miss me when I'm dead and gone."

Seeking respect and sympathy, Annie bends close to granddaughter, Mary Anne, 7, and tells of her misfortunes. Annie's first husband, a fireman, was killed when his horse-drawn fire wagon collided with a train. Their son, also a fireman, died of a heart attack. Her second husband, a foreman in a gas works, died of heart disease. "Maybe when it's too late somebody will take pity on me," says Annie. "Every night I wash my feet before I go to sleep because I may not wake up."

189

"...ecause I'm 80 years old, ...body wants to listen to me. ...have nobody to talk to."

CONTINUED

191

"I'm not against the woman, but I'm never alone with George"

Enjoying a favorite topic, Annie reminisces after breakfast about George's childhood and claps her son affectionately on the head while Mary sits silently.

"I have very good eyes and ears; I don't miss very much"

Keeping track, Annie sits in her personal easy chair and listens to Mary in the dining alcove singing while she feeds Francis, age 1. Diane, 4, watches.

"There's no peace at all here . . . just no peace at all"

After Jackie, 12, ignores commands to stop bouncing ball, Annie angrily seizes it. Mary Anne, 7, tries to grab it back. Diane aims toy gun at light bulb.

"I'm a no-kissing, no-hugging type, but I'm an old hand at this"

Tending Francis, Annie juggles rubber lamb. Until a recent illness, she helped with housework. Now she just cooks her own food, cleans her own room.

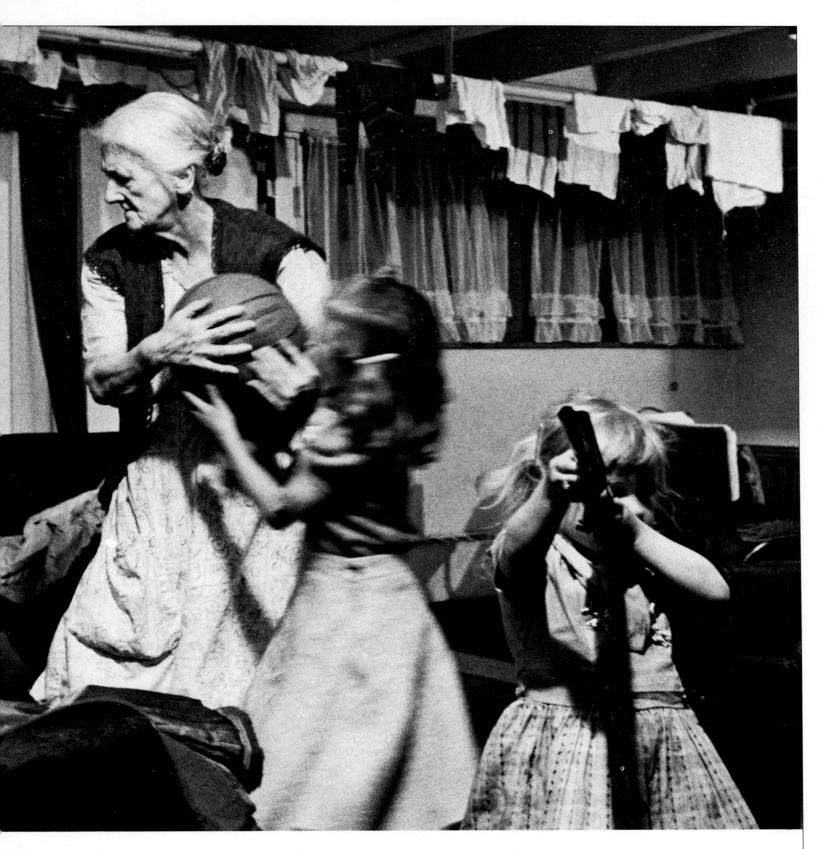

A CONSTANT TUMULT FROM THE KIDS

Often in old age the sense of helplessness and uselessness turns inward, killing the will to live. Or it turns outward to a testy struggle against the world. Annie Mahaffey has chosen to struggle. And her understanding son and daughter-in-law find reassurance in her fighting stance, knowing that a dimming of her spark would mean an approach of the end.

The Mahaffey children, four boys and three girls, aged 1 to 12 years, have become the focus of Annie's struggle. She feels they compete with her for importance in the family and that they refuse her the peace she feels she needs.

They swarm noisily through the house, bringing in their friends, leaving the outside doors open, helping themselves at the icebox, bouncing balls on the floor, "deviling" Annie or else ignoring her. Though Annie complains about the excitement, she also craves it. She loves the children and courts their affection. They always wind up sharing her one indulgence— bizarre foods like crabs, mushrooms, roe, eels. The children can also count on a constant supply of candy and occasional 25¢ pieces, the payment for running her errands to the store. To them, "Gram" is transparently a pushover.

Annie's ancient nerves snap easily and she shunts the blame to the children's parents. "If only George would use the strap to make them leave me alone," she says. When the tumult or the disobedience becomes unbearable, she often takes action herself. She did this over a trifling piece of mischief by Jackie, who is both her favorite grandchild and her chief tormentor. When she finally appealed for help to her daughter-in-law, Mary told Jackie to behave. But then she turned back to Annie with a what-do-you-expect-they're-only-kids remark which brought the tearful scene on the next pages.

"I'm just as independent as they are. But when I get hurt I cry . . . I can't hold anything in."

"I know I have a bad temper,
but I only tell them how I would do it.
Can't I open my mouth?"

195

CONTINUED

REVERIES, SAD MOMENTS

While Mary talks on the phone to her own mother, there is, as always, the presence of Annie, missing nothing. The only privacy Mary and George have is when Annie retreats upstairs to her own room. There she dreams of the days when she had her own home. It gives her a feeling of independence, bolstered by the fact that with her $42.60 a month old-age assistance she is no financial burden.

Between Annie and 37-year-old Mary lies an unbridged gulf, the gulf separating a bygone, rigid way and today's lenient life. "I don't want to tell her how to run her family, but . . ." says Annie. Says Mary, "I'm so busy and she's always finding fault."

But Mary's mildness helps her to hold her tongue—most of the time. Despite her burdens, Mary still can say, her eyes glistening, "You know, I'm the envy of every girl on the block because of George, the way he is toward me and the children." There is no thought of sending Annie to a home for the aged. "George would not do it and I would not want him to," says Mary. "It would break his heart."

"I been sick so much . . ."

Annie takes comfort in her heart pills and in the keepsakes of her lifetime. On bureau is a picture of her late son, Willie, wearing his fireman's uniform.

"My house had no stairs"

After finding the peace of her own room upstairs too lonely, Annie struggles complainingly down the stairs to get back into the thick of family activity.

"I just sit and think how I had it"

Surrounded by the prized furniture from her old home, Annie sits reading in the sanctuary of her immaculately kept room. Nobody can come in without her permission and sometimes she even barricades the door against the children.

"To live too long is a nuisance"

In the evening Annie sits in her easy chair, while Mary, who is pregnant, talks long and fondly on the telephone to her own 61-year-old mother who lives alone. At such times Annie, who is hungry for love, feels suddenly sad and left out.

The Spirit and Frenzy of Olympian Efforts

July 18, 1960
Photographer: George Silk
Designer: Edward K. Thompson

Once in a while a photo essay succeeds despite the best editorial efforts to assassinate it. That was the case here, where the photographer, George Silk, had worked out what he thought was an original way to photograph the U.S. Olympic trials — but everybody else thought he was crazy.

Silk, a sports photographer of outstanding ability, was getting bored by the routine photographs he was constantly being ordered to make. Noticing the strange distortions that were produced by photo-finish cameras at racetracks, it occurred to him to put the principle to work in photographing other sporting events. He talked his idea over with George Hunt, then assistant managing editor, and persuaded him to allocate $1,000 for the modification of a standard Leica into a "strip camera," one that has an extremely narrow slit for a shutter, past which the film is run by a motor. This procedure is backwards from that in an ordinary camera, in which the film is still, but the shutter moves.

Silk took his camera home and practiced with it over Halloween, getting strange, distorted pictures of his children and their friends running about in masks, squat protoplasmic little goblins straight from hell. Encouraged, he experimented some more, and quickly learned that the critical factor in controlling the distortions he was getting was film speed. If the film went past the shutter slit at a relatively faster speed than the subject was moving, the resulting image would be crowded together, narrow and tall, like that of the pole vaulter on page 205. If it went by slowly, the figure would be stretched out like that of the high jumper on page 203. He had just time to get the rudiments of this in his head when the tryouts started and he joined a large team of *Life* photographers and reporters in California. He spent one day in Los Angeles making test shots of the athletes practicing, then all that night in a processing lab, where he had a terrible time with the technicians, who thought there was something wrong with his camera and couldn't be persuaded to make the enlargements he wanted. He was also having trouble with his camera slit, and realized it would have to be narrower if he was to get really sharp pictures.

Nevertheless he turned up for the trials themselves the next day in San Francisco, confident that he had his distortions under reasonable control. His troubles were just starting. Waiting for him was a message from Edward Thompson ordering him to stop his experiments and join the team of "straight" photographers. He ignored it. Next he learned that tripods were forbidden in the stadium. Inasmuch as a strip camera will not

work without one, he hurried downtown and bought a tiny collapsible one that could be folded almost out of sight on the bottom of his camera. That sentenced him to nothing but low-level shots, but it did allow him to work all day without anybody's realizing he was using a tripod.

The trials over, he flew to New York with his film and had it processed that night in the *Life* lab, again encountering total bewilderment with his pictures on the part of the lab crew. By morning he was bowlegged with fatigue, having had no sleep for two nights running. But he did have a set of pictures that were satisfactory to him, and he rushed them upstairs just in time for a general showing in the editor's office of the work of all the photographers who had been in San Francisco.

Silk was aware that his job was on the line for having disobeyed Thompson's instructions. That was rubbed home when Thompson refused to speak to him as he came in the room. Scowling, Thompson sat down at his table and did a silent Billings-like run-through of all the regular photographs. Then he did the same with Silk's. Following that, he emptied his office, slammed the door, and remained alone inside for the better part of an hour. Presumably he was trying to decide how to reconcile a pile of routine pictures he himself had ordered with a few far more spectacular ones that had been made in contravention of his orders.

Those who thought so had underestimated Thompson. What he was actually doing was trying to rearrange the mock-up, which already had several large stories in it, to find eight pages for Silk's pictures, which he had instantly recognized as spectacular. When he opened the door again he not only had the mock-up problem solved, but he had also decided how to lay out the story. His solution — combining conventional and distorted work — was ingenious. He was absolutely right in playing Silk's pictures big. Not only are they the story, but they also need maximum width or height for maximum effectiveness. He was also right in realizing that they needed small conventional ones next to them to explain them. The end effect is not particularly graceful but it is literally eye-popping. *Life* published hundreds of sports stories, but none came even close to this one in visual effectiveness. And that was in spite of the fact that several of Silk's best pictures were not used. They were of unimportant or non-record-breaking events. In his only layout mistake that day, thinking too much like a newsman, Thompson had tossed them aside.

The Spirit and the Frenzy

The muscles of the mightiest track team on earth—one that will represent the U.S. in the Olympics at Rome next month—had a herculean look. The weight throwers, emitting gargantuan grunts, seemed to grow extra arms and legs as they whirled. The spindly-legged foot racers gobbled up ground as though wearing seven-league track shoes. The vaulters soared up, up, up.

In the Olympic tryouts at Palo Alto, Calif. the U.S.

athletes exploded in a chain reaction of power and agility. To capture the essence of the most classical of man's athletic endeavor, LIFE's George Silk employed a portable version of the photofinish camera. His camera has no shutter. The film is drawn past a narrow .004-inch aperture, catching the athletes as they move into and across the camera's narrow field of vision—and bringing about the dramatic flow of motion in these pictures.

An elastic pirouette
in hammer throw

Pivoting on one foot, 232-pound Ed Bagdonas, Army lieutenant, becomes a straining four-armed dervish. Arms and hammer (*shown at extreme edges*) appear twice because they twice passed by camera aperture and were caught in two positions on moving film. In conventional photo above, Bagdonas' heave of 205 feet 11 inches won him team berth.

# of Olympian Efforts

Providing Silk with superb models was the frenzied competition among 220 athletes for 53 places on the U.S. team. Records fell right and left as Silk's camera, powered by a spring-wind motor from an old phonograph, kept grinding. After every burst he paused, got out a hand crank and rewound the motor.

His photographs accent a particular mood for each event—sheer power for the hammer throw (*above*),

fluidity for the jumpers and high-striding knee action for the runners. After the emotional ordeal of gearing themselves for the supreme effort, there was utter dejection among those who failed. When unofficial world record holder Bill Nieder (LIFE, June 27) failed to make the team in the shot-put he strode from the field, leaving his iron ball where it had fallen. But Don Bragg staged a jubilant dance after his historic vault.

Precision ballet
by a hurdling trio

Symmetrical tandem is formed by Willie May, Hayes Jones and Lee Calhoun in hurdles. They were photographed separately—first Calhoun, then Jones, then May—as they took off for hurdle, just out of picture. At right Calhoun wins in tryout record time: 13.4 seconds.

A high jumper's
unprecedented orbit

In mid-air at a record height of 7 feet 3¾ inches, John Thomas of Boston U. forms attenuated arc. His hands are shown at left, the number (93) on his shirt is clear but legs are mostly out of picture (*bottom right*). Conventional photo left catches open-mouthed strain.

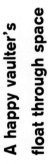

A happy vaulter's
float through space

While propelling himself a
breath-taking 15 feet 9¼ inches
to beat the official world's record,
Army Private Don Bragg made
two images on Silk's film (left), once
going up and once coming down.
Camera's slit was aimed at point
just below bar. Bottom image at
left shows him almost to bar, hands
still on pole. Top image at left
shows him, free of pole, on way down.
Conventional pictures above show
him at peak of vault and,
after landing, staring up in disbelief
at the bar he had just cleared. Then
he grabbed fiancée Terry Fiore, who
had run onto field, and, whooping,
carried her around stadium.

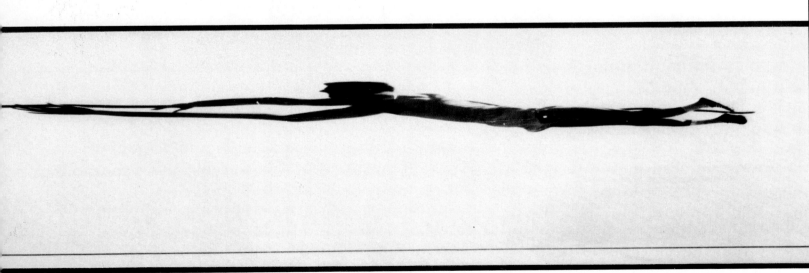

Game-legged fling
with the javelin

Bill Alley's bandaged right leg looms larger than left as he digs in on it (*below*) for throw. He had tripped and spiked himself severely on a previous try. Earlier the Kansas U. star made throw of 269 feet 7½ inches (*left*), earning an Olympic berth by finishing second.

A broad jumper's
bizarre jackknife

About to land heels first after 25-foot 9½-inch jump, Antony Watson of Oklahoma University throws the upper portion of body forward. Because his chest is moving faster past camera's slit than the rest of him, it appears slimmer. Conversely, his hips and legs, which slowed down when shoulders were thrown forward, appear thick and stubby. In smaller picture Watson is shown by normal camera.

The Era of Sentiment and Splendor

October 24, 1960
Photographer: Clarence John Laughlin
Designer: Bernard Quint

In its early days the first story in *Life* each week was a small feature called "Speaking of Pictures . . . ," one of the many devices employed by Billings to salvage interesting photographs that did not qualify as news, did not fall into clear departmental categories like science or fashion, were too insubstantial to be made into photo essays, and yet — as pictures — were too arresting to be ignored. My first job at *Life* was as "Speaking of Pictures . . ." editor, and one of the first stories I managed to get into the magazine was a set of photographs of ornamental ironwork on old New Orleans houses, taken by a young southern photographer, Clarence John Laughlin. It was, by Billings's standards, a static little story. He used it only because I could produce nothing better that week.

What happened to some of *Life*'s attitudes and skills during the next twenty years is nowhere better illustrated than by comparing that grudging little feature with this full-scale essay by the same photographer. The change is not to be explained by artistic development in Laughlin himself. He was a sensitive and gifted photographer already in 1942, interested in decaying old plantation houses, in Victorian architecture and design, in the echoes of bygone life and tastes that such artifacts carried. Laughlin has been faithful to that interest throughout his distinguished professional career, and his evolution as a photographer has been mainly in expanding the number and variety of his pictures in that genre.

It was not Laughlin, but *Life*, that had changed. By 1960 its editors had managed to produce photo essays of so many different kinds that it is not too much to say that they felt confident in their ability to turn any set of photographs into a photo essay so long as the photographs were of high quality and numerous enough that somewhere among them a common theme could be found. So it was that when a friend showed Bernard Quint some of Laughlin's pictures in 1958 Quint immediately began thinking "photo essay." He was captivated by the controlled elegance of Laughlin's pictures, all of which are made meticulously by large view-cameras. Although it was not his job to hustle up stories, Quint got in touch with Laughlin and asked to see more of his work. This was difficult, for many that Quint most wanted were scattered about the country in private hands. As a result, it was two years before the layout seen here could be made. To the best of my knowledge, it is the only set of pure salon photographs ever to appear in *Life* bearing the label of photo essay. What qualified them for the label was Quint's skill in selecting, from a large and heterogeneous collection, the pictures that emphasized most strongly strange architectural patterns, heightened by Laughlin's ability to capture extraordinarily delicate surface textures and shadows. Concentration on those elements — intensification by careful selection — supplied the theme.

When Thompson was shown the story he agreed to run it, although it violated most of the photojournalistic canons by which he lived. He could not resist its elegance, particularly that of the opening page, which is a minor layout masterpiece, with its delicate gray background, its reverse printing, and a white-bordered picture that actually gains in effectiveness by being played small.

Thompson did shorten the essay by a couple of spreads. If he was going to be tempted by salon photography, he was not about to be seduced by it. He was surely right. We, the readers, not knowing what he threw out, do not miss it. What we see here seems just enough.

The Era of Sentiment and Splendor

BYGONE BUILDERS HAD A FANCIFUL HEYDAY

Photographed by CLARENCE JOHN LAUGHLIN

Amidst the current plethora of stereotyped modern buildings, the fanciful patterns of an old freewheeling era are sights for sore eyes. The snail-coil stairs above, built during the 1880s for the Louisiana state capitol at Baton Rouge, and the structures on the following pages are picturesque survivors of a period in which architects and amateur builders let themselves go, freely indulging their taste for Gothick gewgaws, wedding-cake woodwork, classical columns and statuary and bizarre mixtures of modes from many lands and ages.

Over the years many of these remarkable creations have perished as hapless victims of progress, but a number have had the good fortune to remain in appreciative hands or in tucked-away corners. Tracking them down all over the country, Photographer Clarence Laughlin has conscientiously recorded everything from tombs to firehouses, building up an album of the whimsical, gracious and grandiose landmarks of American individualism.

Fireman's Folly

Turning a fire station into a fun house was not at all frowned upon in San Francisco 80 years ago. Station No. 15, one of the oldest in the city, was a jaunty burlesque of Gothic Revival architecture. Along with traditional crenelations, pointed arches and quatrefoil carvings, the building was embellished with hydrants and a fireman's hat as pinnacles, watchful owl and wide-awake fire chiefs as corbels. Modern San Francisco, apparently more concerned with practicality than whimsicality, tore the building down last year.

Garlands and Faces
in Unexpected Places

Captain's Paradise

Festooned like a ballroom (*above and right*), this eight-sided house in New Orleans is a final fancy fling of Steamboat Gothic architecture. It was built in 1905 by a nostalgic Mississippi River pilot named Milton Doullut who equipped it with outside staircase, promenade deck, metal smokestacks and, to top it off, a pilothouse. With a nautical man's penchant for the exotic, Captain Doullut further adorned his dreamboathouse with flaring fretwork around the roof, a feature he observed on a Japanese pavilion in the St. Louis exposition of 1903.

A Moorish Mansion

Crisply carved and carpentered, the airy arcades of this home in Galveston, Texas were designed to suggest a Moorish palace. Though the over-all effect is intricate, the patterns are in fact of the simplest order, revealing the builder's understanding of what could be achieved with repeated arrangements of wood. The house was begun in 1885 but the extensive woodcarving—from the faces on the inside of the columns to the ornamental crest atop the rooftree—was laborious and costly. Before it was finished, the owner went bankrupt and work halted until the house was sold in 1912.

214

Stately Shapes,
Shaded Arches

A Buttressed
Temple

Sunlight slanting across
the buttresses of the Masonic
Temple (*left*) in Galveston
highlights its stately geometry.
The temple was originally a
synagogue, built in 1870
in the Perpendicular style of
medieval English churches.
The brick structure was later
covered with cement and
stucco and painted white. Taken
over by the Masons in 1955
after the synagogue had moved
on, the temple sometimes serves
as a shadowy nook for children
at games of hide-and-seek.

A Classical
Iron Front

The slim, finely fluted
pilasters framing the doorways
(*above*) of the Amstoy Building
in Los Angeles gave it a
classical air, even though the
pilasters were of cast iron
and the building itself
was used for offices. The brick
structure was built in 1876
as a commercial venture
by a former Basque shepherd
who struck it rich in California
and went into real estate.
In 1958 the building was torn
down in order to make way
for a parking lot.

Crypts
and Crosses

In a cemetery
near Cut-Off, La., the
bright light and opaque
shadows of crypts
and crosses create
complex patterns
resembling roof tops
in a whitewashed
Mediterranean village.
As in many Louisiana
cemeteries, the plastered
tombs are built high
to keep coffins out
of the swampy soil.

A Preacher
Enshrined

Amid spectral wisps
of reflections in his
glass-walled tomb, the
statue of Carl F. W.
Walther retains its
stalwart air. A
Lutheran minister who
settled in St. Louis
in 1838, Walther became
a leader in his church.
After his death
in 1887, this marble
statue was installed
in Concordia Cemetery
in a setting
of ornate stained glass.

An Only Son
Remembered

Caught in a snare
of reflections, a marble
angel hovers like a
phantom over the statue
of Nelson Blocher in his
mausoleum in Buffalo,
N.Y. When Blocher died
in 1884, his grieving
parents commissioned an
Italian sculptor to carve
this monument, complete
with pleat-winged angel
holding a wreath
above their
elegantly mustachioed
only son.

216

217

Haunting Perspective
of a Distant Past

Receding into the distance, shaded rows of old slave cabins line a long alley on Evergreen plantation near Edgard, La. Now empty and gently dilapidated, the cabins with their square-framed porches create a haunting perspective of a long-vanished past.

The Lash of Success

November 16, 1962
Photographer: Grey Villet
Designer: Robert Clive

I have noted the importance of the researcher as trouble-shooter, information-gatherer, and general hand-holder during the making of photo essays. Seldom, however, did she play a role in the actual conception. That makes "The Lash of Success" a rarity, for a researcher not only thought up the idea for the story, but also found its principal actor, shaped the story as it went along, had a great deal to do with the kind of pictures that the photographer took, and finally played an important role in the layout sessions.

The researcher was Barbara Cummiskey, then working in *Life*'s text department. She had the idea that the American dream could be expressed symbolically in a series of three separate essays labeled respectively Fame, Success, and Wealth. Encouraged by her superiors to develop her idea further, she settled on Marilyn Monroe as the subject for an essay on fame. The approach to Monroe was entrusted to a patient, low-key staff writer, Richard Meryman, known for his ability to get close to unapproachable people and encourage them to talk freely to him. The world at that time knew Monroe only as a beautiful and presumably happy sex goddess. Meryman, in a series of startlingly candid interviews, succeeded in discovering the true Monroe for the first time, as a terrified and neurotic woman whose hideous childhood and early life, followed by sudden, unparalleled, unmanageable fame, were more than she could handle — enough to explain her later collapse and suicide.

Meryman's story was a sensation. It was published as a text article — which it obviously was destined to be from the moment Meryman was assigned. That left Barbara free to turn to Success (the wealth theme was another, more complicated, story). Chatting one evening with a friend who worked in public relations, she found herself listening to a sour complaint about one of the friend's clients, a driven, insatiably ambitious businessman. Although up to that moment her thinking had not been in the direction of a What-Makes-Sammy-Run type whose only reality was expensive clothes, Cadillacs, and business deals, Barbara suddenly realized that a tremendous story might be built around such a person. That led to a phone conversation with the P.R. client. He was Victor Sabatino, head of a chain of thinly financed foam-rubber stores. A photographer, Grey Villet, was assigned to the story, and all three met for the first time in California. Sabatino, his ego stroked by the prospect of public exposure in *Life*, agreed to the terms of the story: a no-holds-barred look at him. This devastating essay is the result.

It was long in the making. Barbara attached herself to Vic like a lamprey, hour after hour, day after day. She discussed the shape of the story with him, went to his tailor's, met his father, his wife, his little girl, his best friend, arranged to be on hand for a session in Chicago where he was planning to chop up some subordinates who were not doing well. She drove at night with him, all over Brooklyn and Long Island, listening to him ramble on about his dreams of success. Anxious not to interrupt the flow, she took no notes. Occasionally on those night drives she turned on a tape recorder, but mostly she relied on memory and on her own small nudgings of Vic in directions she hoped he would go.

Villet was a silent third party to all this. He never said a word, just watched and shot everything. He is a big man, six foot four, but with a surprising ability to melt into the woodwork, particularly with Barbara up front doing the talking.

Consequently, when Vic went after a hapless Chicago employee, Villet was able to shoot right over Vic's shoulder, his camera becoming Vic. The subordinate was so demoralized by the inquisition to which he was being subjected that he never noticed as Villet shot the strip of terrified faces that the designer, Robert Clive, has played so effectively opposite Vic's own. The bullying continues on the next page with an even bigger picture of another cowering man. We no longer need Vic's face; we have had that. The gesturing hand is more effective. This was a story that had to be shot right on top of its subjects to bring out the sweat, and Villet, instead of normal lenses, used 90mm and 180mm telephotos. The faces had to be big, and Clive made them so. That, of course, ate up space at a reckless rate; the story is one of the two longest in the book.

It is hard to say how credit for this essay should be divided. One way of evaluating the respective contributions of its two makers is to try to weigh the long text blocks against the pictures. Doing that, one quickly realizes that the essay is unique in that neither is anything without the other. Each must have the other, very much as Barbara and Grey did. She was on top of the story all the way. She guided it. Grey would have had a hard time without her. On the other hand, she had to have somebody who could work self-effacingly alongside her, never speaking to interrupt what was going on, in effortless synchronization with her for weeks and weeks. They were, in fact, the perfect team for this extremely difficult, highly intellectual story, one of the most intriguing ever made for *Life*, all of it told in faces.

It is to designer Robert Clive's credit that he stuck to faces, starting with one that speaks volumes about Vic: a shot of him in the rear-view mirror of his Cadillac, the beautiful white machine that he can control better than he can control people. He is a man who drives and drives, and gets nowhere because he lives only in the reflections of others.

It should be no surprise that two people who found themselves as closely attuned to each other as Barbara and Grey should get married — which is what they did not long after they completed "The Lash of Success." The went on to other collaborative stories in which she again did all the arranging, leaving him free for the total concentration on mood that is so effective here. Their most ambitious effort was one on three generations of a patriarchal family living in Vermont. It ran in several installments in *Life*, and took so long to finish that the Villets rented a house in Vermont and settled down there for the winter. Subsequently they left *Life* and have been living in upstate New York, where Grey has been building log houses. Recently they decided to put the team together again and have been working on assignment for *Quest* Magazine.

So vivid was Vic in the Villet essay that, like McCombe's career girl, many readers have wanted to know what happened to him. I did myself when I sat down to write this commentary. But the Villets could not tell me. Understandably, Vic did not like the image of him that emerged, even though he had shaped it himself, and he did not keep in touch with them. I had to inquire around in the foam-rubber industry, and eventually ran down a man who remembered him and his Forcite chain of companies. Forcite, it seems, was already stretched perilously thin when *Life* met Vic. It disappeared shortly afterward. So did Vic. Nobody, today, seems to know where he is or what he is doing.

221

A modern parable:
Vic Sabatino's fierce
vision of money and power

THE LASH OF

SUCCESS

Standing narrow as a knife, Victor Sabatino talks confidently about ingredients of his success— sales shrilly advertised in newspapers and emblazoned store windows, customers who come to a Sabatino store opening to eat free canapés and cream puffs, and look at the furniture. Sabatino knows they will come back and buy because he knows where they are vulnerable, what they long for. To explain, he goes back to his childhood. "I used to watch the chicken hawks, circling over the henhouse at grandfather's farm. The little chickens, with white feathers coming through the soft yellow, wouldn't know enough to hide. And the hawks would dive and take them. Sometimes I look at the people and I think of the chickens."

The Super Selle

Coaxing in His Chickens

"What I want," says Victor Sabatino, "is to be a winner. People remember winners."

One year ago, by this standard, Sabatino at 33 was already a man to be remembered. Starting from nothing, the son of a baker in Brooklyn, he already had: a $5.5 million business, a pile of money, a white Cadillac convertible, a handsome blond wife, a 5-year-old daughter he adored.

Not enough. For Vic Sabatino there is no way to say "enough." Committed to a fierce vision of success, he knew only one thing to do: keep pushing everything to the limit—and finally beyond. Because he is a strong man, he was able to push hard, seven days a week, 16 hours a day.

Five years ago Sabatino was a foam rubber furniture salesman in New York, who had bounced around, dissatisfied, from job to job. Then he got a backer for his own Foam Rubber City store. He soon added others—in Miami, Chicago, Los Angeles.

He was a super salesman who knew how to handle customers—"chickens," he calls them, half affectionately—because they shared his own hungers. They wanted class: he gave them Danish modern. They wanted respect: he gave them deferential salesmen. "Give them value," he said, "but always move them, turn them, twist them."

His Forcite chain grew to 83 stores, owned or franchised. Vic sold fast, kept his profit margin to a perilous 3%, trimming ruthlessly to beat any competition. "I'll do anything for a friend," he said. "But come at my business and I'll cut you up."

A cold-eyed autocrat hunts for a rebel employe

Everything in Vic Sabatino's stores was done one way—Vic's way. He knew it was best and the growth of the chain proved it. Anyone who tried other ways without permission found himself facing a cold-eyed boss. It wasn't just that disobedience endangered the business. It was striking directly at Vic.

In Chicago, where there were seven stores, somebody began to do things differently. Profits fell. Vic flew in to find the trouble.

He called in the key men one by one. Many admired Vic. They had found him warm and helpful and talked freely. Others were afraid of him. Carl Bartolott (*left*), who handled franchises, talked reluctantly. Vic, a master at twisting men, was bitingly impatient. "I'm on your side, Vic," said Bartolott ingratiatingly (*at top*). "Don't be on my side," snapped Sabatino. "Like tell me how it is."

Bartolott, stalling (*center*), said, "I have a feeling . . ." Sabatino cut in roughly, "A feeling I don't want. I want a fact." Bartolott wilted (*bottom*), said, "One day one man is boss—the next day the desks moved around—another man tells me he's boss and I'll be fired if I don't do what he says."

Having squeezed all he wanted from one man, Vic went on to question the next (*following page*).

Shrewd inquisition leads him along the trail

Talking to Herman Horowitz, a manager on the administrative side in Chicago, Vic was a butterfly collector wielding a pin.

His hand stirring the air, his voice unctuous, he asked, "Herman, the general morale of your people—you feel you have a closeness with them?" "Oh, yes," said Horowitz. "After all, I was a student of psychology in college and I know human nature. I know I have their confidence and can accomplish a lot. That's so important."

"When you took over your job here, Herman, did you find you needed a little more organization?" "Vic," answered Horowitz, "within six months we would have had a monster if I hadn't gotten everything really organized—if I hadn't taken over." "Okay, Herman," Vic suddenly snapped. "I'll talk to you more later."

That night Vic walked the streets of Chicago, a fist of anger hard inside him. These men should have followed his explicit orders. He'd practically shown them what shirts to wear. This mess wasn't his fault. They were the ones who had lost money.

He had always thought that if all his instructions were detailed enough, if he set things up precisely, he could plug his men into the jobs, and business would run smoothly. Now Victor had learned men did not work like that.

In the end, Sabatino shook up the Chicago staff and brought several of the men back east where he could keep an eye on them.

Vic knew whom he took after: his grandfather (*far right*) who ran the family bakery. "Working, working," the old man used to say, "that's all I care about—eat and work." But Vic hated the bleakness of his life in Brooklyn and tried to wipe out those memories with expensive things.

"Some people like to drink, some go out with women," says Victor. "I buy clothes. It's good when you're a little depressed." On a Los Angeles business trip Vic tried on a $200 sport coat in the dark, narrow-cut style he always wore. It was good to look in the mirror and see Victor Sabatino, the winner, impeccable and rich.

Leaning against the mirror and watching him was Tony Viola, a store manager. He wore a narrow-cut suit like Vic's—so did all the managers. When Vic wore double-breasted suits, most of them did too. When he changed to single-breasted, he was amused to see them change too.

As a boy he seldom had any new clothes. Home had been one room over the bakery. "My mother when she was young," says Vic, "she was very beautiful, and her hair was combed just so. Her way of dressing was very meticulous. Then she had to go and wait on my aunts and uncles and on my grandmother, cooking for them and sweeping up all day. I used to get so mad that my mother should wait on them."

Now Vic throws away a pair of shoes the minute the sole wears down. His father is a vice president in Forcite's furniture factory. Vic is too busy to see his mother more than five or six times a year.

The winner in clothes that say money
escapes his harsh and glowering past

Talking back,
a friend asks
'Why, Vic, why?' . . .

VICTOR: Why can't you come back, Terry? How could you get so involved in the business, and then you wake up one morning and say, 'That's it'?

TERRY: The business was something new then, something I wanted to do. But couldn't I get much more out of life? That's the point.

VICTOR: But you're so capable in business. What's the matter with doing that?

TERRY: Why, Vic, why?

VICTOR: It's something you know you can do.

TERRY: What do *you* want to do, Vic?

VICTOR: I want to go far. There's no limit. I know what this company can be built to.

TERRY: So you're a General Motors, a DuPont. What do you do then besides think of more ways to make money?

VICTOR: Look down at the city, Terry, it's beautiful to look at something from above it all. You can see the lines down there, the streets, patterns that mark off places. They all have some meaning, a direction. Everything is planned, it's going somewhere. You can't escape it. All there is is finding out where it all leads you.

TERRY: Remember, Vic, what you once told me? You only have X heartbeats in a lifetime.

...but a lonely search
finds no answer

Standing on a bluff overlooking Los Angeles, Vic Sabatino pleaded with a man named Terry Popek to come back to Forcite. He had once been Vic's chief in Chicago but had quit a year ago. Vic needed him not just for business reasons but because Terry was his only close friend, the one man Vic could talk to, the one man who talked back, made Vic laugh, made Vic stop and see himself.

Terry Popek refused to come back to work. He could not take Vic's kind of life and (*far left*) he questioned whether Sabatino himself could stand it.

Vic returned to New York without Terry, without anyone he could really talk to. His only safety valve was to drive the streets of Brooklyn alone. He would hear the voice of his mother saying, "You're

burying yourself in money, Victor." And there were the miles of graveyards. "As I drove past those cemeteries," says Vic, "I started to ask myself, 'What is the end?'" Parking at a peaceful spot on the bay, he would sit, high on the back seat of his Cadillac, staring out at the water. "I watch it move, I lose myself in it," says Vic. "And you can hear the planes that keep going, going, going."

On an impulse Sabatino hired a genealogy tracer who managed to produce an ancient Italian Senator Sabatino and a family crest. He studied it in his office (*right*) at his big desk backed by an abstract painting he picked out himself. As soon as Forcite was really big, Vic insisted, "I'm going to school and I'm going to learn about art, books, how to talk right."

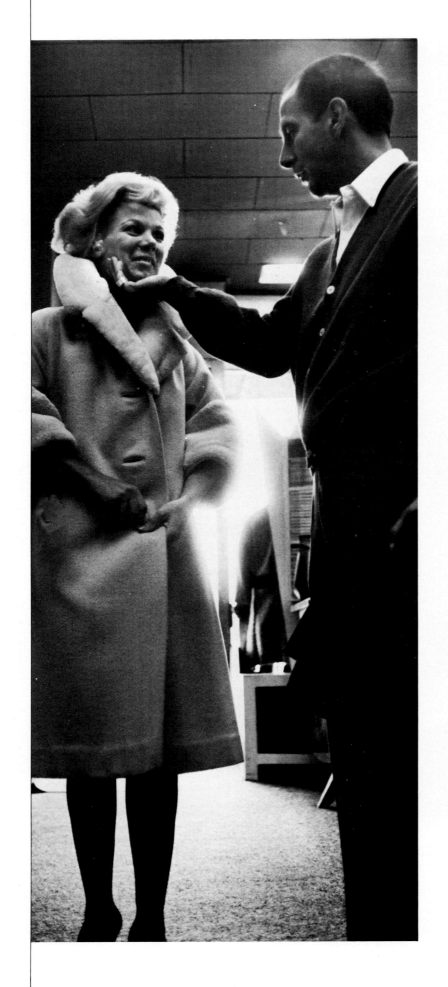

A new coat and a chuck
under the chin pay his family
for too many goodbys

I'd tell myself sometimes that I was doing all this for Lillian and Donna," Vic said, "but I knew it wasn't so." He, his wife and 5-year-old Donna lived in a middle-income housing project, partly because Vic wanted his capital for business ventures, but even more because Lillian felt too unsure of herself to face a new neighborhood.

When they were first married, Lillian had worked while Vic went from job to job. "Go ahead, Vic," she said. "Find what you want."

But as Vic grew successful, he made Lillian feel she was failing him. And sometimes when Vic was home her hands shook so badly that she spilled her coffee as she raised her cup. Once he told her she could have any automobile she chose, any in the world. She picked a Cadillac exactly like his.

Vic almost never made it home till late at night. Buying Lillian presents made him feel a little less guilty about leaving her always alone. Once he rushed home, took Lillian and Donna out for 30 minutes, bought Donna a bicycle and Lillian two coats. Then (*above*) he said another goodby.

Still a success— and a loser

Vic's business trouble in Chicago was only the beginning. Suddenly the whole fabric of his life began to rip.

There was Lillian: she asked for a divorce. "I know what Lillian wanted," says Vic. "She wanted me to see her—look at her. She wanted me to watch her make a dress or care for Donna. But I had to do what I had to do."

They were divorced and it is a relief to Vic not to face Lillian and his guilt. But Donna is all pain. He used to say goodby to her each morning, gently waking her and getting a small, sleepy kiss. Even this had stopped in the last months when he started going to work at 6:30 and she began losing too much sleep. One day Donna had played a game. She pretended to go to sleep on the floor. "Wake me, Daddy," she said. After Vic knelt to her (*left*) she broke into tears.

"I love my little daughter," says Vic in a tight voice. "Now sometimes at night, I feel crazy to go over just to look at her sleeping, just to smell her hair, her cheek, to kiss her. I want to give to her, protect her. I never felt this way about anyone else. From everybody else I always *wanted* something."

Then Forcite, Inc. ran into deep trouble. Its branches were losing money. There was not capital to keep them going until they showed a profit. Vic had expanded too fast. He could not run all branches himself by long distance, and his managers could not operate close enough to the bone. "They didn't have the passion I did," says Vic. "Everybody told me, 'Walk away, Victor. Take what you can and walk away.' But I wouldn't. I fought and I talked and I fought."

Here his great power of persuasion saved him. He talked several banks into going along with him and giving him loans. He cut back costs ruthlessly and sold off or franchised everything but his 16 New York stores and his wholesale business. Today Forcite is making money again. "I couldn't have let my business go too," says Vic. "What would I have had left? God, what would it all have meant?"

We Are Animals in a World No One Knows

February 26, 1965
Photographer: Bill Eppridge
Designer: Bernard Quint

Like "The Lash of Success," this essay relies heavily on the interplay between reporter and photographer. More heavily, in fact, because this one could not have been done at all without the work of its principal architect, writer James Mills, whereas Grey Villet probably could have managed something without Barbara — not as good perhaps, but something.

Here, however, the subject was drug addiction. In covering it, *Life* was in the rare and uncomfortable position of operating outside the law. The entire scene was extremely dicey. It required Mills's constant presence, all his powers of persuasion and cool nerve to keep the essay's fidgety subjects from wrecking it.

Mills is a deceptive man. He comes on like a fresh-faced, innocent college boy, sympathetic and friendly, able to gain the confidence of almost anybody in a few minutes. He is, in fact, a steely, unshockable reporter who knows exactly what he is doing all the time. It was he who tracked this nightmarish essay from one street corner to another, in and out of grimy hotels, in and out of hospitals, in and out of jails, watching calmly when Karen and John got high, got low, got desperate. He was waiting out in the hall while Karen turned a prostitution trick, standing by while John robbed a parked taxicab. He just watched while Karen struggled to keep another junkie who had taken an overdose of heroin from falling into a fatal sleep. He never lifted a helping hand, never took a note, but remembered everything, and wrote a chilling story.

If there was an innocent participant in this gruesome tale it had to be the photographer, Bill Eppridge. This is odd, because Eppridge looked the part that Mills was supposed to play, and Mills didn't. Whereas Mills wore neat suits and button-down shirts, Eppridge was a product of the 1960s, a seemingly flaky young man, given to blue jeans and motorcycles. He looked like somebody whose friends dropped acid, if he didn't himself. Of all *Life* photographers, he seemed the most likely to be able to slide easily and unobtrusively into the drug scene.

He slid, but it was an eye-opener to him. Nevertheless, he kept his head, and shot a story the like of which had never before appeared in a national magazine. It was an absolute shocker. Like Villet backed up by Barbara in "The Lash of Success," Eppridge was so strongly backed up by Mills that he could concentrate all his energies on photographs. He stopped worrying about being busted by the police; Mills would look out for that. He could forget about the possibility of being stuck up by take-off artists — tough junkies who supported their habit by ripping off other junkies — Mills would handle it. He just took pictures, and he took some horrifying ones.

Quint's layout is very strong. It has none of the grace notes of some of his others. It is angular, full of sharp corners and juts, befitting the jagged up-and-down lives of its principals. As he so often did, Quint found an unusual and arresting opener. By itself it would have been a routine picture, but with its headline it engages the reader's curiosity: why are these nice young people animals? The page is turned, and the answer is provided with brutal directness. From then on the story skids sickeningly from one horror to another, and ends on a scene of total desolation.

This essay also has in common with "The Lash of Success" its dependence on text. Quint had to find space for a lot of it, and he did it ingeniously, providing a full page of it at the beginning of the story, and extra-long captions on most of the other spreads. Even more text was packed into an article that Mills wrote to follow the essay. It was as riveting as Eppridge's photographs.

The drug addiction essay, with its big pictures and its flood of activity, runs as long as "The Lash of Success" — sixteen pages. Barring that, and the other similarities mentioned, the stories could not be more different. One is all action, the other all mood. If they appear to bear a surface resemblance, it is in the remarkable freeing-up of the essay form that had been achieved by the mid-1960s, with the gradual blurring of the boundaries that had previously separated text stories and picture stories, and an increasing use of pictures played so large and so close that they draw the reader right into the embrace of their subjects.

'We are animals in a

Pretty girl named Karen, pleasant young man named
John—they could be hurrying to a movie,
a supermarket, a college classroom.
But they are drug addicts, headed for heroin,
for a pusher with a fix. This series, reported
and written by Associate Editor James Mills, tells
what their lives are like and, in next week's
instalment, what more could be done—to
help the addict, to halt the flow of drugs,
and to clean up a tragic and tenacious social evil.

Photographed by BILL EPPRIDGE

240

world no one knows'

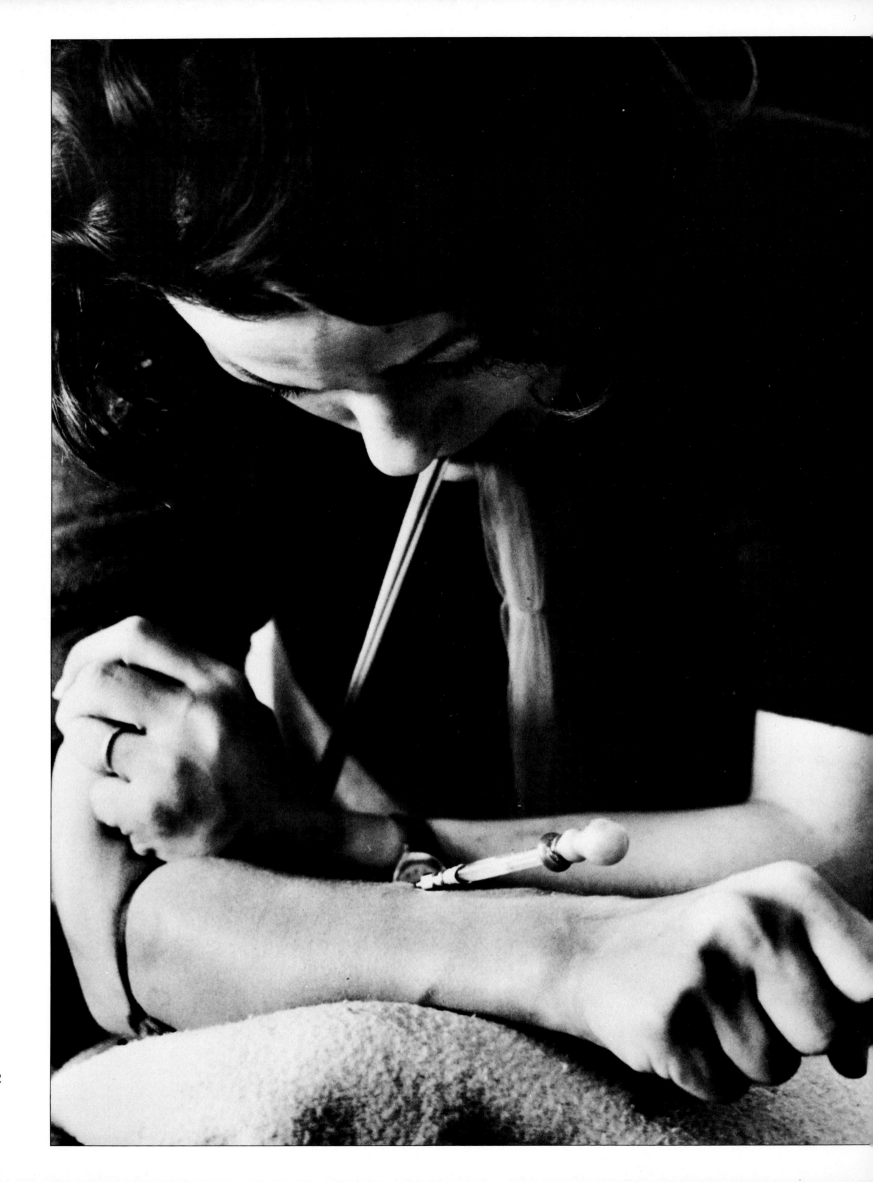

John and Karen, Two Lives Lost to Heroin

Four times a day, this is John and Karen, holed up with heroin. Faces desperate and intent, teeth pulling tight the tourniquet, grimy fingers squeezing fluid into the bloodstream, and then—peace. This is everything they live for— this is what heroin is all about. With this shot their problems vanish, and the world they cannot handle fades to leave them in solitary bliss.

No "square"—the addict's word for anyone who does not use drugs —can imagine the strength of heroin's hold. The addict will beg for it, walk miles for it, wait hours for it, con for it, stay up days and nights on end to pursue it, steal from those he has loved for it, risk death for it. Heroin, more than any other drug, leads the greatest number of addicts to squalor and desperation.

The frightening power heroin holds over John and Karen is the subject of this essay and the article that follows. To outsiders, they sometimes seem to stroll (*preceding pages*), but always they are driven by the drug—he to thievery, she to prostitution, and both to "pushing" heroin to pay for their own supply. The drug urges them, as the story shows, to murky streets and ill-lit corners, through shabby rooms and in and out of hospitals and jails. It is their jealous lover, and their wrathful god.

Every day heroin wins a few new converts to its ranks, and now there are more addicts in America than authorities can successfully count. The Federal Narcotics Bureau estimates that the U.S. has 60,000 heroin addicts, but other less official counts climb into the hundreds of thousands. Half of the country's addicts live in New York City, and almost all the others are in the slums of Detroit, Chicago and Los Angeles. Half are Negro. Only 20% are women. They commit an enormous number of crimes—more than 15% of New York City's burglaries (but less than 2% of its felonious assaults). Few are violent. Contrary to popular belief, it is not heroin that may lead to violence, but the excessive use of other drugs: amphetamines, barbiturates, cocaine, Doriden, marijuana.

The heroin addict is a very busy man. For those who would separate him from his heroin he has no use and no time. When he awakes in the morning he reaches instantly for his "works"—eye-dropper, needle ("spike," he calls it), and bottle top ("cooker"). He dissolves heroin in water in the cooker and injects the mixture. This is his "wake-up," a morning shot to hold off the anxiety and sickness of withdrawal and get him "straight" enough to start the day. If his habit is costing him $20 a day, and that is not a large habit by any means, he must now start out to steal at least $100 worth of goods, knowing that a fence will give him only one-fifth the true value of his loot. When he has stolen something, he must haggle with his fence over the price. The argument seems interminable to him, for it has now been hours since his wake-up and he is getting nervous again, his eyes are watering and he is beginning to feel like a man coming down with a bad case of flu.

Finally he gets the money and begins his search for a "connection"—someone with heroin for sale. Not just any connection, but a connection who deals good quality stuff—"dynamite," not "garbage." Once the addict has bought his fix (has "copped" or "scored") he is faced with the risky business of getting it to his cooker and into his arm without getting caught and "busted" (arrested). When he has finally injected the heroin— he calls it "shooting up," "taking off," "getting off"—he may or may not go on a "nod,"—his eyelids heavy, his mind wandering pleasantly—depending on how much heroin his body has become accustomed to and how much actual heroin was in the powder he injected.

He hopes that the shot will be at least strong enough to make him straight for a few hours. He can judge immediately the quality of the shot. If it is strong enough, he calms down, the flu feeling leaves, and he instantly begins looking for money for the next shot.

What haunts the addict are anxieties, which only heroin can relieve. In the shaky families and oppressive environment of big-city slums, anxieties pile up fast—and it is in the teeming slums that heroin is handy. From friend to friend the drug spreads inexorably among the emotionally weak and unstable.

John and Karen have much in common with other big-city junkies. Karen is 26, John 24. Both had broken the law before they started on heroin—she as a prostitute in the Midwest, he as a thief in New York. Karen is the first in her family to use illegal drugs; but John has two addicted brothers, and a third died of an overdose.

Both John and Karen have used many drugs, but they prefer heroin to all the rest just as a gourmet prefers wine to beer. Both have been to jail (he 10 times, she twice) and to hospitals (he 4 times, she twice)—and have emerged each time to start their habits fresh.

John and Karen have been together—sleeping wherever they can find a place to lie down— for three years. They use the same last name, but never got around to formal marriage ("We did get a blood test once," says Karen). Karen's earnings as a prostitute also support John's habit, and he occasionally contributes a little money by breaking into parked cabs, in which drivers may have left coin changers.

Both John and Karen are at times all but overcome by revulsion for their habit and for the horrifying, unseen world it forces them into. "We are animals," says Karen. "We are all animals in a world no one knows."

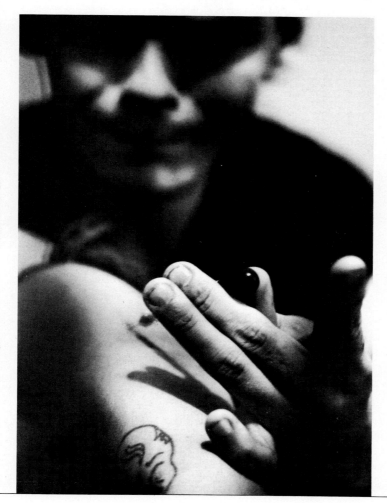

A stocking wrapped around her arm to make the vein stand out, Karen (left) waits for blood to start backing into the eyedropper—a sign the needle is in the vein. To get more pressure, she has replaced the dropper's small bulb with a nipple from a baby pacifier. John (right) also shoots directly into a vein (a practice known as "mainlining") but he does it further up his arm.

243

Keeping a furtive eye out for detectives, Karen passes a pusher $5 for a bag of heroin. Sometimes, like most junkies, she earns money for heroin by selling it herself. One such time, when a pusher gave her a small supply of unusually pure heroin on consignment, she went quickly into business on a corner (below). Soon junkies were rushing up to her to arrange buys.

*A*lmost all female addicts support their habit by prostitution, and Karen is no exception. After a $10 "trick" with a "John" (customer) in a hotel, she leads him down back stairs (above, right), then stands lookout while John rifles cabs (below). Asked how many cabs he has "boosted," John said, "How many are in New York? I guess I make more off them than the owners."

To get money, Karen prostitutes and pushes, John loots cabs

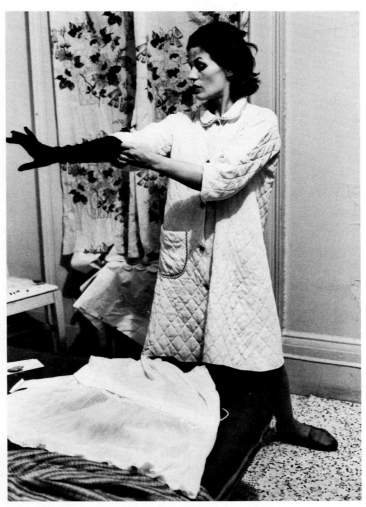

*K*aren, once a show girl in a New York nightclub, grows nostalgic after a heroin shot (right) and begins to model clothes stolen from a friend's wife. Earlier she sat with John (below, right) while he tried to fix a radio taken from a cab. He gets many radios from taxis, and once turned up $500 hidden under a seat—but was himself robbed of half of it by other junkies.

245

He visits her in a hospital: 'Stop nodding, they'll throw me out'

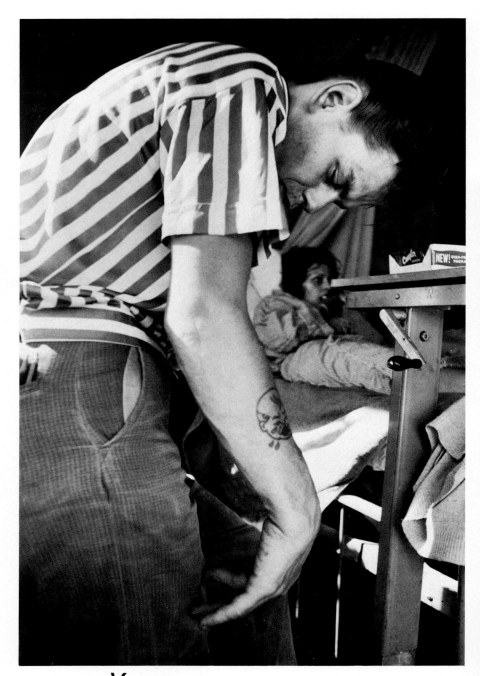

Visiting Karen in the hospital, Johnny showed up high on heroin and spent most of his time there nodding (above). Afraid that he would get her in trouble with the nurses, Karen yelled at him to stand up straight (right). "You're stoned, buddy! Stop that nodding before they throw me out!" He grumbled that he was not nodding, just awfully sleepy from not having had a place to lie down for three days. On several *later visits John brought her heroin and the needle and eyedropper needed to inject it. Why was she using stuff if she was there to kick the habit? "I just felt like getting high like any other human being would. I was bored. I'd been lying there in that hospital for a week, and when you're kicking and they're giving you methadone [a drug hospitals use to withdraw addicts from heroin] you just feel so normal."*

*L*eaving for a hospital, Karen kisses a customer goodby, while John looks away. Her body had built up such a high tolerance to heroin that she was having trouble getting enough to hold off withdrawal symptoms. She knew that after a couple of weeks away from the drug in a hospital, she would be able to start her habit afresh—getting a stronger "high" from a smaller dose.

*T*o win admittance to the hospital, Karen pretends to be in great pain from heroin withdrawal, while a nurse fills out forms. After a few questions and a quick search for drugs in her belongings, the hospital finally let her in.

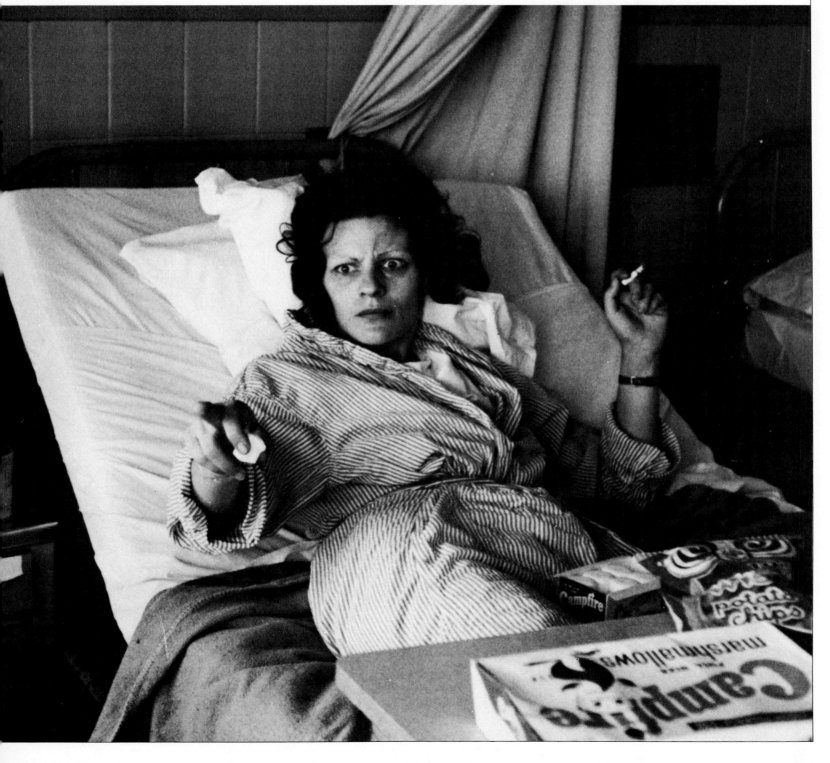

The cops search them— and John gets locked up

A few days after she left the hospital, Karen stood with John on a street corner, unaware that they were closely watched by two narcotics detectives (one is behind the mailbox in the top picture at left). The detectives had heard that John and Karen were selling drugs and, for an hour, stayed near enough to watch what they were up to. Then when another addict walked up, brushed against them and kept on going, the detectives assumed that drugs had been passed, and moved in. One questioned Karen (center picture) while the other searched John's pockets and cuffs. Karen broke into tears (bottom). "Whenever the cops come around," she explained later, "I right away start crying and yelling, especially if I've got stuff on me. Usually they don't want too much to do with a screaming, hysterical broad, so they lay off." John tries never to have any drugs on him. When he is pushing heroin, he usually follows the general practice and hides the bags between the pages of a phone book in a public booth, or under a trash can or behind a radiator in a hotel hallway. Then he simply takes the customer's money and tells him where to look.

Jailed for disorderly conduct, John stares through the bars, then sits on his bunk yawning and holding his stomach as he goes through withdrawal. A policeman arrested him when he balked at moving off a corner where he and other junkies were loitering. He was locked up for 18 days. John admits that often during withdrawal the nervous anxiety is far worse than the physical discomfort. "When I'm kicking in jail," he says, "I just gotta have someone to talk to. Once I was lyin' there kicking and this other guy was in the bunk over me and he was sleepin' and sleepin'—like a baby. I shoved hard on the bottom of his bunk and threw him clean out onto the floor. Man, he was scared, his eyes was wide open. And I said to him, 'Okay, man, now talk!'"

John out of jail: 'Don't play with my brains!'

Meeting Karen his first day out of jail (above), John bawls her out for not writing. Later in a hotel (below) he gets affectionate, his drug-free days in jail having restored desires dulled by heroin.

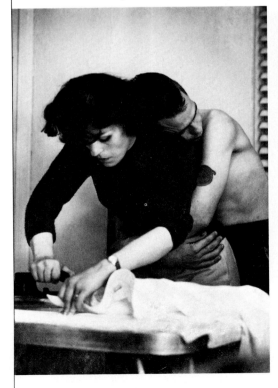

Go ahead and shoot it all up! You're a pig junky, just like you always were and always will be!" Karen screams at John as he takes a shot (above) minutes after his release from jail. Before he was arrested he had hidden 30 bags of heroin in a hotel hallway. Just after meeting Karen, he retrieved his stash, collected some friends and went to another hotel to "turn everyone on" —give them all heroin. In jail, off heroin, his body lost its dependence on the drug, and he uses it here not to fight off withdrawal, but only to get a high. But Karen still has a physical need for the drug and is furious at him for not giving it all to her. He shouted back at her, "Don't bug me, Karen! Don't play with my brains!" All 30 bags were gone by that night. A friend went for more and returned with a connection from Harlem, whom Karen paid off (right). Frightened that the men in the room were about to rob him of his drugs and money, the pusher was in a rush to get paid and did not complain about being photographed. Nevertheless, since his identification might encourage him to retaliate against John and Karen, his face has been retouched.

252

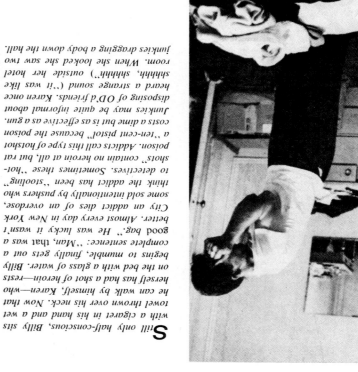

One of the junky's natural enemies is the overdose, the ''OD''—a shot that unexpectedly contains more heroin than his body can survive. In these pictures, taken while Johnny was in jail, Karen works to save the life of a young addict named Billy. Her expressions (right) mirror the danger, hope and final victory of her two-hour struggle. Billy collapsed in a hotel room after swallowing five Doriden tablets and then mainlining a shot of heroin. Though he is nearly unconscious, Karen holds him on his feet and keeps him walking.

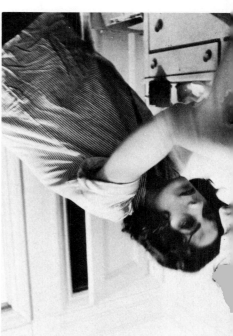

Open your eyes, Billy. Try to wake up. You took too much stuff, Billy. Don't go to sleep—you might not wake up. You got to fight it, Billy. Do you hear me, Billy? You got to fight it. Billy? Billy?'' Exhausted and hot from walking him around the room, Karen has dumped him into a chair and removed her sweater. Then, afraid that if he sits down too long he will slip into a fatal coma, she walks him some more. Finally, she sits him down in a chair again and shouts into his ear. He begins to come around. ''That Doriden is something,'' she explains. ''It makes you feel like you were almost clean, almost like you'd never had any heroin before. And then you take the heroin and, man, it really sends you.''

Still only half-conscious, Billy sits with a cigaret in his hand and a wet towel thrown over his neck. Now that he can walk by himself, Karen—who herself has had a shot of heroin—rests on the bed with a glass of water. Billy begins to mumble, finally gets out a complete sentence: ''Man, that was a good bag.'' He was lucky it wasn't better. Almost every day in New York City an addict dies of an overdose. Sometimes these ''hot-shots'' contain no heroin at all, but rat poison. Addicts call this type of hotshot a ''ten-cent pistol'' because the poison costs a dime but is as effective as a gun. Junkies may be quite informal about disposing of OD'd friends. Karen once heard a strange sound (''it was like shhhh, shhhhh'') outside her hotel room. When she looked she saw two junkies dragging a body down the hall.

John out of jail: 'Don't play with my brains!'

Meeting Karen his first day out of jail (above), John bawls her out for not writing. Later in a hotel (below) he gets affectionate, his drug-free days in jail having restored desires dulled by heroin.

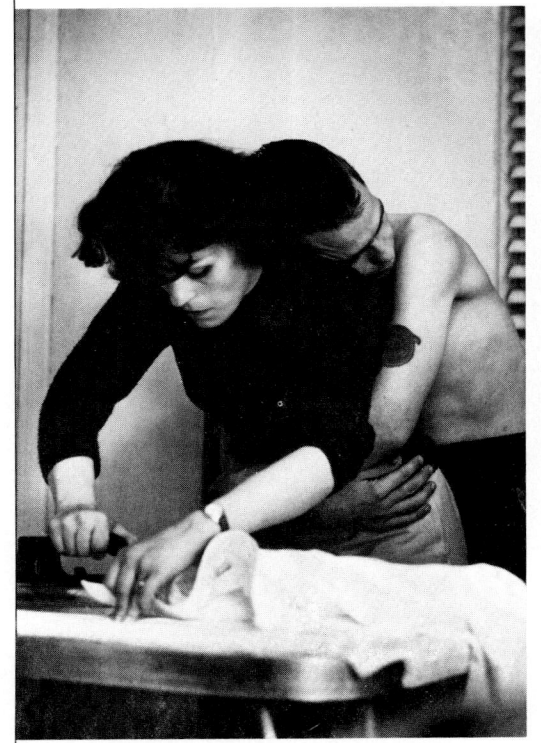

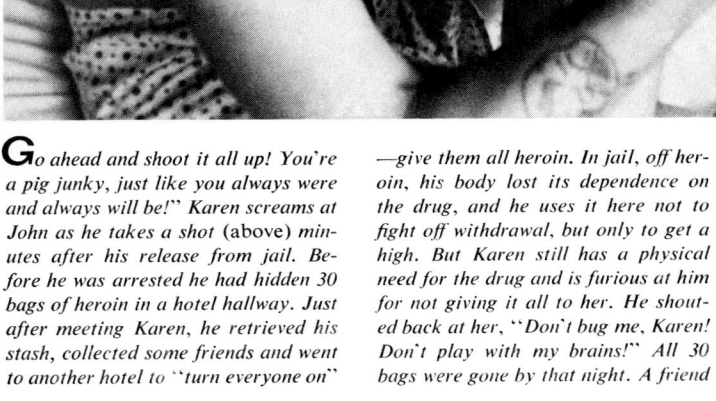

Go ahead and shoot it all up! You're a pig junky, just like you always were and always will be!" Karen screams at John as he takes a shot (above) minutes after his release from jail. Before he was arrested he had hidden 30 bags of heroin in a hotel hallway. Just after meeting Karen, he retrieved his stash, collected some friends and went to another hotel to "turn everyone on" —give them all heroin. In jail, off heroin, his body lost its dependence on the drug, and he uses it here not to fight off withdrawal, but only to get a high. But Karen still has a physical need for the drug and is furious at him for not giving it all to her. He shouted back at her, "Don't bug me, Karen! Don't play with my brains!" All 30 bags were gone by that night. A friend went for more and returned with a connection from Harlem, whom Karen paid off (right). Frightened that the men in the room were about to rob him of his drugs and money, the pusher was in a rush to get paid and did not complain about being photographed. Nevertheless, since his identification might encourage him to retaliate against John and Karen, his face has been retouched.

252

The deadly
overdose:
'You got
to fight
it, Billy!'

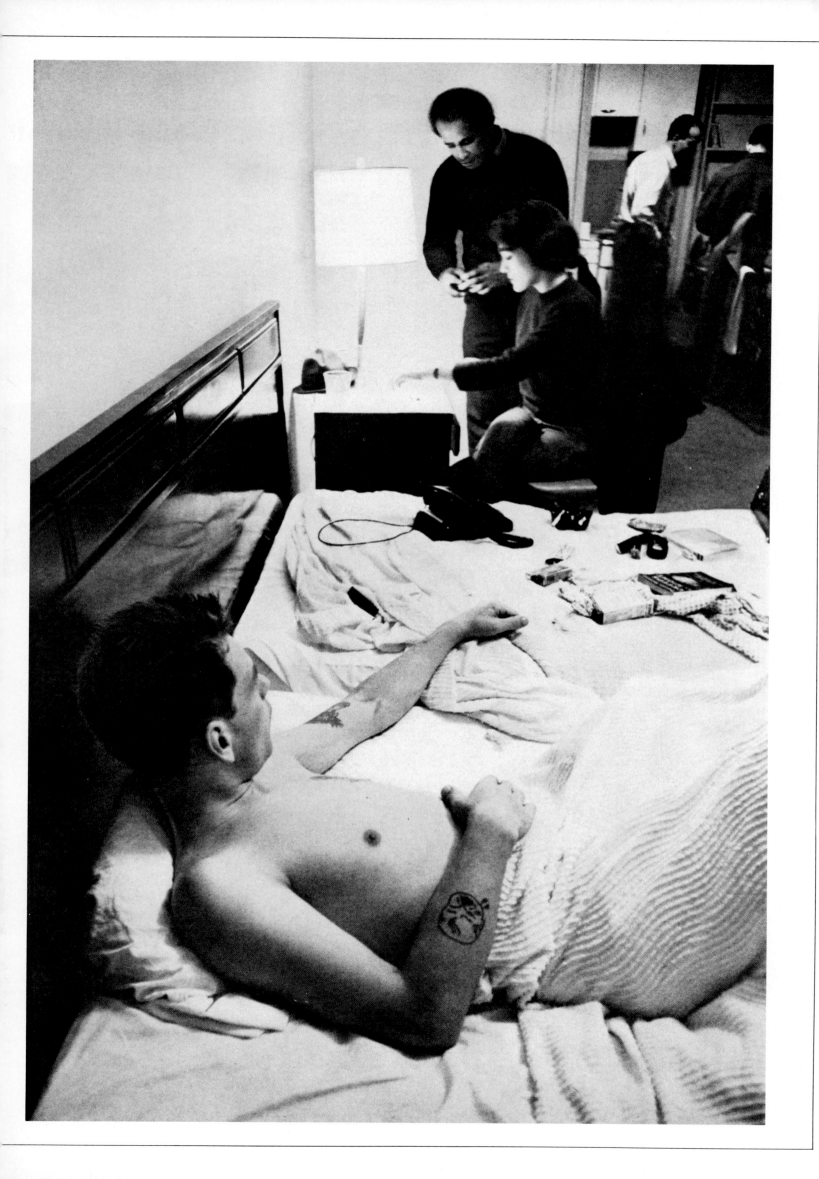

*H*er arms around Johnny and his brother, Bro—also an addict—Karen lies hopelessly on a hotel bed. On the table next to her rests a glass of water for dissolving heroin, a bottle-top cooker and burnt matches.

The Shakers

March 17, 1967
Photographer: John Loengard
Designer: Bernard Quint

Like Eugene Smith, John Loengard is a printer at heart. He loves rich dark prints, and will keep making them darker and darker, pulling magnificent ones 16 × 20 in size that are very impressive to editors. Ralph Graves points out, however, that almost anything that size, printed dark enough, will impress, and goes on to say that Loengard was sometimes the despair of editors. Once, sent to Hollywood to do a color story on fading movie queens — Paulette Goddard, Betty Hutton, Myrna Loy, Joan Blondell — he came back with six transparencies, all of them nearly black. On the other hand, he once produced a sensational shot of Washington policemen trying to cope with demonstrators during a march on the Capitol. This was a lowering dawn-lit picture, full of depth and menace. It was only when someone looked at the contact sheet that it was learned that Loengard had taken it at ten o'clock in the morning.

Loengard prefers to work in black-and-white, where negatives can be manipulated in the darkroom until he has exactly what he wants. He is a highly intellectual, studious man who likes quiet subjects and takes infinite pains with them. Given time and the right assignment, he can find things to photograph that others do not see. His approach to a story is slow, reflective, almost melancholy. No better choice than Loengard could have been made for an essay on the Shakers.

Here is a subject built on stillness, solitude, past energy, things no longer used, on sunlight streaming through empty rooms, on echoing silences, on pervading peacefulness, but sadness too, because the Shakers are a dying sect. Celibates, they must depend on recruiting to replenish their numbers, and their quiet life does not attract new members these days. No one has joined the sect in years. Once they had eighteen communities and a membership of six thousand people. When Loengard photographed them in 1967 their active villages had been reduced to two and their membership was down to eighteen, all of them women. The last male member had died six years before.

"I like to take simple pictures," says Loengard. "I don't go for the grand view. I prefer to try and build it up piece by piece." He has done that here with exquisite taste, in a series of photographs that gain in beauty from his predilection for rich printing. A hallway, a chair, a face, a fence, a basket, the side of a barn — the Shaker life, now only a memory.

The memory is preserved in a serene layout whose needs are once again served by Quint's meticulous attention to details: an appropriate type face; subtle changes in the amount of white space around the pictures; just enough movement among them to banish any sense of dead formalism that otherwise might have crushed such a quiet story; finally an ingenious introduction of prints from another day that wind like a thread through the essay to remind that Shakers were once a vital sect. But those pictures are played very small; that way, they also remind that all that activity is now far off.

What of the Shakers today? The two communities that Loengard visited are still functioning, although their membership, through death, has fallen from eighteen to nine. One village, in Canterbury, New Hampshire, is now the parent ministry of the sect. Its two leaders, Eldresses Bertha Lindsay and Gertrude Soule, still live there, as does one other sister. All are in their eighties. Six sisters live in the village at Sabbath Day Lake in Maine. One is in her fifties. The others are all old women. It is only a matter of a very few years before these last two surviving communities will wink out. Plans exist for turning them into Shaker museums, as has been done with three other communities after the deaths of all their members. One is in Massachusetts, two in Kentucky. The remaining Shaker communities have been put to various uses. One is being used as a Catholic seminary; another, in Mt. Lebanon, N.Y., is now the Darrow School. Part of the University of Indiana was once a Shaker village. The one in Enfield, Connecticut, is a prison.

Serene in their faith, the aged women sit in silent communion. They are Shakers, stalwarts of an all but extinct sect whose members only a few decades ago were numerous enough to fill their meeting halls (*right*). In 1774 their predecessors fled to America from England, where they had been called, derisively, "Shakers" for their custom of dancing in a frenzy to express religious ecstasy. In time they too adopted the

name. To Shakers, work is also a form of prayer, and in America they prayed long and hard. Inventive as they were pious—their many innovations included the flattened-out broom and the circular saw—Shakers became most famous for the beauty locked in the simplicity of design of their furniture and handicrafts. Theirs was the most successful of all communal experiments in the New World and at their peak, during the decade just before the Civil War, they had 6,000 members in 18 communities. Because all Shakers are celibate and rely on conversions to replenish their numbers, their order began to disintegrate. Today just two active communities exist with a total membership of 18, all women: the one at Sabbathday Lake, Maine (*above*) and another at Canterbury, N.H. Said one sister who died last year: "We are not defeated as a people, but intend to be true to our trust, valiant to the end with heads lifted, hearts courageous and colors flying."

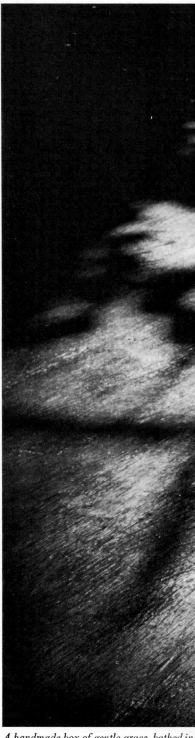

A handmade box of gentle grace, bathed in

Serene twilight of a once-sturdy sect

The Shakers

streaming sunlight at Shakertown Museum, Pleasant Hill, Ky.

Photographed by JOHN LOENGARD

Neat as a toy town, the still-active Shaker village at Canterbury, N.H.

Doorway to a sisters' room

A brethren's retiring (bed) room

Segregated stairs at Pleasant Hill, Ky.

Restored Shaker parlor at Hancock, Mass. museum

Picket fence and 1850 building at Sabbathday Lake, Maine

"Mother Ann" Lee, founder and spiritual leader of the movement, believed that sex is the seed from which all earthly evil springs. To keep the mingling of the sexes to a minimum, Shaker houses even had separate doors and stairs for the brethren and sisters. Whenever a family joined the village, the husband and wife would part and so would their sons and daughters. If, somehow, a Shaker boy and girl fell in love, they were put on six months' probation. Then, if they still wished to marry, they were sent into the "world" with a sack of flour, a horse, $100 and a blessing. Brethren and sisters ate in the same dining rooms, but at separate tables, and they never touched, even during the spirited dances. This same discipline carried over into their meticulously ordered homes. Ubiquitous wooden pegs studded every wall and virtually everything hung from them: clothing, utensils, even furniture when the floor was being cleaned. And that was often, for Mother Ann lectured, "There is no dirt in heaven." Though a central ministry set down general rules, villages were self-supporting and self-governing. A village was divided into "families" of from 30 to 100 individuals each, including the children whom Shakers took in and reared. Recalls a Canterbury sister: "People think we've missed a lot by not having our own families, but I think I've loved these adopted children more than I would my own." In each village two elders and two eldresses handled family matters and gave spiritual guidance, while deacons and deaconesses dealt with the "world," what lay beyond the neat white fences and pampered crops. And every village raised its food, built its houses, made its furniture. A typical Shaker village, at Pleasant Hill, Ky., is being completely restored and, in June, will be opened to the public.

261

The last Shaker brother died nearly six years ago. The surviving sisters—six at Canterbury and 12 at Sabbathday Lake—are, says one, "reaping the results of labors of the past." They have leased out most of their farm acreage and locked all but a few of their buildings. As each of the other 16 villages has succumbed, its land and property have been sold and the proceeds passed along to the remaining communities.

The sisters are resigned to the death of the sect, for Shakers never believed that everyone would or should follow their ways. "There is as little chance of that," says one sister, "as all flowers becoming daisies." Mother Ann herself had predicted that the order would decline until there were not enough Shakers to bury their dead, but that someday, some place, Shakerism would arise stronger than ever. Meanwhile, both Canterbury and Sabbathday Lake are keeping open their small museums and gift shops, largely because the sisters enjoy talking with the "world's people" whenever they drop by.

Two of six sisters who live at Canterbury village

Mt. Lebanon, N.Y. brethren and sisters, 1875

A Shaker sister in meditation, in Sabbathday Lake meetinghouse

Barren trees, empty barn at Pleasant Hill, Ky.

262

Sister Mildred Barker, one of 12 sisters at Sabbathday Lake

Shaker cemetery at Harvard, Mass.

263

Round stone barn at Hancock, Mass.

Sturdy barns, Canterbury village

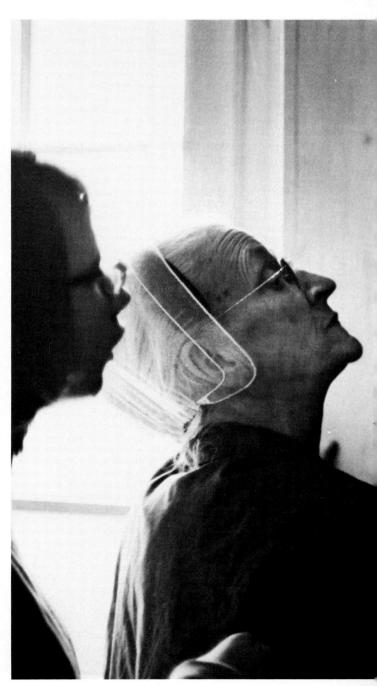

The flat broom, invented by a brother

264

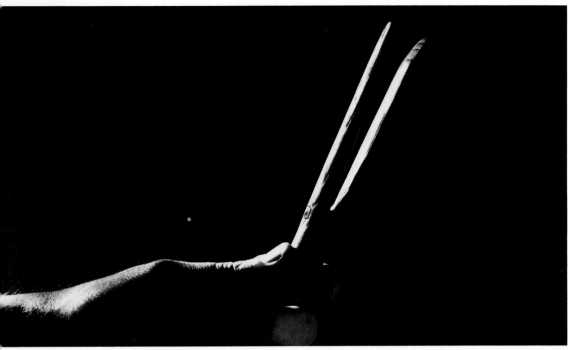

An early clothespin, claimed as a Shaker invention

School at Mt. Lebonon, N.Y., 1875

If mystical in their religion, Shakers were shrewdly practical when it came to figuring out ways to do their work faster and better. They were such innovators, in fact, that there is probably not a well-swept home in America that does not contain a replica of the flat broom that a Shaker brother designed in 1798. Sawmillers and do-it-yourself craftsmen owe much to the Shaker sister who discovered she could buzz through wooden shingles with a notched tin disk attached to her spinning wheel.

Shakers drove the first one-horse buggies in America. They made a static-electricity generator and, using it, were the first to practice shock therapy—for rheumatism, not psychiatric disorders. They made significant improvements in the Franklin stove and the washing machine. The clothespin and the metal pen point are claimed as Shaker inventions, as are the screw propeller, the harrow, the threshing machine, the pea sheller, the apple corer and cut nails. The first patent medicines and herbs on the market bore Shaker labels, and for a century Shaker-produced garden seeds were the finest available.

Eldress Marguerite Frost and visitors at Canterbury dispensary

265

The dog Wiggles, cranberries and Sister Bertha in Canterbury kitchen

Though Shaker sisters still hold services, they no longer indulge in the dancing and marching that in early days provided recreation as well as a way of displaying reverence. Today television antennas sprout from their roofs and every sister has seen the movie *Sound of Music* at least once. The stark and spare furniture once used by Shakers is now a rarity in their living quarters. Collectors have grabbed up most of it and, anyway, the sisters prefer the comfort of soft upholstery. Yet, while embracing the good things that modern times have to offer, the sisters enjoy such old-fashioned pleasures as sorting cranberries and on a winter's afternoon they love to gather in the sewing room to gossip and giggle. "If anyone pities the Shakers for the life they lead," says one 90-year-old, "they don't know what they're talking about. I've never been bored a day in my life."

Shakers in a solemn march, palms uplifted to receive blessing

Sister Mildred in Sabbathday Lake sewing room

266

A Family of His Own

December 17, 1971
Photographer: Leonard McCombe
Designer: Robert Clive

Some picture stories anyone can edit. They consist of half a dozen whizbang supershots surrounded by garbage. The good pictures literally leap off the contact sheet. It is when all of them are good, sliding imperceptibly from there through the very good to the great, that trouble starts. Peggy Sargent admits that, of all photographers' work, Cartier-Bresson's was the hardest to edit. The next, she thinks, was Leonard McCombe's. McCombe seldom took obvious smashers, but then he very seldom took poor pictures either. The smashers only revealed themselves when they were separated from all the near-smashers that surrounded them. That was not easy because his photographic ideas often were all tangled together. The pictures tended to lean on one another, each becoming explicable only in the context of several others. Like John Loengard, McCombe prefers to build up stories in bits and pieces. Unlike Loengard, his pieces are not of objects, of still faces, but of people doing things, of small confrontations growing, of emotions being discharged. One picture touches another, and another —

That kind of take is very hard to come to grips with. McCombe and Peggy Sargent, as a sort of game but basically to make a tough job easier, sat down more than once to edit duplicate sets of contact sheets, and then compared the result to see who had marked what for printing. More often than not they marked the same ones, proving that even with complex takes it is possible for two different people to agree on what are the significant pictures. When that happens, there is a great surge of reassurance. Each knows that there is indeed a strong story lurking somewhere in the pile of selected prints. It is up to the designer to find it and organize it. The temptation, with a McCombe take, is to duck the hard weeding down and print far too many pictures. That simply shifts the burden to the designer, and he drowns.

That did not happen here. A manageable set was handed to Robert Clive and he found a straight story line.

McCombe's faculty for edging into a story and catching it on the fly is thoroughly tested in this essay on a troubled, homeless boy who has had a series of foster parents but who has proved to be too much of a handful to stick with any of them. Now he is about to move again — this time into a real family, a couple willing to adopt him permanently.

It is that moment in the life of a loser — a loser already although he is only nine — that McCombe has caught so well. At the last moment Donny is scared. He doesn't want to be tested again, and fail again. He stares at photographs of his new brother and sisters, five of them. Will they like him? Will they tease him? Are they bigger than he is? Suddenly the farm couple he has been living with, and their dog Bullet, become almost too precious to leave; at least he knows what life with them is like.

But the case worker comes in a car, and in another car are his new parents. He hides behind a tree, hugging Bullet. With two wonderful pictures selected from forty or fifty (and not from a couple of hundred) the story gets off winging. Donny bids a tearful good-bye to his foster mother in another near-smasher (someday I will have to ask Peggy Sargent what is hard about finding a picture like *that*), gives a last hug to Bullet, and is whisked off to a new world and a new family.

He meets them all. In an emotion-packed picture he looks hopefully at them and they look indulgently back at him, the mother biting her lip in the background. Then, with everybody still staring, the oldest daughter, a leggy teenager in short shorts and bare feet, breaks the ice by leaning forward to give him a kiss. The last picture in the essay is an anticlimax used to segue into a text trailer written by Betty Dunn.

It all seems so easy. The story is right there, in the pictures. Only fourteen were used. But the devilish thing about a McCombe essay — or any first-rate photo essay — is that those fourteen could be thrown out, and several entirely different-looking essays, almost as good, made with the reject pictures.

Almost as good. Only those who worked on this story, and on the twenty-one other essays in this book, know how difficult striving for the best was, and what an extraordinary feeling spread out to all when it all seemed to come together.

270

Donny, age 9, is adopted at last

A FAMILY OF HIS OWN

The snapshots spread out on the table were of some people named Anadell from a place near Milwaukee. When he studied the pictures in the kitchen of his current foster home, a farm in upstate Wisconsin, the boy, Donny, 9, had never met the Anadells. The caseworker had asked him: "Do you know what will be different about the Anadell home?" "It's another move," said Donny, "but I'm going to stay there forever, I hope." "But this will be different from a foster home," said the caseworker. "This will be an *adoptive* home, Donny."

A ward of the state of Wisconsin, Donny has lived in lots of surrogate homes in the past four years—11 in all, counting two stays at psychiatric centers and a year at a live-in school for disturbed children. He went through three foster homes in four months before he was taken to the farm where he now lived. At each home, memories of Donny remained on scratched furniture, decal-decorated walls, bedsprings sprung from jumping. He stole candy, told lies, walked uninvited into neighbors' houses. Once he poured shaving lotion down a toilet—just mischief, but just one prank too many for people who did not know their exasperation level. Donny showed them where it was, and they turned him back to the state that night.

The caseworker went back into town to fetch the Anadells, and Donny lined up the color pictures, leading off with the group picture that showed the whole Anadell family together. "This one has to be first," he said, "because my Mom and Dad are in it." Then he arranged the children in order of their ages—Cindy, the oldest, then Linda, Mike, Pamela and Terri Lee—and figured out which two he would fall between; Pamela and Terri Lee. There were a lot of girls in this family. All of them had brown eyes. His own were blue. "How old is Mike?" he had wanted to know. Mike was 13. He memorized the ages of all the Anadell children and knew that their father—his father—managed a supermarket. Finally, Donny put away the pictures. He went outside for a while, and ran to his foster mother when she called him. His new parents were coming.

the farm kitchen of his foster home, year-old Donny looked at snapshots the family that was going to adopt m and said, "Oh, how I wish all ese kids were younger than me!"

Photographed by LEONARD McCOMBE
Text by BETTY DUNN

He worries lest the Anadells say:

The first car was familiar. It belonged to the caseworker. But the station wagon following it had to be the Anadells', and at the moment of arrival Donny lunged for the security of a tree to hide behind and a dog, Bullet, to cling to. This was the meeting that the caseworker had tried to prepare him for:

"The Anadells want to adopt you, Donny."

"I thought the Gregorys were going to adopt me. How are the Shermans? My mother there —does she want me to come back?" (The names Sherman and Gregory are fictitious.)

The caseworker thought for a moment: "Mrs. Sherman said she was happy that you're getting a real mom and dad."

"But the Anadells could say, 'We don't want Donny.'"

"The Anadells could say, 'Because of the type of people we are, we can't handle him,' but I hope they have that little something extra —that they'll keep you even if you misbehave."

Terry and Delores Anadell, both 37, thought about adopting an older child a few years ago and then forgot about it. Last spring, when they heard about another homeless boy, also 9, also disturbed, they became serious again. But the psychiatric tests on the boy they had in mind were too negative. Would they like Donny instead, the agency wanted to know. "When we

Donny hid when his new parents drove up (left), but emerged immediately to chat with Terry and Delores Anadell (above) about horses and dogs. "You throw a stick for this dog," Donny said, "he'll run and get it." Delores said they had three dogs, four girls and, now, *two* boys. Below, Donny conducts a tour of the farm.

'We don't want him'

went into this," said Delores Anadell, "we didn't realize there were kids who *were* trouble. After we thought about it, it didn't make any difference." The Anadells consulted their own children and said a prayer. Sure, they'd take him. "We just like kids," said Delores. But although they had read the "record" on Donny, they didn't know what to expect when they got out of the car to meet him. The first thing Donny said to them was, "Do you have any horses?"

It is a wrench to leave the farm and Bullet, but he is glad to go

Wrenched by the leavetaking at the farm, Donny gave Bullet a rough squeeze (above) and then yanked at his new mother's necklace (right) in the car. "I know why they gave me your pictures," he said. "So if I have to go away I can take them with me." Reassured that he would not have to leave the Anadell home, Donny (below) finally relaxed enough to fall asleep.

"Bye, Mommie," said Donny (left), trying not to cry, then hugged and kissed his foster mother when she asked him to. From the car he shouted, "Send me a cabbage when my garden grows!"

aying goodbye to his foster family didn't sound too hard when Donny talked about it with the caseworker the day before: "Donny, how do you feel about going with your new parents tomorrow?"

"I'd like that. I'm ready. I'm ready anytime."

But leaving the farm wasn't easy. In two months there Donny grew from a size 10 to a size 14. He had been given warmth by foster parents who would have liked him to stay on indefinitely, but who realized they were too old to adopt. Of all the places where he had stayed, the farm was the best, and Donny was the expansive young master that afternoon. He showed the Anadells the barn, the cows, his own garden, his hand-me-down bike and particularly the horses: "Molly is 20 and we used to use her to plow. We just got Shawn a few years ago, I think." Tense from trying to please, Donny at one point threw "his" dog in a mud puddle, then cried when Bullet nipped him. He jauntily invited the Anadells to stay overnight ("We have an extra room"), as if to insure that they wouldn't back down on their bargain. "To turn him back then would have been like turning back one of your own," said Terry Anadell. "We'd made a commitment." The next morning the Anadells came back to drive him home to Milwaukee. "What is your name, Donny?" the caseworker said. "I think it's going to be Donald Edwin Anadell Jr.!" he replied.

The first thing Donny saw when the car pulled into the driveway was the homemade welcome sign pasted on the garage doors.

'I'm going to stay here forever!'

Arriving home with the Anadells in the Milwaukee suburb of Brown Deer, 350 miles and a world away from his life on the farm as a foster child, Donny faced his new family and announced loudly: "I'm going to stay here forever—even if you don't want me!" Then he saw the garage welcome sign made by the Anadell children. "We like you," Linda, 15, told him, weeping. "We just hope you like us." In moments, Donny was swept into the whirlwind life of an active family. Cindy, 17, had stayed home as long as she could; she said she was too happy to cry and rushed off to her part-time job as a bakery girl at a supermarket. Donny measured himself against Pamela, 11 (he was taller), and told Terri Lee, 6, to say "please" to her mother, not "gimme, gimme." Mike helped Donny carry his clothes to the room they would share on the top floor of the split-level house. The Anadells' aboveground swimming pool was inspected, and the undeveloped woodland in back. Then the doorbell rang and the neighborhood poured in.

Delores and Terry Anadell swallowed tears at the moment of first meeting (above) between Donny and their own children—Cindy, Linda, Mike, holding onto Scarlet, and Pamela. (Terri Lee had vanished.) Then Linda gave Donny (right) a warm hello.

276

A few fights, a lot of acceptance

Before the Anadells took Donny they were told he would test them somehow to see if he would be sent away if he did something really wrong. Thus braced, they weathered his bullying of Terri Lee, his tantrums, his swearing, his moments of gushing affection and his fake crying. Collectively, the Anadells experienced a letdown. They had been prepared for worse.

In the parlance of social workers, Donny had never been "socialized." He had never lived in a family that had older children and was accustomed to ordering younger ones around. He couldn't swim, couldn't throw a football, couldn't understand family teasing. Now, after three months with the Anadells, he swims better than Terri Lee and not long ago threw his

first good pass in a fury because he wanted to equal Pamela's skill. A third-grader, he's a year behind in school and is taking speech lessons to improve his enunciation and sharpen his lisping "s"s. "I haven't had any complaints from school, and he hasn't been thrown off the school bus," said Delores, whose relaxed attitude has always been: "If you accept everything as the will of God, then anything that comes into your life, you just don't let it drag you under."

The Anadells, who will file to adopt Donny in February, are Baptists, and Donny, like the other children, belongs to a church youth group, where he made his mark recently by accidentally beaning a little girl while he and another boy played catch with a doorstopper. He told

Delores recently, "You're mean sometimes, Mommie, but I like you." Delores slaps him when he fibs and restricts after-school playtime for misbehavior. He never mentions his foster homes, but the Anadells sense he has yet to accept their home and family as "his." On the other hand, they have accepted him completely. "It seems like **we've always had** him," Cindy said recently. Terri Lee, with whom he fights regularly, is listing his misdeeds in her diary for his nostalgic reading when he grows up. Recently, while engaged in a friendly rock and dirt fight, he broke four windows in a new house (the first hit was accidental) and he is saving to pay for them from his share of Mike's predawn paper route. Mike pays him 20¢ a day.

One of the family, Donny rides behind his new brother, Mike, on a neighbor's minibike. As the only Anadell boy, Mike approved all along of adoption as a means of upgrading the household, but his first question about Donny before meeting him was, "How big is he?" Donny asked the same thing about Mike. He doesn't mind being shorter because Mike is older.